WICKET WOMEN

*Cricket & Women
in Australia*

WICKET WOMEN
Cricket & Women in Australia

Richard Cashman and Amanda Weaver

with research assistance by Sandra Glass

PRESS

Published by
NEW SOUTH WALES UNIVERSITY PRESS
PO Box 1 Kensington NSW Australia 2033
Telephone (02) 398 8900   Facsimile: (02) 398 3408

© Richard Cashman and Amanda Weaver
First published 1991

This book is copyright. Apart from any fair dealing
for the purpose of private study, research, criticism or
review, as permitted under the Copyright Act, no
part may be reproduced by any process without
written permission from the publisher.

National Library of Australia
Cataloguing-in-Publication entry:
Weaver, Amanda, 1963–
    Wicket women: cricket and women in Australia.

    Includes index.
    ISBN 0 86840 364 4.

    1. Cricket for women–Australia–History. I. Cashman,
    Richard, 1940–   . II. Title.

796.358082

Design & production by Di Quick
Typeset by Adtype Graphics, North Sydney
Printed in Singapore through GlobalCom

Contents

Abbreviations	vi
Preface	vii
Acknowledgments	ix
Foreword by Betty Wilson	xi
Chronology	xii
1. Belles and Novelties: The Era Before 1900	1
2. Organising Clubs and Associations: 1900–31	26
3. The Evolution of the Uniform	51
4. Expansion and Acceptance: The Golden Decade of the 1930s	70
5. Post-war Revival Followed by Stagnation	101
6. Revival in the 1970s	127
7. Expansion in the 1980s	148
8. The Media	174
9. The Future of Women's Cricket	198
Statistics of Australian Women's Cricket prepared by Erica Sainsbury	215
Notes	235
Select Bibliography of Woman and Sport in Australia	239
Index	241

Abbreviations

ACB	Australian Cricket Board (Men's)
ACTWCA	Australian Capital Territory Women's Cricket Association
AWCC	Australian Women's Cricket Council
IWCC	International Women's Cricket Council
MCG	Melbourne Cricket Ground
NSWWCA	New South Wales Women's Cricket Association
QWCA	Queensland Women's Cricket Association
SAWCA	South Australia Women's Cricket Association
SCG	Sydney Cricket Ground
TWCA	Tasmanian Women's Cricket Association
VLCA	Victorian Ladies' Cricket Association
VWCA	Victorian Women's Cricket Association
WACA	Ground of the Western Australian Cricket Association
WAWCA	Western Australian Women's Cricket Association
WCA	Women's Cricket Association (England)

Preface

The number of books written on Australian sport is immense but almost all of them are about men, with books about animals in sport (horses in particular) as the next largest category. Sporting books entirely devoted to women are exceedingly rare in spite of the considerable achievements of women in many sports in 20th century Australia: in athletics, swimming, tennis, squash, netball, softball and cricket — where the Australian women have been almost unbeatable for more than a decade.

It is time then to rectify this balance. Sports involving women are some of the fastest growing in the country. Softball in the 1960s and netball in the 1970s and 1980s have expanded at a greater rate than most men's sports and cricket is beginning to become very popular among women and girls.

The rapid growth in women's sports has occurred for a number of reasons. Many women and girls no longer accept that sport is male territory and have been participating in increasing numbers in an ever widening range of activities. Government, recognising that women and girls have been denied access to many sports, have introduced positive discrimination in favour of women playing sport. Sponsors are also slowly beginning to recognise the untapped market potential of women's sports.

A second central purpose of this book is to explore the prejudice against women playing cricket, and sport in general. The issue of bias against women's sport has attracted much attention in recent times with articles, books and government reports appearing on the subject. The team game of cricket is an ideal case study of the historical roots of this prejudice. Cricket has for more than a century been regarded as a male game — cricket and football provided tests of manliness — and those women who played the game achieved little recognition at best and ridicule at worst.

The bias against women playing cricket has been long and deep-seated. Public prejudice, which can range from outright hostility to apathy, has stymied the past development of the game in this country. For the players it has diminished their enjoyment of the game and they have achieved far less recognition and financial reward than might otherwise have been the case.

There have been no national histories of any women's sport in Australia which have looked at the wider context and broader issues. However, there have been some books on sports in individual states, such as hockey in NSW, and cricket in Victoria and Western Australia.

This book includes details of important international games and tours along with the careers and achievements of star players and the statistics of the game. It also investigates the broader context of cricket as played by women — the puzzling high and low points over the past century. It looks both at the issue of women playing cricket, the involvement of women in the men's game, and also the changing relationship between men and women administrators of cricket. No sport is played in isolation; therefore an understanding of women's cricket can only be appreciated in the context of other sports. This book examines women's participation in other fields and the impact this had on women's cricket — how the rise of softball for instance represented a threat to the game.

The term 'women's cricket' is used in the text because it has been an accepted name — both by those within and outside the sport — for what has been a minority sport for the past century. With greater cooperation between the men and women administrators of cricket there is every chance that men's and women's cricket will not be seen as two games in the not too distant future. It will become one game — cricket played by men and women.

Acknowledgments

A lot of credit for this book must go to Ann Mitchell, President of the AWCC who has long pushed for this history, to help put women and cricket more on the sporting map. She encouraged us to write this book, commented on drafts, enthused others about the project and provided photographs. Some past and present members of the AWCC have been equally helpful and enthusiastic: these include Christine Brierley, Betty Butcher, Menna Davies, Coralie Towers, Sylvia Faram, Lyn Morling, Leonie Seebohm and Ray Sneddon.

Erica Sainsbury, official statistician and scorer for the AWCC, has contributed a valuable and comprehensive statistical appendix, the first complete one ever published, and has helped reduce statistical errors in the text itself. Betty Wilson, the most outstanding Australian woman cricketer, kindly consented to write the Foreword. Sandra Glass assisted with research.

A number of individuals have freely loaned their scrapbooks and other historical material. They include Mollie Dive, Ruth Irwin, Karen Price, Ann Mitchell, Hazel Pritchard (loaned by her son Terry Scanlon) and Dawn Rae.

Many others have provided information and read parts of the manuscript. They include: Denise Annetts, Peggy Antonio, Betty Archdale, Peter Bakker, Philip Barclay, Joyce Bath, Pat Bleazard, Don Blunt, Averil Condren, Pat Cremer-Roberts, Jill Crowther, Neil Dalrymple, Lawrence Deane, Stroy Donnan, Ross Dundas, Denise Emerson, Graeme Errington, Lyn Fullston, Christine Garwood, Stephen Gibbs, Zoe Goss, Belinda Haggett, Brian and Margaret Hall, Rebecca Hawke-Weaver, Karen Hill, Margaret Hollis, Amy Hudson, Ruth Irwin, Margaret Jennings, Kay Kearney, Jill Kennare, Miriam Knee, Lyn Larsen, Mary Loy, Annette Lucas, Louella McCarthy, Tom McCullough, Nell McLarty, Mary Martin, Chris Matthews, Pat Mullins, Ben Mout, Henny Oldenhove, Grant Parker, Ross Peacock, Muriel Picton, Lorna Purfleet, Leonie Randall, Kit Raymond, Lindsay Reeler, Edna Ridley, Neil Sherring, Kath Smith, Val Stiles, Lorraine Taylor, Lorna Thomas, Hilda Thompson, Raelee Thompson, Sharon Tredrea, Peta Verco, Judy Warring, Norma Whiteman, Debbie Wilson, Veronica Wood and Kaye Wyvill.

Material on cricket was collected from a wide range of institutions including the Archives of the University of Melbourne, Melbourne Cricket Club Library, Mitchell Library, NSW Cricket Association Library and the archives at Abbotsleigh, PLC (Sydney) and Ravenswood.

Many have loaned individual illustrations which are acknowledged in the text. Thanks are due to Max and Reet Howell and Jack Pollard who made available a number of illustrations from their collections. Anthony Weate took the photograph of the authors and helped reproduce a number of other illustrations.

Illustrations are published courtesy of the *Bulletin*, E S Marks Sporting Collection, John Oxley Library, *Sydney Morning Herald* and *Wisden* Annual.

One of the more difficult tasks in the final stages of the manuscript was discovering an appropriate title and the authors are appreciative of the suggestion of Gloria Nicol.

Thanks also go to the Mayor and staff of North Sydney Municipal Council for their help and support.

Julia Tanguy of NSW University Press has given us great support and sensible advice at every stage of the project and the book has been enhanced by the attractive cover and layout of Di Quick.

Foreword

To be invited to write the foreword to this long awaited publication on the history of women's cricket in Australia is indeed an honour, and my appreciation and best wishes are extended to Amanda Weaver and Richard Cashman for their forethought in presenting this book.

Only those women who played in my time will appreciate the sacrifices we made to play cricket. We had to raise large sums of money for the privilege of going on tours, which were few and far between, and we were also required to assemble an immense wardrobe before any tour which was very costly and time consuming.

Opportunities to play Tests were far more restricted than today and I only played in eleven Tests in about ten years. Although women cricketers got a lot of publicity in the 1930s, there was less public recognition of us in the 1950s. We also had the problem that we were forever being compared with the men — unlike other women's sports such as hockey.

There are many colourful stories of women's struggle to play and their battle for recognition. Despite being patronised and ridiculed, women have persisted and have enjoyed their cricket while many administrators have worked hard and long and at personal cost for the game they love. It is encouraging to me to read that the prejudice against women playing cricket is now starting to diminish.

The fine illustrations in the book convey to me how much women got out of cricket: friendship, travel, and even the occasional chance to play cricket on some of the great Test grounds.

This book will be enjoyed by past and present cricketers alike and by all open-minded people interested in women being fairly represented in sport. I commend both authors for their careful research and lively writing.

Betty Wilson
Australian International and Hall of Fame Representative 11

Chronology of Women and Cricket

1745 26 July	First account of a women's match published in the Reading Mercury
1747 13 July	First women's match on a major ground (Artillery Ground, London)
c 1807	Christina Willes, originator of round-arm bowling
1874 7 April	First recorded match in Australia at Bendigo
1886 8 March	Fernleas play Siroccos at the SCG
1896 October	Tarana scores the highest total in any women's match (567) against Rockley NSW
1890 26 & 27 December	Rosalie Deane scores 195 & 104 at the SCG
1891 17 & 18 March	NSW versus Victoria, the first intercolonial, SCG
1905 11 July	Victorian Ladies' Cricket Association formed
1906 17 March	First interstate match between Victoria and Tasmania
1923	Victorian Women's Cricket Association formed
1926	Women's Cricket Association formed
1927 January	NSW Women's Cricket Association formed
1929	Queensland Women's Cricket Association formed
1930	South Australian Women's Cricket Association and
1930	Western Australian Women's Cricket Association formed
1931 20 March	Australian Women's Cricket Council formed
1931	First interstate tournament
1931	Formation of the Pioneers, for former Victorian players
1934 28–31 December	First women's Test match, Exhibition Ground, Brisbane
1937	First Australian tour of England
1948	Largest crowd at Test in Australia
1948	Women admitted to men's change room at the SCG
1948–49	Australian women win the Ashes for the first time
1948–49	First Test played against New Zealand
1948–49	Una Paisley, first Australian woman to score a Test century
c 1954	Wattle Club formed for past and present Australian players
1958 7–10 February	Betty Wilson's Test (7–7, a hatrick, 11 wickets and a century)
1958	International Women's Cricket Council formed
1963	Queensland Women's Cricket Association becomes defunct
1973	England wins First World Cup
1973	Australia's first tour of the West Indies
1976	Queensland Women's Cricket Association reformed
1976	First women's international at Lord's
1976	First Test played against the West Indies
1977	Australia plays first Test against India
1977–78	ACT Women's Cricket Association formed
1978	Australia wins Second World Cup held in India
1982	Tasmanian Women's Cricket Association reformed
1982	Australia win Third World Cup held in New Zealand
1984	Women entitled to full membership at Melbourne Cricket Club
1984	Formation of The Waratahs, for former NSW players
1984 February	Australian record Test score (525), Ahmedabad (India)
1984 October	*Between Overs*, magazine of the AWCC, first issued
1984–85	Jubilee Test series against England
1987	Denise Annetts scores 193 — a Test record
1988	Australia win Fourth World Cup held in Australia
1991	Christina Matthews breaks world wicket-keeping records
1991	MCC (England) vote against the admission of women

CHAPTER ONE

BELLES AND NOVELTIES

THE ERA BEFORE 1900

Beginning of club and intercolonial cricket

Women's cricket made an enthusiastic start in Sydney at the Association Ground (later known as the Sydney Cricket Ground [SCG]) on a Monday afternoon, 8 March 1886, before an estimated crowd of over 1 000. The Siroccos,[1] captained by Miss Nellie Gregory, were dressed in a cardinal and blue outfit and the Fernleas, led by Miss Lily Gregory, sister of Nellie, were attired in black and gold. The game began at 2.00 p.m. and when stumps were drawn at 6.30 p.m. the Fernleas 41 and 8–93 required just four runs for an outright win over the Siroccos 83 and 54. Trophies which were awarded included two gold watches, a diamond and pearl brooch, gold rings and other jewellery. £215 was raised for charity and the spectators were entertained by the Burwood Band.

The promoter and manager of the match, Fred Ironside, was one of the identities of Sydney cricket who was prominent in the organisation of junior (Moore Park) competition. It wasn't his first involvement in women's sport: an 1879 publication reported that

'*Frisquette* or Ladies' Cricket, an Australian winter game' had been 'invented' by Ironside and first played in Sydney in July 1878.[2] Ironside's reflections on the 1886 game were included in the *Sydney Mail* of 13 March:

> This is the first match of its kind played on the ground. I took the idea about two months ago. By advertising in the papers I got sufficient names. Miss Gregory gave me most valuable assistance in the matter. The young ladies have been practising almost every morning since we organised, from 6 to 8 o'clock, and in the evening from 6 to 7 o'clock. They have been very enthusiastic in their work. . . . This is the inauguration of what I hope will be an annual affair. It is entirely complimentary.

Newspaper comment of this game in the same source was generally fair. Miss Rosalie Deane, player of the match, was praised for 'excellence in all departments of the game' while both wicket-keepers were 'very smart behind the sticks, and at times brought the house down with [their] dexterity'. The fielding was 'generally good' though it was noted that most of the players could not throw. The bowling was mostly roundarm.

Ironside must have been sufficiently pleased with the first game that he organised another in April 1886 at the SCG which was a 'great success, both as regards the play and the attendance' of at least 3 500. This game was again between the Fernleas and the Siroccos and was played for a 'deserving charity' as were so many of the first women's cricket games. Playing for a worthy cause presumably reduced the potential for criticism of women involved in competitive sport. The match reporter was again fair in his comments praising Nellie Gregory, the star of the match, with 12 wickets and scores of 35 and 47 not out. The complete scorecard of the match was published in the *Sydney Mail* of 10 April 1886.

While there was support in some circles, other male cricket scribes treated women's cricket with disdain. 'Censor', who wrote a regular cricket column for the *Sydney Mail*, was biting in his comments of 17 April 1886:

> They are attempting a ladies' match at Melbourne. At least, the firm of Boyle and Scott are trying to advertise their business by the promotion of such an absurdity. We have had a ladies' cricket match in Sydney, but it is to be hoped that we shall never have another, for as a spectacle it was not edifying. However, if the Victorian ladies will allow themselves to be the means of cheap advertisement for a cricketing depot by all means let them.

'Censor' undoubtedly reflected what the vast majority of males, and probably many females as well, thought about women's cricket — it was something of a joke. Newspaper items, which

---

THE UNIQUE GREGORY FAMILY

The famous cricketing Gregory family contributed a great deal to the beginning of women's cricket in Sydney from 1886 to 1910. Nellie and Lily Gregory obviously played a lot of backyard cricket with their brothers — they were daughters of Edward James 'Ned' Gregory, who played in the first Test match in 1877 and sisters of another Test player, Sydney 'Syd' Edward Gregory. Without the benefit of school and club cricket before 1886 women had no other place to learn to play the game. Test player Harry Donnan, who married Nellie Gregory, added his support to the cricketing family by umpiring some of their games.

It is highly unlikely that any other state side, male or female, has ever before or since been represented by five members of one family. When NSW met Victoria in the first match of the 1910 series the NSW side included three Gregory sisters and two of their nieces.

They were Mrs Nellie Donnan, Mrs Meagher and Mrs Clymer and the two nieces were Miss Varley — daughter of Mrs Varley, another sister of Syd Gregory — and Miss Donnan. By 1910 the Gregory sporting dynasty could boast that over twenty children had represented NSW in a variety of sports — cricket, football, sailing and athletics.

Nellie Donnan became the first President of the NSWWCA, which was founded in 1927.

Table 1.1

FERNLEAS v SIROCCOS

FERNLEAS

First Innings		Second Innings	
Miss F Brown b N Gregory	0	c Farrar b N Gregory	1
Miss Stubbin how b N Gregory	0	b N Gregory	0
Miss R Deane not out	39	c M Stubbins b N Gregory	36
Miss L Gregory b N Gregory	5	b N Gregory	2
Miss L Baylis c Lewers b A Gregory	4	b N Gregory	0
Miss L Farrar b N Gregory	4	b N Gregory	3
Miss S Varley c & b N Gregory	0	b A Gregory	2
Miss E Somerville b A Gregory	1	b A Gregory	0
Miss S Mannix b A Gregory	3	b A Gregory	4
Miss S Rowley how b N Gregory	3	c Thompson b A Gregory	0
Miss M Thompson b N Gregory	2	b A Gregory	0
Miss J Lloyd b N Gregory	0	not out	2
Sundries	2		3
Total	63		53

	O	M	R	W	O	M	R	W
A Gregory	16	7	17	3	10	2	18	5
N Gregory	15	2	37	8	10	0	12	6
Matterson	1	0	6	0				

SIROCCOS

First Innings		Second Innings	
Miss Matterson run out	9	b Baylis	3
Miss R Englestoff b Deane	1	c Deane b Baylis	0
Miss A Gregory c Stubbin b L Gregory	27	c L Gregory b Deane	2
Miss N Gregory b L Gregory	35	not out	47
Miss S Matterson b Deane	4	c Stubbins b Baylis	0
Miss M Lewers b L Gregory	3	c Baylis b Deane	3
Miss E Farrar b Deane	1	b Deane	5
Miss Lewis b Deane	0	not out	3
Miss J Jeffrey not out	1		
Miss M Stubbins c Stubbin b L Gregory	2		
Miss Edney b L Gregory	0		
Miss R M Thompson b L Gregory	0		
Sundries	3		2
Total	86	6 wickets for	65

	O	M	R	W	O	M	R	W
Baylis	8	0	41	0	9	1	38	3
Deane	13	3	22	4	9	3	25	3
L Gregory	7	1	14	6				

Notes:
1. Miss Stubbin's dismissal of 'how' was probably hit own wicket.
2. Each side batted twelve players.
3. The runs allocated to each bowler do not tally with the batting totals in a number of instances.

One of the Gregory sisters, probably Nellie. Note the cricketing footwear. (Courtesy SCG Trust)

> **ASSOCIATION CRICKET GROUND.**
>
> THIS DAY (MONDAY), 5th APRIL,
>
> **LADIES' CRICKET MATCH.**
>
> Proceeds to be charitably used.
>
> Gates open at noon.
>
> Play to commence at 1 o'clock p.m.
>
> Admission to the Ground, 1s; Stand and Lawn, 1s extra.
>
> S. H. FAIRLAND,
> Secretary A.C. Ground.
>
> Office, 99, Elizabeth-street.

Sydney Morning Herald 5 April 1886.

appeared from time to time, pandered to this popular perception that women playing cricket could not be taken seriously. A year after the first women's match the *Sydney Mail* of 19 March 1887 referred to a game played in Lahore between men and women in which the former played with broomsticks and the women played with bats.

The women cricket players were not put off by such criticism and the Fernleas and Siroccos again met at the SCG on Friday 15 April 1887. The worthy cause this time was the Bulli Relief Fund and the Vernon Band entertained the spectators. The estimated crowd on this occasion was only 500 — it seems that some of the novelty of the women's game was starting to wear off.

Fernleas team (1886) with Rosalie Deane front left. (Courtesy Pat Mullins)

Cricket.

SWEET GIRL CRICKETERS.
LADIES' MATCH ON ASSOCIATION GROUND.

The Association Cricket Ground, Moore Park, was the scene on Monday of one of the most interesting cricket matches—as it certainly was the most novel one—ever played in this country. The players were all young ladies (whose ages range, perhaps, between 13 and 18), residing in Sydney or the suburbs; and most of whom are connected with what, to use the language of another popular sport, might be called cricketing families. It is to Mr. F. J. Ironsides, an enthusiast in all that pertains to cricket, that the credit of organising the match on Monday is entirely due, and it was upon his invitation that the spectators assembled to witness it. The attendance, which numbered about 1500, was thus select, and the contestants may have derived some encouragement from the consciousness that they were playing in the presence of friendly critics. Mr. Ironsides has had no little difficulty in working up the match. He had to bring together a number of young ladies, many of whom had little or no acquaintance with each other previously; but, having a very large circle of cricketing acquaintances, and his name being a sufficient guarantee for the propriety with which the contest would be conducted, he succeeded, after some months' correspondence and superintending of practices, in bringing the match off. The costumes worn were very pretty indeed, and appropriate—close fitting bodices with loose skirts, and small, peakless, cricketing caps. The dresses of the "batsmen" appeared to be less "in the way" of the ball than might be supposed; and the gentlemen who acted as umpires were never once placed in the delicate position of having to give an lbw decision; indeed, the rule with regard to this essentially masculine way of getting wickets would appear to have been by common consent suspended, much to the relief, no doubt, of both players and umpires. The two sides were severally designated "Siroccos" and "Fernleas." These designations, however, were purely complimentary, representing neither locality, age, nor any other feature, the sides having been chosen by Mr. Ironsides with a view to bringing about as even a distribution of cricketing talent as possible, and so, if possible, securing a close contest. The Siroccos appeared in blue and cardinal colors; the Fernleas in black and gold; and the effect of the uniforms was charming. The celebrated Gregory family was represented by three daughters of that famous veteran of the cricketing field, Ned Gregory; and the sides were captained respectively by Miss Gregory and Miss L. Gregory. The play was, of course, not what would be considered first-class in the ordinary sense of that term as applied to male cricketers; but we can assert without any fear of contradiction that it was first-class ladies' cricket. Some of the "sweet girl cricketers" displayed a knowledge of the game and a proficiency that could only have been acquired by long and regular practice. Miss Dean, for example, showed really superior cricket. In batting she exhibited a good defence against the dangerous bowls, and opened her shoulders at and hit freely and cleanly the loose ones, while her bowling (roundarm) was highly effective, and she made a number of exceedingly smart catches in the field, some of them off her own trundling. She did excellent all-round service for the Fernleas. The three Misses Gregory also worthily upheld the family reputation, distinguishing themselves both with the bat and the ball. Miss Gregory, captain of the Siroccos, made several very smart catches in the field, besides performing well with the bat. She made top score, her runs being got by clean, hard hitting, and including several hits for 4.

ROSALIE DEANE (1866–c 1955) was born into a large family (she had eleven siblings) with a keen interest in sport and played cricket with her brothers in the backyard from an early age. One of her brothers, Sid, represented NSW in cricket in two matches in 1888–89. Her nephew, also Sid, was a prominent Rugby League player who captained Australia in Rugby League in 1914 in the famous Test known as the 'Battle of Rorke's Drift'. Another relation, Hal, was a notable referee.

Although Rosalie Deane played club cricket for only two to three years, her unique performance of two centuries in a match in 1890, resulted in her becoming the first Australian woman to be mentioned in *Wisden* — a brief note appearing in the 1897 annual.

Rosalie Deane was a talented individual who was also a prominent Sydney musician. She was trained as a violinist at Leipzig, Germany, and performed publicly in Australia and Europe.[5] Her uncle Edward had been a famous cellist in his time.

When questioned about her cricketing achievements late in life Rosalie Deane put her fingers to her lips and replied: 'In those days it was considered quite unladylike to play cricket.'

Town and Country Journal *13 March 1886.*

Rather than being discouraged by limited acceptance, female cricketers raised their sights, and by the season of 1890–91 organised a more ambitious program. There were matches between city and country sides, the first intercolonial clash between NSW and Victoria, and there were even plans for a women's cricket tour to England.

A match began on the SCG on 26 December 1890 between the Probable Intercolonial Team (of NSW) and the team of the Sydney Club. Indicative of the development of the game was the fact that the match was a long way short of completion after two days with the Probable Intercolonial Team scoring 321 and 239 and the Sydney side scoring 121. Rosalie Deane produced a truly remarkable performance scoring 195 in the first innings (17 fours). When she reached 180 one of the umpires had the temerity to suggest that she get out: 'Miss Deane, I think the crowd have seen enough of you to-day. Don't you think you could get out?' She sacrificed her wicket a little later.[3] In the second innings she scored 104, contributing more than half her team's two innings total.

She later described what it was like to walk out on the vast expanse of the SCG: 'I felt like a little mouse when I walked on to the field for my first game . . . I had the impression that everyone was looking at me.'[4]

Although there was great praise for Rosalie Deane the press and the public were beginning to cast a more critical eye over women's cricket. *The Sydney Mail* of 3 January 1891 reported that the attendance was small at the SCG, the bowling was 'slightly erratic' at times and throwing from the boundary required a relay of several fielders. The players, while being familiar with the game, had a long way to go: 'with practice [they] may acquire at it [cricket] as much skill as ladies obtain at lawn tennis'.

It was reported in the *Town and Country Journal* of 10 January 1891 that the President of the Sydney Ladies' Cricket Club had left for Melbourne on Tuesday 6 January to make final arrangements for the first ladies' intercolonial to be played in Melbourne on the '16th and 17th instants'. An eleven to represent NSW was announced. The report added that 'a qualified matron will journey and take charge of the ladies while away from Sydney'. No record of this match has been found and it appears that the arrangements fell through.

Meanwhile the enthusiasm of city women for cricket was taken up by some country women. A True Blue Cricket Club was established at Morpeth and an intra-club game played on 26 January 1891. In the following month the team from Morpeth played against a Sydney side, who were reported to 'be about to visit England', at West Maitland in front of about 1 000 spectators. Rosalie Deane rattled up her third century of the season, 139 not out, as the city women 2–243 easily defeated their opponents 55 and 89.[6]

Such was the enthusiasm of women for cricket that a second scratch match between the two sides was played in Newcastle in what the reporter of the *Sydney Mail* of 7 March noted was 'an almost continuous downpour of rain'. In spite of the dismal weather, there was 'a very good attendance'.

When a Victorian team travelled to New South Wales in March 1891 to play the first ever intercolonial the women cricketers might have expected great public interest in the series. New South Wales 99 and 154 defeated Victoria 38 and 105 at the SCG on Tuesday and Wednesday, 17 and 18 March. The second

Table 1.2

THE FIRST INTERCOLONIAL MATCH

17 & 18 March 1891

NSW

1st Innings		2nd Innings	
Miss E Harper b McDonnell	4	b McDonnell	20
Miss Overlock b McDonnell	0	b Fox	17
Miss M Tunks b McDonnell	2	b McDonnell	11
Miss Edmondson c Flyger b McDonnell	0	c Fox b Carrall	34
Miss Harvey c Fox b McDonnell	14	not out	20
Miss Inglestoff run out	25	b McDonnell	1
Miss M Harper c & b McDonnell	31	b McDonnell	40
Miss Moyle not out	0	b McDonnell	0
Miss A Tunks	d.n.b.	b McDonnell	0
Miss Porter	d.n.b.	b Fox	0
Sundries	23		11
Total	99		154

VICTORIA

1st Innings		2nd Innings	
Miss Carrall c Inglestoff b Edmondson	12	b E Harper	62
Miss McDonnell c Inglestoff b Edmondson	10	b M Harper	17
Miss Fox b Edmondson	2	c Inglestoff b Edmondson	3
Miss Henderson run out	2	b M Harper	3
Miss M Rennison b Edmondson	1	b M Harper	2
Miss Flyger run out	4	c Harvey b Harper	8
Miss Somerville c Harper b Edmondson	2	not out	0
Miss Langley b Edmondson	0	c Inglestoff b Edmondson	3
Miss A Rennison b Harper	2	run out	1
Miss M Flyger not out	1	c Harper b Edmondson	1
Sundries	2		3
Total	38		105

Source: *Sydney Mail* 21 March 1891.

Notes:
1. The scores add up to 103 in the Victorian second innings.
2. It is possible that the apparent absences of three players from the NSW side, and one from the Victorian team, in the first innings, may represent inaccurate newspaper reporting. However, a similar scorecard was published in the *Sydney Morning Herald* and the same totals were quoted in the *Town and Country Journal*.

intercolonial at Parramatta on the following Wednesday appears to have been uncompleted with NSW 34 and 6–65 as against Victoria 41 when time was called.

But clearly all was not well with the women's game. There were no worthwhile crowds at the games and there was far less reporting of the intercolonial series than the first club games in 1886. Male journalists became even more openly antagonistic to the women's game: 'Cricket Gossip' of the *Sydney Mail* of

21 March 1891 stated that 'from what we have seen of the bowling ... we feel sure that it will never be of any value until the distance between the wickets is reduced to 20 yards, as the full length cannot be achieved by ladies with anything like certainty'. The first intercolonial also was something of a bizarre event as NSW batted three short in the first innings and Victoria were one short. The NSW side had no Rosalie Deane, who had retired from cricket, and none of the Gregory sisters — presumably they could not get time off work.

A reporter of the *Sydney Mail* commented on 4 April 1891 on the proposed tour of England and threw a very wet blanket over it:

The matches played by teams of lady cricketers of Sydney have been, so far as public attendance was concerned, little short of a complete failure. Presuming it is definitely decided to go on with the proposal to take a team to England, it would be very well to know what arrangements are to be made to guarantee the young ladies their passages back in case the tour does not turn out to be a financial success.

Despite the continuing media sniping it seems that there was much enthusiasm for an England tour and that it was seriously considered. Following the intercolonial games a match was played between an 'Australian Eleven' and a 'Combined Team' at the SCG on Saturday 21 March. Presumably this was a trial game for a touring team which never left Australia.

The failure of the tour to get off the ground, the limited response to the intercolonials, and the continuing press and public criticism eventually took its toll on the supporters and players of the women's game. This short five year boom for women's cricket in Sydney — when it obtained a public profile for the first time — was followed by a longer lull of fifteen years before the game really surfaced again in the media in this city. Women's cricket virtually disappeared from the Sydney newspapers until the next proposed interstate series in 1906.

The trials and tribulations of women's cricket in Sydney from 1886–91 established a pattern which was repeated again and again in many other places over the next century. The first games of women's cricket invariably attracted some general interest and a reasonable crowd but once the novelty of the game had worn off there was not much public support. Although women's cricket had a few strategic allies in the male cricket world, there was very limited media and public acceptance. Women cricketers were simply not taken seriously. In the opinion of the majority cricket was a man's game and women playing cricket was by definition something of a sideshow. Worse still, those women who persisted in playing the game seriously became the butt of ridicule. Rosalie Deane later summed up the attitude of the public to women's cricket: 'You had to love the game very dearly to stick to it because you were ostracised by society and hands were lifted in horror when you walked on to the field showing an inch of stocking above the ankle.'[7]

Women's cricket also suffered because it had a shallow base. There were only a handful of clubs and there was no cricket played in schools or universities by women. Women cricket players came from one source and one source only — backyard cricket. The Gregory sisters had gained a lot of expertise playing with their cricket-playing brothers. Other names familiar in men's cricket — Blackham, McDonnell and Trott — also featured in the early history of Victorian women's cricket. By the turn of the century women had gained an informal acceptance as backyard players rather than as cricketers in their own right.

Women and sport in England

Australia inherited many British sporting institutions and attitudes towards sporting participation. Along with games and rules, Australia imported sporting ideologies including notions of the appropriate participation of men and women in sport. British sport, according to Richard Holt, had always been a male preserve:

with its own language, its initiation rites, and models of true masculinity, its clubbable jokey cosiness. Building male friendships and sustaining large and small communities of men have been the prime purpose of sport. Women have been banished to the sidelines both literally and metaphorically.[8]

In the 19th century the ideal of manliness was a much-touted concept which developed many wider meanings and associations. Sport was seen as a way in which boys could develop character: the virtues of courage, stoicism, discipline and, through team games, cooperation with others and working towards common goals.

Sport has always been associated more with male than female culture. Medieval sports such as archery and jousting, which were linked with military endeavour, were almost exclusively male though females were amongst the spectators. Women also took little part in the more violent sports, such as folk football. However, in the 18th century and before, many sports were far less gender specific than they later became. Recent research has indicated that women participated freely — though never as much as men — in a number of pre-19th century sports including cricket, stool ball, trap ball, golf, foot races, pugilism, rowing, swordfighting, swimming and dancing.

Female monarchs had set the lead for aristocratic women in

that they were prominent in sport as patrons, participants and spectators. Elizabeth I, Anne and Mary Queen of Scots were noted hunters. Anne Boleyn was an archer and Mary Queen of Scots was also fond of playing golf. Queen Anne, a great lover of horses, played a role in the laying out of the Ascot course. Other women followed the royal example: the Marchioness of Salisbury won a national reputation as a daring rider and was a master of the Hertfordshire foxhounds from 1775 to 1819.

At the popular level there was a sizeable female involvement in a number of sports in the 18th century. In athletics there were almost as many smock (shift or chemise) races for women as there were running contests for men. From the 1740s to the 1770s there were many inter-village cricket games involving peasant women, particularly in the counties of Surrey and Sussex. With an increasing number of teams, clubs and competition, the rise of more organised cricket for women paralleled that of the men's game though admittedly on a smaller scale.[9]

Women's games were also played in a similar spirit to the male version. The scene at women's cricket matches of this time was 'robust, colourful, boisterous, sometimes rowdy and certainly often inelegant, with spectators of both sexes drinking, shouting, swearing and gambling'.[10] There are many hints that women cricketers achieved more acceptance in this century than at any subsequent time. The leading matches were advertised in the press, gate entry was charged and sizeable crowds watched. Women's matches were scheduled on the leading arena of the country, the Artillery Ground. Some of the leading patrons of the men's game, such as the 3rd Earl of Dorset, were sympathetic to women playing cricket. He quipped: 'What is human life but a game of cricket and, if this be so, why shouldn't ladies play it as well as we?' The Duke of Hamilton, another patron, attended a ladies' match in 1777 and fell in love with, and married, Elizabeth Ann Burrell, who top-scored in this game.

'The frequent recording of boisterous matches for women by predominantly male authors,' noted Brailsford, 'may well reflect interests that were not wholly athletic.'[11] It was reported in 1744 that the twenty-two gentlemen who played in a game at Walworth Common:

have subscribed for a Holland smock of one guinea value, which will be run for by two jolly wenches, one known by the name of The Little Bit of Blue (the handsome Broom Girl) at the fag end of Kent Street, and the other, Black Bess, of the Mint. They are to run in drawers only, and there is excellent sport expected.[12]

It is true, too, that even in this era there were some men who criticised women's sport — in the manner which women fear and resent most — by ridiculing it. Thomas Rowlandson produced his caricature of women playing cricket — a painting entitled 'The Cricket Match Extraordinary' — in 1811. Rowlandson depicted women, wearing bunched up dresses, romping around in what was then an undignified manner. The artist also conveyed an atmosphere of rollicking decadence, a character surprisingly absent from paintings of the often boisterous men's game.

New definitions of femininity which were developed by the reforming middle class resulted in the virtual exclusion of women from most sports. The ideal which reached its zenith in the Victorian era stressed that women were passive, gentle, emotional and frail creatures and that vigorous physical exercise was to be avoided. Sporting competition was defined by doctors as undesirable for the emotional, physical and mental well-being of women. The medical theory which supported such a view was the 'theory of finite energy' which suggested that too much physical and even mental exercise would dissipate energies required for reproduction. Prominent medical authorities, such as Henry Maudsley, Professor of Medical Jurisprudence at the University College, London, argued that 'Nature is a strict accountant and if you demand of her in one direction more than she is prepared to lay out, she balances the account by making a deduction elsewhere'.[13] Such widely-held beliefs provided justification for restrictions both in sport and in other arenas, such as the area of higher education. Changed living conditions and work practices in urban society also helped to reduce opportunities for women to participate in sport.

This does not explain fully, however, why 19th century sport not only excluded women but became more male-centred than ever before. Nor does it account for why some of the popular sports of the Victorian era, such as golf, were, as Lowerson put it, 'powerfully anti-feminine' and offered men 'yet another escape from domestic demands'.[14] Nor does it provide an answer as to why the Victorians placed so much emphasis on the cult of manliness.

In addition to creating greater social stratification, the city sharpened, and even exaggerated, existing gender differences. An expanding and more complex media set about redefining gender roles in a more complex urban society. Richard Holt has suggested that this involved not only new definitions of male and female, but also new attitudes towards male homosexuality, which came to be seen as the antithesis of 'manly' behaviour and was defined as a criminal activity in 1885.[15] There was no more interesting illustration of the sharper gender boundaries and alternative ideas of manliness than the celebrated clash between the Marquis of Queensbury, the inventor of the modern rules for the manly art of boxing, and his son, Lord Alfred Douglas, who became Oscar Wilde's lover. Since it was largely the men who were defining the gender territories — whether as doctors, clerics, educationists, writers and so forth — males were provided with the more attractive roles and with greater access to sport.

In his study of children's literature J S Bratton[16] has provided a convenient illustration of the sharper gender boundaries. Bratton demonstrated how the greater demand for and commercialisation of children's literature after 1850 produced greater market segmentation and greater role differentiation. Prior to 1850 most books were written for children in general and were not gender specific. With the growth in the market after that time there developed more specific genres: more specialised books for boys and books for girls. Books encouraged one set of attributes for boys — adventurous, ambitious, assertive — and another for girls — obedient, domestic and generally passive.

Despite the many restrictions on women playing cricket in the 19th century some were very obviously keen on the game. Christina Willes, sister of John Willes, a Kent bowler and sports patron, was a very good bowler in the early 19th century. It was said that 'Willes, his sister and his dog could beat any eleven in England'.[17] Finding it difficult to bowl underarm because she wore a full skirt, she developed a higher roundarm action when she bowled to her brother in a barn at their Tonford home. Her style of bowling impressed her brother who took it up himself even though it was not until 1835 that the action became legal. John Willes helped pioneer an important change in bowling although Bill Frindall has noted that 'it is generally accepted that she [Christina Willes] originated roundarm bowling'.[18] Since the roundarm revolution was an important step towards the overarm technique, a woman contributed to the most important technical change in cricket in the 19th century.

Some women writers had more than a passing interest in cricket. Mary Mitford wrote with considerable understanding and charm on village cricket in the early 19th century though she despised one type of passive feminine presence: she scorned those cricket dandies 'where they show off in graceful costume to a gay marquee of admiring belles'.[19] One of the characters in a Jane Austen novel — Catherine Morland in *Northanger Abbey* — 'was fond of all boy's games, and greatly preferred cricket not merely to dolls, but to the more heroic enjoyments of infancy, nursing a doormouse, feeding a canary-bird, or watering a rose-bush'.

Many mothers played an important role in encouraging and even coaching their sons in cricket. There was none more famous than Martha Grace, mother of W G (William Gilbert) and his cricketing brothers. She was as keen on cricket as her husband, Dr Henry Grace, and coached her five sons in the family orchard. Martha Grace attended every cricket match she could, closely followed the game and was not reticent in offering advice. When W G was dismissed on one occasion she was overheard to comment: 'Willie, Willie, haven't I told you over and over again how to play that ball?' She also maintained logs and scrapbooks of all her sons' doings. When a telegram announcing the death of Martha Grace reached Manchester, a cricket match between Lancashire and Gloucestershire, involving two of her sons, W G and E M, was abandoned. As such she was the first woman to appear in the hallowed cricket annual, *Wisden*. The four Grace girls were given less encouragement to play sport: emphasis in the Grace family was placed firmly on the boys and the girls figured only 'as occasional fielders and marriage fodder'.[20]

English women's cricket, which had been in a state of decline for much of the 19th century, showed signs of revival in the late 1880s with the foundation of the 'first women's cricket club', the White Heather, in 1887 — one year after the establishment of the Sirocco and Fernlea clubs in Sydney. Although there were plenty of clubs around in the 18th and 19th century, this appears to

Thomas Rowlandson, 'The Cricket Match Extraordinary' in England in 1811. The treatment women fear most — ridicule.

have been the first formally constituted club. The White Heather Club had specific colours — pink, white and green on the ribbon round the hat, silk tie and blazer braid — a leather bound scorebook, membership lists and presumably a constitution. Its organisation was also sufficient for the club to last from 1887 to 1951. Unlike many of the 18th century games, which were between peasant women of one village against another, this was decidedly a club for women of high status: 'its players were all women of independent means and most were of aristocratic birth'.[21]

The revival of interest in women's cricket, according to Flint and Rheinberg, was related to the growth of interest in the 'emancipation of women' amongst the more educated.[22] It was also obviously related to the 'games revolution' in men's sport in the 1870s and 1880s. Team sports, such as cricket, were becoming more popular and more widely organised, with new forms of competition, new heroes, international matches and the encouragement of the game in schools. It was not surprising that a number of women also wanted to participate in the sporting revolution.

Women and sport in Australia in the 19th century

While the women's game took more than a century to emerge on a more or less regular basis after European settlement, men were playing cricket from 1803 and regular inter-club competition was established by the 1830s. While the men engaged in tough competitive contests, the women's one option was to join the crowd of spectators. A crowd of 2 000 who watched a match at Hyde Park on 18 June 1832 included 'many respectable females'. The 'fair sex', as they were referred to, were welcome as they added 'colour and adornment' and provided extra copy for many a 19th century journalist. A newspaper reported in 1832 that 'a numerous and respectable circle of visitors were on the ground, and many well-dressed belles added liveliness to the scene and inspired the players with more than ordinary energy'.[23]

Women were also welcome at cricket games because they inspired the men to play better. Such was the view of the media at this time. The Sydney *Gazette* noted the benefits for men of being skilful at cricket in 1832:

Let no man henceforth set up for a sporting character whose name is not enrolled among the 'gentlemen cricketers' of Sydney. Let no adoring swain hereafter think to 'dangle at a lady's apron string,' or
— feast upon the smiles
From partial beauty won,
unless he can boast of excellence in handling a bat, or sending up a ball — the former will reject his company, the latter his addresses.[24]

The role of women as cricket spectators was recognised later in the century when Ladies' Stands were built at most of the major cricket grounds including the SCG (in 1896) and the Gabba. The principal reason for such areas was to separate the male smokers from the female non-smokers.

In the male-dominated colonial society of NSW, cricket was a sport which came to be valued as a 'manly' game which strengthened all the virtues of the Victorian concept of manliness. As in England, the opinion that competitive sports were not for women was supported by the male medical profession.

In addition, cricket and football involved violent and real physical danger which society defined as character-building for men, but dangerous for the 'gentler' sex. Although cricket may appear a gentle slow-moving game to some, there was even in the era of underarm bowling the very real possibility of physical injury due to the poor quality of the pitches and the lack of protective equipment. While there were some slow underarm bowlers, many others bowled at a fast pace and injuries were common.

Although the cult of manliness did not fully emerge until the later 19th century, rank prejudice against women playing cricket was evident from the earliest times of the game in Australia. When a split occurred in the Australian Cricket Club in 1835 'Tom the Native's' opinion on the other faction (which included the Hardy brothers) appeared in the *Sydney Herald* of 12 March. He poured what must have been seen as the ultimate scorn on his enemies: 'The natives [native-born] will play these *hardy, immaculate, lady batsmen,* £100 to £50.' Echoes of this stereotype were alive and well in the 1980s: one prominent Channel 9 commentator was fond of repeating what was regarded as the ultimate criticism of the male cricketer — that he was batting 'like a woman'.

Some of the barriers against women playing sport began to be removed by the 1880s. The medical profession, which had been totally against any form of sporting activity for women, began to accept that some forms of physical activity were beneficial for the general health of women. There is also abundant evidence that many women were keen to pull down some of the sporting barriers and to participate in the 'games revolution'.

Swimming was one of the first sports to gain public acceptance, because it was initially non-competitive and it was segregated: men and women swam at different times and even in separate baths. It was also seen as potentially beneficial to women's health. One of Australia's famous swimmers, Annette Kellermann, was advised to take up swimming in the 1890s to correct weakness in her legs dating from childhood.

Lawn tennis, croquet and golf for women became popular in

There was a substantial gathering of women in the Ladies' Reserve (in front of the Ladies' Stand) for a men's match at the SCG in December 1901.

the 1880s and 1890s. Tennis competitions for women dated from 1884 and there was a national golf championship for women by 1894. Although there was a competitive element to these women's sports, most female involvement was social rather than competitive. Tennis gained wide public acceptance as a 'ladylike' and even an appropriate mixed sport because many games were played on private tennis courts and represented an attractive new form of outdoor home entertainment as much as a sport. Women played all three sports in long skirts, which must have greatly restricted their mobility, but satisfied even the most morally conservative.

Women were an important though controversial part of the cycling craze in Australia in the 1890s. The involvement of women in this sport created public debate because cycling was a much more public sport than any of the more accepted 'ladylike' sports and it provided women with a greater mobility and an increased access to public space. But the central issue of debate revolved around costume and dress reform. The issue of whether women should cycle in a full-length dress, which greatly restricted the ability to cycle and to enjoy this sport, or wear more rational attire, such as bloomers, was not fully resolved in the 1890s.[25]

It was fashionable for women to watch cricket but less acceptable for them to play. The scene is the SCG.

Beginnings of women's cricket in Australia

Women's cricket was played occasionally and on an informal basis in various parts of the country before the 1886 match between the Fernleas and the Siroccos. There is an unconfirmed report of a match on the outskirts of Sydney in 1815.[26] There are reports of matches between two gold mining towns in NSW, Sofala and Hill End, in 1855, and another match at Yass on 7 December 1878 between the North and South when a Miss Jenkins scored 68 for the North. There must have been many other informal games, scratch matches, and even mixed games in the country which have not been recorded.

The first substantial account and scorecard of a women's game is of a match played in the Victorian gold mining town of Bendigo in April 1874. The match was clearly related to the 'cricket mania' which was sweeping the country with the visit of a third English men's team to Australia — it was the first tour for a decade and it marked the first visit of W G Grace to the country.

The *Bendigo Independent* of 24 March 1874 reported that a committee had been set up to organise a match for the Easter Fair with the object of raising money for the 'Hospital and Benevolent Asylum'. A committee was elected and thirty-five women

The new sporting woman viewed as a symbol of progress. Melbourne Punch 1897.

declared their intention to participate.

There was considerable media interest in this event though there was more copy on the procession to the match and the women's outfits than the actual cricket. The women participants travelled to the ground in three buggies, following a mounted Grand Marshall and a Volunteer Band. The 'lady cricketers', commented the *Bendigo Independent* of 7 April 1874, looked 'so pretty' in their dresses. The *Bendigo Evening News* of the same day gushed about 'the bevy of beauteous damsels, the sight of which for the moment fairly turned the heads of the onlookers'. Not a great deal was recorded about the match itself although the scorecard, published in full, indicated a win for the Blues over the Reds by 21 runs. There was an 'immense crowd' around the fence.

The women who organised this match had no intention of organising cricket on a continuing basis; they set up a committee for a particular match rather than forming a club. It was also stated that the calico dresses would be handed over to the Asylum after the match. The appeal of the game was as a novelty match as the *Bendigo Evening News* freely admitted:

Each year some new attractions and leading features are being brought out, and on this occasion the Ladies Cricket Match by two elevens ... is one of the prominent attractions ... Next Easter Fair, we will probably see a still greater advance in novelties, and teams of spinsters, or widows perhaps challenging our first elevens of B.U.C.C. or any other [men's] club to the contest.'[27]

The women's 'Australia' v 'England', East Melbourne, 1895.

Novelties, by definition, are not so successful subsequently. There was a report of another match in 1875, which featured a Miss Midwinter, sister of the Test cricketer Billy Midwinter, but there is no record of any further games.[28]

Inspired by the tour of the English men's team to Australia in 1894–95, a women's match was played between two local teams titled 'Australia' and 'England' on 13 March 1895 at the East Melbourne Ground. The match — Melbourne's first important women's game — was similar in many respects to the first game in Sydney between the Fernleas and the Siroccos. There was a sizeable crowd, an estimated 2 000, and some £200 was raised for charities. Sisters of male Test cricketers were prominent — Annie and J Trott, May McDonnell and Miss Blackham. Albert Trott was one of the umpires.

Although media coverage was extensive, it was not very encouraging. The most positive report appeared in the *Weekly Times* of 16 March which stated that top-scorer McDonnell batted 'like a veteran' and Miss A Trott 'bowled overarm in a manner which showed that the boys of the family do not monopolise all the skill in that direction'. But the other press reports were far more critical. *Illustrated Australian News* of 1 April stated that 'as an exhibition of cricket it must be allowed that the display was disappointing'. The *Australasian* of 23 March ridiculed the game and its players:

> After carefully watching the match that took place on the East Melbourne cricket ground last week, one is driven to the conclusion that Nature even in her most thoughtless moments, never intended woman to play cricket, least of all to run. . . .
>
> It is said that at practice Miss Trott, the roundarm trundler, bowled well. But when at play the ball sometimes pitched half-way up the wicket, and rolled to the batswoman, at other times only dropped a few feet away from the bowler, even lacking force to run down the wickets, which, by the way were only 18 yards apart. The fielding was just as bad as the bowling and batting and for the same reason.

The women of the Victorian western districts — where there were several active women's clubs in this decade — were rather damned with faint praise by the *Bulletin* of 27 February 1897 which stated that 'some of the ladies have already acquired such proficiency that they can throw a ball without hitting themselves behind the ear'.

It was in the country area of Warrnambool that the first clubs were established in Victoria. Teams with decidedly uncompetitive names were formed at Allansford ('Forget-Me-Nots'), at Garvoc ('Snowflakes') and Nirranda ('Seafoams') and played in a series of matches in 1897 and 1898. The games, according to one newspaper, blended sport with social life: 'Ladies' cricket in the Warrnambool district combines sport with social functions in a happy way.' There must have been some competitive edge to the games as the Seafoams and the Forget-Me-Nots played a series of five matches in 1897. The Seafoams, who won the last match, and claimed the series by 3–2.

Country women were certainly very keen to play cricket. When the Seafoams met the Snowflakes on their home ground, they had to travel twenty miles on horseback through rough forest country. The game started as soon as the visitors arrived at the ground.

Novelty and social games were also an important part of the calendar of country women's clubs. The Forget-Me-Nots took on the men of the Avoca Fire Brigade in March 1898. The men were handicapped: they had to bat, field and catch with their left hands (presumably the opposite to their normal side for any left-handers) and were permitted to bowl only underarm. The Forget-Me-Nots also took on another male team, the Victorian

Parliamentary team, at Allansford in the same year. When stumps were drawn the Parliamentarians had just failed to reach the total of their female opponents.

An even more absurd game watched by 1 000, was played between the Forget-Me-Nots at Warrnambool in 1898, and 'antique heavyweights of other days'. Their male opponents had to be either fifty years or over fifteen stone — and many qualified both ways.

There are hints in the brief reports of a handful of matches that there were not enough women playing cricket to sustain the interest in competitive cricket, or perhaps the acceptance of serious games was always conditional and limited. For whatever reason the novelty game was a prominent feature of women's cricket before 1900. Although novelty games drew crowds, they probably harmed rather than helped the cause of women's cricket.

There were some localities, such as the NSW Blue Mountains–Bathurst region, where some effort was made to organise girls' and women's cricket on a continuing and more serious basis. The *Mountaineer* of 27 December 1895 referred to the 'indefatigable efforts' of J Still O'Hara who was keen to provide 'healthful amusement for growing girls'. As an inspector of conditional purchases he travelled extensively and was responsible for setting up some fifteen clubs involving 320 girls from Katoomba to Bathurst. Girls from these clubs played in regular cricket matches. High scores were often achieved in these matches and Edith Wilson had the distinction of scoring six centuries. O'Hara had plans to take a team to Sydney but there is no record of any such visit.

Two of the teams organised by O'Hara, Tarana and Rockley — rural villages in the Bathurst–Oberon district — participated in a memorable game in October 1896 at Rockley. The visitors hit up the huge score of 567, which represented the highest total in any women's match and which had not been bettered by 1990.[29]

There are also occasional references to cricket in schools in this era. The school magazine of the Methodist Ladies' College, Melbourne, made reference to a 'girls' cricket match in New Zealand and argued that 'girls' could play cricket 'scientifically and heartily, thereby gaining health and muscle, without loss of a girl's greatest adornment — modesty'.[30] An intra-school cricket match occurred between two teams, the Possums and the Kangaroos, in November 1891. There was no reference, however, to the formation of any club or continuing competition.

Hit and giggle. Ladies and gents play at Duchess, Queensland, 1924. There must have been many other games like this. (Courtesy John Oxley Library)

The beginnings of women's cricket in Tasmania

The first known women's cricketing activity occurred at Clemes College where a team was formed in 1891. A Girls' Cricket Club, known as Atalanta, was formed in the same year at the Friends' School, and the first known match was organised between Clemes College and Hobart Ladies' College in 1892.

There was very active school competition from 1902 to 1911. When a Hobart Girls' Cricket Association was formed in 1902 three schools joined: Friends' School, Girls' High School and Queen's College. *Echoes,* the magazine of Friends' School, reported in 1903 that 'we are very keen on cricket at present and so far, we have been very successful in our matches'. During this decade Friends' School played against the above teams and others including Wahroonga and Leslie House.

Cricket appears to have been best organised on the north-west coast around the Devonport area and it was from this area that a team was recruited to play Victoria in 1906.[31]

The first matches in Queensland

One of the first descriptions of women's cricket in Queensland is of a match between the Brisbane Girls' Grammar and All Hallows' schools played at Albion Park Race Course in the early 1890s:

The Elevens were captained respectively by Miss M Aherne and Miss J Hall. The Grammar School captain, winning the toss, sent her opponents to the wickets.

The Convent girls' first innings totalled 32, to which Miss Ivy Nolan contributed 11 and Miss C Forrest 9. The Grammar School made 6 in its first innings, Miss Anderson contributing 4 of the number. There were

THE CRICKETRESS

FOR THE BULLETIN

I gazed up at the scores and read.—
"Miss Mabel Mellowflower 20"
"I might have made some more," she said
"But I concluded that was plenty
You see, the crowd are so obtuse".
(She spoke like one who ill presages)
"It may be that some awful goose
Will think those figures mean our ages

Bulletin *1885*.

no fewer than 9 ducks in the Grammars' innings. The main cause of this collapse was the fine bowling of Misses Knapp and Nolan, the former getting 5 wickets for one run, and also getting the hat trick. The Grammars, on going to the wicket for their second innings, made 20, the Convent girls thus winning by an innings and 6 runs.[32]

Queensland also had some novelty games in the 1890s. The *Bulletin* of 17 April 1897, reporting on a game played at Rockhampton, was not reluctant to comment on the worth of the game. 'The men played with the left hand and the orthodox pick-handle bat; the ladies had the use of right hands, skirts, feet, and umpires. After most grotesque cricket on both sides, the horrid men won by 4 runs.'

Other games were played to raise funds for charity. A Town versus Country game was held by the 'ladies' of Bundaberg in April 1908 and £100 was raised for the Lady Chelmsford Hospital. A return match was scheduled for Maryborough in October.

Members of the cricket team and their teacher at Friends' School, North Hobart c 1900. (Courtesy Gillian Unicomb)

Conclusion

Although there were more frequent reports of games in the 1880s and 1890s, women's cricket was not in any sense organised by 1900. There were no known continuing clubs or regular competitions though it is likely that unreported games (probably occasional) were organised in city and country areas. The future of the game was far from assured, given the generally hostile media response, though more and more women and girls in the city, country and schools showed an interest in participating in this sport.

CHAPTER TWO
ORGANISING CLUBS AND ASSOCIATIONS: 1900–31

The new woman

In the last decades of the 19th and the first decade of the 20th century a number of influential, mainly middle-class, women began to push for greater rights and freedoms in a variety of areas: in education, employment, politics and sport. From the 1880s there were some concessions to the demand for greater female rights. Women were admitted to universities at Sydney and Melbourne in 1881. During the 1880s and 1890s women also gained legal ground in terms of property rights, the raising of the age of consent to protect young girls and the right to file for divorce. Australian women received voting rights in 1902 in the federal sphere after the right had been conceded in colonial parliaments a decade before — South Australia led the way in 1892. Vida Goldstein was a prominent figure in pushing for reform and founded the Women's Federal Political Association in 1903 to support her own candidacy for the Senate in that year. Employment opportunities for women widened after 1900: there were new positions in business for telephonists, typists

Riding a bicycle with this costume was not easy but Dunlop recognised the potential of women's sport back in the 1890s.

and secretaries, and more opportunities in teaching, nursing and the civil service.

Since the arguments over women's emancipation were body-centred — whether it related to the intellectual, political or physical — there was an overlap between the various causes for female reform. Miss Evelyn Dickinson at Sydney University cycled, wore rational dress, believed in political equality and, it was rumoured, also smoked. She was the founder of the Sydney University Women's Boat Club in 1897 — one of the first bodies to bear the name 'women' rather than 'ladies'.[1] The new sporting woman was a popular focus for the wider debate about women's rights. H G Wells' Anna Veronica, a symbol of the 'New Woman', rode a bike, wore trousers and was arrested for suffragette activities.[2] A number of women who supported progressive political causes also lent their weight to advancing women's sport:

> **Victorian Ladies Cricket Association.**
>
> **First Annual Cinderella**
>
> AND PRESENTATION OF TROPHIES.
>
> MASONIC HALL, COLLINS STREET,
> WEDNESDAY 14TH AUGUST.
>
> **Single Ticket, 3/=**
>
> BENJAMIN'S BAND.
> AGNES E. PATERNOSTER,
> Hon. Sec.

Vida Goldstein became first President of the Victorian Ladies' Cricket Association (VLCA) in 1905, while prominent Sydney woman, Rose Scott, was President of the NSW Ladies' Swimming Association. Ruby Durrant, who captained Victoria in cricket in 1907, was a teacher with strong Labor views.

> **Victorian Ladies' Cricket Association.**
>
> **Grand Picture Night**
> AT
> West's Picture Theatre,
> ON
> Wednesday, 21st October, 1914.
>
> **TICKETS 6d.**
> A. McDONNELL,
> Hon. Secretary.
> This Ticket must not be sold on night of Party.

Women were equally keen to enjoy greater access to sport as they were to enter universities, politics and find new avenues of employment. After the bicycle boom of the 1890s competitive swimming came to the fore as one of the more popular sports. By 1905 some five 'ladies' swimming clubs had been established in Sydney with several hundred young women involved in regular competition and by 1907 the number had jumped to 700. By 1912 Australia had produced a number of world-class swimmers and three superstars: Fanny Durack who won the gold medal at the 1912 Olympics, Mina Wylie who won the silver in the same games, and Annette Kellermann who was a world record-holder, an outstanding long-distance swimmer and featured in aquatic exhibitions. All three stars helped to promote the cause of women's sport.

Women cricketers in Australia were as keen and enthusiastic as their counterparts in other sports to take up the new sporting opportunities. The magazine *Cricket*, reporting on the English scene — but it could equally have applied to Australia — commented in 1895 that the 'new woman is taking up cricket, evidently with the same energy which has characterised her other and more important spheres of life'. A cartoon, published in *Melbourne Punch* in 1897, chose a cricketer as a symbol of the new sporting woman clean bowling the elderly male Father Time.

Ruth Preddey, who came into the NSW cricket side at the age of nineteen, was a symbol of the exuberant new woman who was enthusiastic about and proficient in all sports. Had she lived in the late 20th century she would undoubtedly have become a triathlete and possibly a female 'ironman'. The *Sydney Mail* of 16 March 1910 was clearly impressed both with her unashamed enthusiasm for sport and her undoubted all-round talents:

This young lady is a remarkable athlete. Besides being a fine cricketer, she plays tennis, goes in for swimming, surf-bathing, and breasts the breakers, rowing, driving, riding, and cycling. In the course of an interesting chat, Miss Preddey said that she can bowl all day long. 'Now, to-day,' she said, 'I started practice at 10 o'clock and did not finish until 5 o'clock, and do not feel tired. If I were a boy I would go in for football. At cricket I am a most inveterate slogger. I have not the patience to play a quiet game. I put all my power into every stroke — probably that is why I have not taken on croquet and bowls. I have been advised to play golf.' A glance at the glow on the cheeks of Miss Preddey and her athletic pose indicates that strenuous exercise does her no harm. In addition to her field games, she goes in for physical drill, and strongly recommends deep breathing exercises as a cure for sleeplessness. She can ride a horse bare-backed, and did not lose her seat when unexpectedly her horse took her over a three-rail fence.

The climate of opinion, which had been hostile to women's involvement in any form of physical activity, was shifting by the turn of the century. Although some members of the medical profession now conceded that some measure of exercise was beneficial as a preparation for motherhood and could also be a means of curing illness, medical myths did not die overnight and some doctors continued to warn about the dangers of women playing sport. British Dr Mary Scharlieb warned of the dire consequences of too much sport in 1911:

Doctors and schoolmistresses observe that excessive devotion to athletics and gymnastics tends to produce what may perhaps be called the 'neuter' type of girl. Her figure, instead of developing to full feminine grace, remains childish, or at most tends to resemble that of a half-grown lad, she is flat-chested, with a badly developed bust, her hips are narrow, and in too many instances there is a corresponding failure in function. When these girls marry, they too often fail to become mothers . . . they are less well-fitted for the duties of maternity than are their more feminine sisters.[3]

Although there was a greater acceptance of women's sport after 1900, there were definite limits to this and only the first small steps were taken towards equality in sport. The great progress made in women's swimming occurred because it developed in a context of sexual segregation — women swam in separate baths from men and mostly in front of female audiences — which did

> HONOURS AND AWARDS
>
> 31 DECEMBER 1982
>
> APPOINTED A MEMBER IN THE CIVIL DIVISION OF THE MOST EXCELLENT ORDER OF THE BRITISH EMPIRE
>
> MISS ETHEL EMILY RUTH PREDDEY
>
> C I T A T I O N
>
> FOR SERVICE TO SPORT, TO JOURNALISM AND TO BROADCASTING.

not challenge contemporary notions of gender. Swimming for women was accepted more easily because it was an individual activity and it was regarded as less masculine than other sports — it was a sport with 'no sweat', it was smooth and the effort involved was hidden — and one in which there was scope for feminine grace. The physique of Fanny Durack was praised by one journalist for its absence of 'ropes' and 'muscles'.

Although there was a relatively wide public acceptance of the value of competitive swimming for women — in the media and from doctors, educationists and entrepreneurs — it was decidedly qualified and the sport 'crept in the back way' as Veronica Raszeja Wood has suggested.[4] Some influential persons, including Rose Scott, believed that Fanny Durack and Mina Wylie should not swim in the 1912 Olympic Games because it involved swimming in front of a mixed audience.

The response to the new woman was decidedly mixed. While women were in some measure accepted as participants even in some forms of competitive sport, the old prejudices remained, however, about women playing in team sports. Although the following comments emanate from a British magazine, *Hockey*, of 13 March 1913, they could equally have appeared in an Australian sports journal. Hockey, it was suggested:

> produces angularities, hardens sinews, abnormally develops certain parts of the body, causes abrasions, and at times disfigurement. It thus destroys the symmetry of mould and beauty of form, produces large feet and coarse hands. Its fierce excitement destroys the serene, tranquil beauty of the features, and its spasmodic climax is most injurious to the fine, keen nervous temperament of women.

While some cartoons of the 'new woman' in sport were positive, many were hostile and ridiculed women. Wood has noted there were many jokes about fashion and matrimonial stakes in press

Champion swimmers Fanny Durack and Mina Wylie. Modesty was the probable reason for the crossed arms. (Courtesy Mitchell Library)

coverage of women's tennis and croquet. The more savage attacks were reserved for women 'who were bordering on the margins of contemporary notions of appropriate male and female behaviour' — those who dared to take up 'male' team sports. Scorn was poured on those women who wore bloomers or trousers and they were 'depicted as large, ugly, or masculine'.[5] The *Sydney Sportsmen* of 13 March 1912 published some scathing 'prophetic sketches' of women's football. The cartoon appeared after a number of young women had written to the Secretary of the Football League requesting that he form a football club for them.

Club cricket

Despite the ridicule and scorn which had been poured upon the first games of women's cricket in the 19th century, a number of women set about establishing clubs, particularly in Melbourne. When the Victorian Ladies' Cricket Association (VLCA) was established in 1905 there were twenty-one clubs in existence. Hopetoun was one of the first clubs formed and from 1902 played in a number of games against the outer suburban team of Dandenong known as the 'Sunflowers'.

The names of the clubs convey the growing sense of purpose and respectability of women's competition in Melbourne. Fewer teams chose to play under delicate names such as 'forget-me-nots', 'snowflakes' or 'sunflowers' — which seemed to mask the fact that women were involved in competitive sport — but now represented suburbs, churches and even a business.

Teams represented at the initial meeting of the VLCA in 1905

Essendon	Coldstream	St James
Maribyrnong	Tally-Ho	Waverley
Hopetoun	Mia-Mia	St Paul's (Ascot Vale)
Brighton	Acacian	Hyde Park
Mayfield Park	Emo	Kew Independents
Sherwood	Loongana	St John's (Melbourne)
Dunlop Tyre (Elsternwick)	Boomerang	St John's

By 1905 games were played on a regular and competitive basis. At the end of the 1905–06 season Emo-Caulfield (81 and 64) defeated Coldstream-Brighton (75 and 40) in the final in May 1906 and became the first premiers in Melbourne. Matches were played on a number of suburban grounds: Albert Park, Ascot Vale, Brighton, East Melbourne, Kew, Malvern, Moreland, St Kilda and Royal Park. The geography of women's cricket — located more in the middle-class south and south-eastern suburbs of the city — underlines the social basis of the game.

Betty Butcher, in her history of women's cricket in Victoria, noted that with the improved organisation and greater seriousness of play, personalities began to emerge. Miss Elsie Simmons, who made 132 not out for Coldstream and had a batting average of 84.3, was later described as the women's 'Bradman' of this era. She must have been a good bowler as well as she took 34 wickets

---

MARGARET PEDEN (1905–1981) was the daughter of Professor Sir John Peden, Dean of the Faculty of Law at the University of Sydney.

After attending Abbotsleigh, where she played cricket, Margaret Peden enrolled at the University of Sydney where she took a degree in Arts followed by a Diploma in Education. Along with her sister Barbara, she founded the Sydney University Women's Cricket Club in 1926 and later formed the Kuring-gai Women's Cricket Club in 1927. The two clubs still participate in the Sydney competition and have provided the state with some of its leading players.

It was largely due to Margaret Peden's efforts that the NSWWCA came into being in 1927 and she was the Association's first Secretary. Within three years forty-two teams were affiliated with the NSWWCA. She was also instrumental in the formation of the AWCC in 1931 and was Secretary at the inaugural meeting.

Margaret Peden captained Australia in the first Test series against England in Australia in 1934–35 and again led the side in the second Test series against England in England in 1937. She was a good cricketer — a steady opening bat and a useful bowler — but it was her leadership potential which secured the captaincy. She had a keen cricket brain and was an astute leader who gained the complete respect of her team. She was regarded by them as a very determined yet supportive person.

Margaret Peden was a teacher at SCEGGS Redlands and served on the Council of Abbotsleigh where a memorial service was held for her when she died. She devoted much energy to cricket coaching and, with the help of her sister Barbara, established what are believed to be the first purpose-built indoor cricket nets in Australia. She was President of the AWCC from 1946–50 and remained a Patron of the NSWWCA until her death.

SOME PROPHETIC SKETCHES.

"When the Girls Play on the Ball."

During the last fortnight a number of letters have appeared in the city press written by young ladies to Mr. E. R. Larkin (secretary to the Rugby Football League), asking him to form a football club for them.—(Press Item.)

FORWARD & FAST

COLLARED

FULL BACK

The UMPIRE will be in for a hot Time.

On fields at last we'll pick the "fast," also the fierce and shy,
We'll also see the forward girls, as for the line they try.
We'll go each day to see them play, in thousands, yes, by Gum!
All pirates bold would give much gold to pack in when they scrum,
'Midst girls with charms and rounded arms, the plump, the short, and tall.
Oh, things will hum, that's, should time come, when girls play on the ball

Women playing 'men's' team sports were not considered attractive. (Sydney Sportsman, 13 March 1912)

The press regarded new women — such as this quoitiste — as 'freaks'. (Sydney Sportsman, 6 December 1905)

for 37 runs in seven matches. Miss 'Curley' Cheeseman, captain of the Boomerangs, scored 103 two months before the century of Elsie Simmons and was the first Victorian centurion.[6]

In this period women's cricket was starting to gain acceptance in Melbourne. The establishment of a Church of England Ladies' Cricket Association, formed in 1906 and with ten affiliated teams, was symptomatic of the growing respectability of the game which had the backing of Rev. E S Hughes, who later became a Canon of St Paul's Cathedral and Secretary of the Victorian Cricket Association.[7] There were also more regular school

> RUTH PREDDEY
> MBE (1891–1985), born on 21 January, was one of the pioneers of women's cricket. When she first represented NSW in 1910 she was aged nineteen. However, as there were then no more state games for two decades, she had to wait until 1930 to play her second game for her state. She was a hard-hitting bat and a 'swerving bowler'.
>
> 'Miss Pred, as she was known, was elected Honorary Treasurer of the NSWWCA in 1928 and was a founding delegate of the AWCC in 1931. She played an important role in the first international series of 1934–35: she was Manager of the Australian team, a selector, and even helped finance the series until sufficient money was raised. During the 1950s and 1960s she served as President both of the NSWWCA and the AWCC and became inaugural President of the IWCC in 1958. She was also responsible for the formation of the Wattle Club, an association restricted to women who have played cricket for their country.
>
> Preddey worked tirelessly on the design of more suitable cricket equipment for women finally succeeding in convincing Slazenger to produce a specially weighted bat.
>
> She was active in other sports, such as hockey, softball and tennis both as a player and as an administrator. When she was Vice-President of the Women's Amateur Sports Council of NSW, she played a role in the acquisition of two large areas of land from the government for use by sportswomen.
>
> Ruth Preddey was one of women's first sports journalists. As the Sports Editor for the *Women's Weekly* in the early 1930s she was able to write extensively on, and provide maximum publicity for, the 1934–35 tour. She continued her involvement in the media in the 1940s and 1950s covering the 1948 London Olympic Games for radio and reporting on the women's events at the 1956 Melbourne Olympic Games.
>
> Awarded the MBE in 1983, she died in Sydney at the age of 94 on 19 August 1985. The Open Age National Tournament was named the Ruth Preddey Cup in her honour.

matches from 1900. The media also gave greater recognition to the women's game and from 1902 the *Australasian* included a female columnist, 'Queen Bee' who reported on women's matches on a regular basis.

By 1906 and 1907 there may have been as many as thirty to forty teams — affiliated to the VLCA, the Church of England Association and schools — involved in regular cricket matches which would mean that 300 to 400 women and girls were playing cricket on a regular basis. Such was the strength of Melbourne cricket in this decade that many mid-week games were played in addition to Saturday matches.[8]

School matches

Inter-school matches, mostly between private schools, became more frequent after 1900. Three matches involving schools were reported in Melbourne in 1902: Church of England Grammar School versus Ladies of Black Rock at Glanmire, Sandringham; and two matches between PLC and Merton Hall, Church of England Grammar School.

A report of the final match by 'Queen Bee' in the *Australasian* indicated that the game was both keenly contested and supported by the school authorities:

The teams of the P.L.C. and Merton Hall met on the Scotch College cricket ground last Saturday morning to play the deciding match of the season. The heavy rain had made the pitch in a very bad state, and it took all the girls knew to get a footing, and sawdust had to be supplied freely to the bowlers. . . . The players wore galoshes over their cricketing shoes, and any fall showed at once on light skirts. The game was contested most keenly throughout, quite as keenly as if it had been a senior match in club cricket. . . .

The game was watched from the pavilion by a few mothers, sisters and brothers of both teams, who encouraged the contestants on more. Mr McLaren, principal of P.L.C. and Mr Vieusseux were also present.[9]

As elsewhere in Australia, in Melbourne the initial impetus to play cricket came from the private schools. This was yet another indicator that the women's game gained acceptance by the more progressive elements in the middle class before it was accepted by society at large. Women's cricket at government schools was slower to emerge, though McDonnell and Ruddell note that there was a club at Melbourne Continuation School (University High) before World War I. In this era cricket was also played at Sydney Girls' High School where Nellie Donnan was a teacher.

Sonja Lilienthal's thesis on women's sport at the University of Sydney 1882–1918 clearly establishes that at the school and university level cricket lagged a long way behind tennis, hockey and even rowing in NSW and probably in other states as well.[10]

PLC vs Merton Hall, 1905, published in the Australasian *22 April. The batting was loose, the ground rough, the bowling underhand, and some of the players were stationary. (Courtesy Betty Butcher)*

This occurred due to the slower acceptance of this game. Women's sport flourished in the more enlightened atmosphere of the university with a Ladies' Tennis Club formed as early as 1887, followed by the Women's Boating Club in 1897 and a hockey club in 1908 all of which were affiliated to the Sydney University Women's Sports Association in 1910. Women's cricket did not emerge at the University until 1926.

Tennis had an advantage over cricket in that it was seen initially as a social game which could be 'participated in by members of both sexes and could be seen as an extension of courting procedures'.[11] However, an acceptance of competitive tennis for women did not take long to emerge: the first Wimbledon Ladies' Championship took place in 1884 and was followed one year later by the inaugural NSW Ladies' Singlehanded Tennis Tournament.

Women's tennis clubs and school teams mushroomed over the next two decades. The University women played against clubs such as Navena Club, Croydon, the Wasps, the Butterfly Club of North Sydney and Kambala School. There was a sufficient network of schools playing tennis to create the need for a Girls' Schools Tennis Association in 1902 to regulate inter-school sport.

The first schools to join were Ascham, SCEGGS Darlinghurst, PLC Croydon, Normanhurst, Riviere, Abbotsleigh and Kambala.

The foundation of the VLCA — the first state association

A meeting of male and female delegates from twenty-one clubs was held at St Peter's schoolroom in Eastern Hill, Melbourne on 11 July 1905 to establish the Victorian Ladies' Cricket Association — the first women's cricket state authority in Australia. There appear to be two main reasons why the VLCA was established at this time: the number of teams playing in or around Melbourne had created the need for an authority to regulate competition and there was also the prospect of more regular interstate competition. From 1906 to 1910 Victoria was involved in three interstate exchanges.

This first meeting must have been very lively, with a great deal of debate about the rules. One male delegate, a prominent district cricketer, was keen to direct the discussions but not all his advice was heeded. McDonnell and Ruddell later recalled that he:

> brought along a 'Rule and Fixture Book' to help us form our Association. Everything went well, until some other Delegate disagreed with a few of his propositions. He immediately folded up the booklet, and returned it to his pocket. Much to the amusement of those present when an attempt was made to carry on without the aid of this particular gentleman, he produced the book again and carried on.[12]

The office-bearers of the VLCA, elected at the meeting, indicated the strength of women's cricket in this state, which could count on strategic support in high places. High profile feminist Vida Goldstein was elected President and among the four Vice Presidents were Sir John Madden (later Lieutenant Governor of Victoria) and Sir Samuel Gillott. The VLCA could also boast of some twenty-one patrons including prominent figures in politics, sport, business, the media and the church.[13]

None of the above were involved in the day-to-day running of the Association which was the responsibility of the Secretary, Agnes Paternoster. It has even been suggested by one commentator — noting that Goldstein only presided over one subsequent meeting of the VLCA on 12 October 1905 — that she used the VLCA to advance her political campaign to gain election to the Senate.[14] While this was undoubtedly true, it would be unwise to underestimate the symbolic importance of her support, and that of the Patrons, for the growing cause of women's cricket. There were many indirect and subtle ways — other than attendance at meetings — in which the President and the Patrons could have supported women's cricket in Victoria. Those who ran the VLCA

AGNES McDONNELL AND THE PATERNOSTER FAMILY

The Paternoster family, with a strong background in cricket, played a very important role in the establishment of the VLCA. Agnes Paternoster (1882-1973), who captained Victoria in 1906 and 1910 and married into the McDonnell family, wrote of her family:

'My brothers all played country cricket, and my sisters also played, so I just lived in a cricket atmosphere. My grand-father was a good wicket-keeper in England ... and a nephew, Harry Paternoster, organised the Victorian Men's Country Week Association and was Secretary for years.'

Agnes McDonnell was a prominent administrator in Victoria holding the position of honorary secretary of the Coldstream Club and also the VLCA from 1905-16. She was later secretary of the Pioneer Victorian Ladies' Cricket Association from 1931-60. Her sister, Fanny (1869-1923) was equally involved in women's cricket.

Agnes McDonnell and Mabel Ruddell, who was Treasurer of the Pioneer VLCA until 1960, produced an interesting essay, 'Women's Cricket: Then and Now', which captured much of the atmosphere of cricket in this era.

must have accepted Goldstein's role because she was still President of the Association in 1908.

Cricket in other states

The development of cricket in other states was far more uneven than in Victoria. Although NSW managed to send a team to Melbourne in 1910, it was reported in one newspaper that while Melbourne had twenty-eight clubs in 1910 Sydney had only four.[15] The fact that the three Gregory sisters of 1886 — all married and well into their 40s — were still representing their state in 1910 suggests that there was not a great number of younger players coming through the club ranks, with a few notable exceptions such as Ruth Preddey. With comparatively fewer women playing cricket in Sydney there was no great need of an association and Fred Ironside was still the driving force behind women's cricket in this city.

There were some occasional press reports of games outside Sydney. Penrith met Emu Plains on the Penrith Show Ground in aid of Nepean Cottage Hospital in October and November 1906. There was also a report of a country match at Narrabri in February 1906 where women's cricket was played 'for the first time' when the local 'ladies' led by Miss Annie Edwards defeated Boggabri captained by Miss M. Grover, by 69 runs.[16] The game was watched by hundreds of spectators.

It is likely that country games were played on an occasional basis and continued to feature novelty games. When a Goulburn team defeated a Yass team at Yass on 6 November 1906 by 16 runs, both sides played in fancy dress. The Goulburn side was drawn from members of the Goulburn Operatic and Musical Society who provided entertainment in the evening for the Yass Hospital.[17]

Beginnings of cricket in Western Australia

Teams had been formed before 1900 in Western Australia though mostly for social and occasional matches. One of the earlier Perth teams was established by the Claremont Mental Hospital staff, who played on their own oval for the entertainment of the patients. A captain of this team, Jean Cameron, became the first state captain.

Women's cricket made an early appearance on the goldfields, with the Kalgoorlie Ladies' Club formed in 1904. The team, coached by Harry Cope, practised twice a week from 5 a.m. to 8 a.m. They played matches on Wednesday afternoons on the Kalgoorlie Recreation Ground against visiting theatrical teams, such as Williamson's Opera and Pantomine Company, and drew

Eumavella Ladies' Cricket Club, Boulder (Western Australia) 1911. (Courtesy WAWCA)

large crowds. Cricket was strongest on the goldfields between 1905 and 1911 when there were also teams at Kanowna, Coolgardie and Eumavella.[18]

Interstate cricket, 1906 to 1910

A team representing Tasmania — recruited from the Devonport area on the north-west coast — visited Melbourne from 15 to 27 March 1906 and played five games against some of the leading clubs and two against Victoria. The tour 'was arranged through correspondence with a gentleman, named Mr. Rodgers'.[19]

The Tasmanians lost four of the five club games — against Sunflowers, Loongana, Mia-Mia, Coldstream and Emo — and both of the games against Victoria. But if the standard of Tasmanian cricket was not up to that of Victoria, the tourists must have been pleased with the public support for the tour. While the Tasmanians scored only 28 runs against the Emo Club, who replied with 6–106, the game was played in front of a crowd of about 3 000 and 'the ground was effectively decorated with flags, and a band played popular airs'.[20]

Victoria had an easy win against Tasmania in their first encounter at Victoria Park, Collingwood, on 17 March. The return match at the Friendly Societies' Ground on 23 March also saw the home side dominant: Victoria 82 and 5–113 declared led Tasmania 43 and 2–21.

Coldstream vs Tasmania, 1905, at the Friendly Societies' Grounds — the home of women's cricket in Victoria — now Olympic Park. Government House is in the background. (Courtesy Betty Butcher)

On the same day as this match there was newspaper talk of a NSW team leaving Sydney for a series of matches in Melbourne in late March and April. The *Sydney Mail* of 14 March noted that Fred Ironside was still the moving spirit behind women's cricket in Sydney and that 'he had an interview with a Melbourne gentlemen in regard to an interstate series between the two states'. The tour does not appear to have taken place.

The future of interstate contests appeared very promising at this time and there was even newspaper talk of a fourth state becoming involved in a women's cricket carnival. The *Sydney Mail* of 14 March 1906 noted that the Victorian 'ladies' were anxious to meet South Australia so that 'in the near future we may have triangular home and away matches'.

Buoyed by the success of the visit of the Tasmanians to Melbourne in 1906, a Victorian team captained by Ruby Durrant of Brighton visited the north-west coast of Tasmania and played at Devonport, Latrobe, Wynyard, Melrose and Penguin in 1907. The tourists won every match. The team left with both a manager (Frank Golley) and a chaperone (Mrs Black) and the fares were 'paid for by a Delegate of the Association'. McDonnell and Ruddell note that in the welcome by the President of the Shire, at one of the towns, they were 'granted the privilege of stopping the Town Hall clock or ringing the firebell'. It was discovered later that this particular town did not possess either a Town Hall clock or a firebell.

Tamworth Cricket Team c. 1900. (Courtesy Dulcie Isted and Muriel Picton)

During Easter in 1910, a NSW team, captained by Mrs Nellie Donnan, again visited Melbourne. After a warm-up game against the Brighton Club on 26 March before 500 spectators, the visitors played Victoria, captained by Agnes Paternoster, at the Richmond Racecourse (now a Housing Commission Estate) on 28 March, Easter Monday. The Victorian side 87 beat the NSW side 78 on a 'disagreeable' wicket — just a 'pitch of cinders covered by matting'.[21]

NSW turned the tables on Victoria in the return match at the same venue on Wednesday, 2 April, dismissing the home side for 68 and passing that score with 2 wickets in hand. The veteran Mrs Clymer (nee Gregory) held the side together with 36 not out but her sister Nellie Donnan was less fortunate. While running between the wickets Mrs Donnan — who must have been well into her 40s — sprained her ankle and 'was carried to the Casualty Room . . . where the injured jockies were treated, and was then attended to by a doctor from Richmond'.

This game was not without its bizarre aspects. For some reason which is not entirely clear, Victoria fielded an almost new side from the first game — May Fielden was the only player who

Table 2.1

Victoria Park, Collingwood, 17 March 1906

TASMANIA

Miss Porter, c McPherson, b A. Bryden	7
Miss Stevens, b McDonnell	0
Miss Lane, run out	9
Miss Martin, b I. Dennis	10
Miss M. Hocking, c W. Coutts, b I. Dennis	0
Miss Peart, b I. Dennis	0
Miss Dunn, b I. Dennis	0
Miss Garner, b A. Bryden	6
Miss Hardstaff, b Skewland	7
Miss E. Hocking, b Skewland	2
Miss Palmer, not out	0
Sundries	8
Total	**49**

VICTORIA

Miss V. Coutts, b Lane	0
Miss I. Dennis, b Lane	5
Miss E. Simmonds, b Peart	9
Miss A. Bryden, b Lane	23
Miss Pattinson, not out	28
Miss Skewland, not out	10
Sundries	3
Total	**4 wickets for 78**

Source: Betty Butcher, *Sport of Grace*.

appeared in both. It was probably a case of giving as many of the club cricketers (and possibly younger brigade) a chance against the visitors. It certainly underlined the strength of women's cricket in Melbourne — they could put not one but two sides which could match NSW.[22]

The account of the game in the *Sydney Mail* of 6 April 1910 also suggests some strange happenings and unusual field placings:

> New South Wales started off very quietly, so quietly in fact, that two draught horses, oblivious that anything out of the ordinary was transpiring in the vicinity, began to browse near the pitch, and were not awakened to a sense of rashness, until a fast ball from Miss Rattigan whizzed past the wicket-keeper, under the skirts of the back-stop, and out of the reach of the second back-stop. Then, startled by the shrill cries of the fields and the screams of the barrackers, the horses tossed up their heels and cantered round the course.

Victoria brought back some of its best players for the deciding game of the series at the East Melbourne Cricket Ground on

6 April and after declaring their innings closed at 7–125 (with Vera Rattigan 62 not out) dismissed the visitors for 88.

In addition to a busy cricket timetable during their fortnight in Melbourne — which included several more games against local sides — the tourists had a very full and lively social calendar as conveyed by McDonnell and Ruddell. The itinerary included:

Met by drag and four horses at Spencer Street . . . afternoon drive . . . Pictures by kind invitation of Mr. Hendry (Wirth's Park) . . . entertained by Mordialloc team . . . Ball at Brighton . . . up the river by motor boat, afternoon tea at 'Glen' Tea Gardens . . . entertained by Church of England Girls' Association . . . Drag trip to Hampton . . . Cinderella Dance . . . Coldstream social at Oddfellows Hall . . . Lantern lecture on 'Ladies Cricket' . . . farewell social.

Another period of decline, 1910–23

It is odd that after such a flurry of interstate competition — three interstate series in five years involving three states — there was a period of twenty years of relative inactivity before the next interstate contest. World War I was the most obvious factor behind this decline. The VLCA was disbanded in 1916 and the Tasmanian Association also ceased operation during the war. McDonnell and Ruddell noted that 'when the 1st World War was declared the [women] cricketers became totally involved in voluntary work (rolling bandages, knitting socks, gloves and balaclavas) and the Association [VLCA] lapsed'.[23]

However, it seems that the bubble of enthusiasm, particularly in Victoria, had burst well before World War I. The number of affiliated teams in Melbourne listed in the minutes of the VLCA from 1905 to 1914 clearly establishes this:

Season	No. of team	Season	No. of teams
1905	21	1910	8
1906	16	1911	12
1907	15	1912	8
1908	11	1913	7
1909	10	1914	5

The Church of England Ladies Cricket Association lasted but a few years, disbanding before 1914.

The pattern of boom and bust — a problem of all minor sports attempting to gain recognition — which was evident in Sydney from 1886–91 appears to have been repeated in Melbourne from 1905–1911. There was an initial burst of enthusiasm, activity and a measure of public acceptance but it did not last long.

The more general reasons for the rise and fall of cricket in Melbourne in this era are not known and are puzzling. Perhaps, as Flint and Rheinberg suggested, some of the players took up other interests or got married — the sport had shallow roots at best which did not assist it to survive tougher years. Agnes Paternoster, Secretary of the VLCA, married in 1910 though it is not known whether this led to any temporary reduction of her activities for women's cricket. Marriage, however, did remove another promising player from cricket in the immediate post-war era. Mary Martin nee Watson (b 1904), who joined the Preston side as a teenager after the team was formed in 1921, played a couple of seasons with the side before she married in 1924, had four children and was lost to cricket forever.

It is likely that while there was a strategic acceptance of women's cricket in Melbourne by some prominent people in high places — certainly a lot more than in Sydney in the 1880s — there was still not a broader social acceptance of women playing the game in a serious and continuing manner. The spectacular decline from 300–400 players to a mere handful suggests some positive social disincentives. McDonnell and Ruddell referred to some of these. There was, first of all, rank prejudice: 'young ladies, at that time, were not encouraged to go in for sport'. Then there was ribald barracking: 'We often came in for quite a lot of that, when we started. To see us playing cricket would bring forth quite a lot of uncalled for remarks.'[24]

When women's cricket revived again in Melbourne in 1921 it was as if the game had to start from scratch with just two teams, Preston and St Peter's, Melbourne. A new association, the Victorian Women's Cricket Association (VWCA) was formed in 1923. Mary Martin, who played in the Preston team, stated that the St Peter's team was not a strong one. An unsourced newspaper clipping in her collection (dating from the early 1920s) confirms this. The match report stated that the St Peter's bowling was 'very weak': Preston were 3–81 at stumps with 38 of the runs coming from wides! Earlier St Peter's had been dismissed for 32.

Revival in the late 1920s

After this period of decline there was a revival of interest in women's cricket in the late 1920s when the game became better organised throughout the country. State associations were set up to administer the game in Victoria (1923), New South Wales (1927), Queensland (1929), South Australia and Western Australia (1930). A national authority, the AWCC, followed in 1931. Interstate competition was resumed in 1930 and a regular annual tournament established in 1931.

There were no doubt many individual reasons for the revival of the game from state to state but there appear to be several broader reasons for the revitalisation of women's cricket. Betty Butcher has suggested that interest in the women's game has always run parallel to and been influenced by the status of the men's game. The 1920s, and particularly the 1930s, were periods of great expansion and popularity of men's cricket. Bradman, the Bodyline series, the introduction of radio commentary and the Depression all helped enhance cricket's status as the national game and undoubtedly some of the popularity of the men's game rubbed off on to the women's game. More girls and women, inspired by men's cricket, became keen to play the game themselves, the elevation of star cricketers providing role models for many youngsters to emulate. Australians, both men and women, couldn't get enough cricket in the 1930s and were willing to watch the game at any level — Test, state and club — played by both men and women.

The other essential factor for growth is that women's cricket developed a cadre of skilled administrators — such as the youthful Margaret Peden in NSW and June Cole in Victoria — who had the enthusiasm and expertise to create a national organisation and the vision to expand the game even though the resources and finances were decidedly limited.[25] June Cole was an enthuasiatic Victorian administrator who later played an important role both in the AWCC and IWCC.

Victoria led the way when it established the Victorian Women's Cricket Association (VWCA) in 1923 with Mrs Vera Cutter (nee Rattigan), who had represented her state in 1910, as President. The woman who was instrumental in founding the new association was the Matron of the Melbourne Residential YWCA, Louise C 'Louie' Mills, who later played a role in the establishment of the AWCC. Although the YWCA did not enter a team in 1923, it became one of the great supporters of women's cricket in Victoria and produced some of the state's prominent cricketers and administrators, such as Miriam Knee and Sylvia Faram. The Association began with four affiliated clubs: St Elmo, Preston, Semco and Essendon. The activities of the VWCA were more modest than its predecessor the VLCA and in its first seven years of operation it concentrated solely on organising inter-club matches in Melbourne.

The new association opted for 'Women' rather than 'Ladies' in its title suggesting that the game was becoming less social and less elitist than previously. The inclusion of the factory team, Semco (art needlework), also indicated another shift in the social bases of women's cricket. This was the first of a number of factory teams which were affiliated to the VWCA in the 1920s and 1930s. Factories encouraged their work force, both men and women, to participate in sport by allowing time off and providing

Port Elliott (South Australia) Women's Cricket Team, 1908. (Courtesy Christine Garwood)

equipment and facilities for doing so.

Associations soon emerged in most of the other states. A NSW Women's Cricket Association was formed in January 1927 with Nellie Donnan, President, Margaret Peden, Secretary and Ruth Preddey, Treasurer. By the end of the year the Association had nine affiliated teams and a Saturday afternoon competition.

Queensland followed suit in October 1929 when the Queensland Women's Basketball Association convened a meeting with the object of setting up a women's cricket association. Most of the players for the twenty cricket clubs which were formed were drawn from the basketball and hockey associations. Dot Waldron and H L 'Elsie' Feige were prominent in setting up a state cricket association.

A South Australian Women's Cricket Association was then formed in 1930 under the guidance of Miss Anne Stanton, a YWCA sports administrator. Mrs Rae Miller (d 1962) was another pioneer of women's cricket in this state and was instrumental in bringing the state into the AWCC in 1934. As Treasurer of the AWCC she managed the finances of four international tours and was Manager of a number of tours: the 1951 tour to England, the 1956–57 Test against New Zealand and the 1957–58 Tests against England.

Cricket developed rather more slowly in South Australia than in the eastern states and it was 'not until after the war [2nd] that we began to make our presence felt'.[26] An interstate tournament was first held in Adelaide in the 1937–38 season though Adelaide did not host a Test until 1949. South Australia was the first state to break the NSW-Victorian monopoly of the interstate tournaments but it had to wait until the 1951–52 season for its first win. Susan Summers, who toured England in 1937, was the first South Australian international representative.

Western Australia was the next state to found an Association. Following a letter to the *West Australian* in November 1930 a meeting was convened at the YWCA by Captain H D Russell and the Western Australian Women's Cricket Association (WAWCA) came into being in December 1930 with Russell as the first President and Miss Marie Jegust, Secretary. Within a comparatively short time the Association had five affiliated teams and a regular competition. The first two teams were rather unusual. The first was known as 'Trotting Girls' (later Trojans) as it was based on friends and connections of the trotting fraternity. The second team was entered by the Claremont Mental Hospital staff. The other three were rather less exotic: a Cambridge side based on women from the Subiaco and Leederville areas and two teams from Fremantle.

With the growth in the number of club teams and associations, interstate competition was resumed in 1930 when a Victorian team was defeated by NSW in April at the SCG No. 2 Ground. A Victorian Second XI, which also made the trip to Sydney, reversed the result. Margaret Peden later recalled that the women enjoyed themselves in these matches:

Certainly a picnic spirit prevailed, and officials of the Sydney Cricket Ground were horrified when several players leapt the picket fence instead of making the conventional sedate exit through the gate to the dressing room. And Victoria took the field like a football team, running on, and passing the ball from one to the other.[27]

The Australian Women's Cricket Council was established on 20 March 1931, during the first interstate tournament at Sydney. Margaret Peden, who was the prime mover behind the new national body, later described how the AWCC was formed. NSW women's cricket authorities were thinking of establishing a co-ordinating body when they heard that a group calling themselves the Australian Women's Cricket Association had formed in Brisbane. NSW administrators then sent the Queensland group a copy of their draft constitution and proposals to hold a triangular interstate series and to create a national association at this tournament. Queensland accepted the NSW initiatives and agreed to change its name to the Queensland Women's Cricket Association. The NSW constitution operated as a temporary constitution to

PROGRAMME
OF
WOMEN'S INTERSTATE CRICKET MATCHES, 1931
Victoria, Queensland, New South Wales

Saturday, 21st March, 10.30 a.m.
NEW SOUTH WALES v. VICTORIA
Cranbrook Playing Fields, Kent Road (opposite Rose Bay Golf Club), Rose Bay.

Umpires—Mr. E. M. Herbert and Mr. W. M. McCulloch.

Monday, 23rd March, 10.30 a.m.
NEW SOUTH WALES v. QUEENSLAND
Sydney Cricket Ground No. 2.

Umpires—Mr. E. M. Herbert and Mr. C. Woodcock.

Wednesday, 25th March, 10.30 a.m.
QUEENSLAND v. VICTORIA
Sydney Cricket Ground No. 2.

Umpires—Mr. M. Carney and Mr. W. M. McCulloch.

TEAMS

QUEENSLAND	VICTORIA	N.S.W.
D. Waldron (Captain)	J. Reeve (Captain)	E. Pritchard (Captain)
L. Connell (Vice-Captain)	M. Roach (Vice-Captain)	A. Wegemund (Vice-Captain)
J. Campbell	J. Day	F. Blade
H. Barty	E. Deane	D. Blake
L. Hoskins	D. Debnam	E. Bloomfield
M. Joliffe	J. Anderson	E. Carpenter
C. Lane	N. McLarty	M. Hannan
E. Little	J. Sutton	P. Knight
B. Marchant	M. Tonkin	M. Lofberg
E. Mateer	R. Tucker	E. Pritchard
Q. Mateer	I. Webster	E. Shevill
M. O'Sullivan	B. Roos (12th)	R. Kenyon (12th)
C. Smith	Miss M. Elvins (Manageress)	
C. Sneddon		
Miss M. G. Wood (Manageress)		

run the first tournament. Delegates from Queensland, Victoria and NSW met in Sydney in 1931 to found the AWCC. Louise C 'Louie' Mills of Victoria was elected first Chairwoman, Dot Waldron, Secretary and H L 'Elsie' Feige, Treasurer.[28] The objectives of the AWCC were ambitious. It aimed:

To promote the development of Women's Cricket in Australia; to make rules for the good government of women's cricket; and to arrange control and regulate visits of teams to and from Australia; representative matches in Australia in which cricketers of more than one state are engaged; and annual cricket matches between State Women's Cricket Associations.

Pioneer Victorian Ladies' Cricket Association
(NON-PLAYING)

President:
MRS. STEWART
(Nee Ruby Durrant)

Treasurer:
MISS MAB. RUDDELL

Hon. Secretary: MRS. McDONNELL,
(Nee Agnes Paternoster)

73 Harold Street,

Tel. Haw. 4897   Hawthorn East, E.3

_____19_____

The AWCC did not waste time promoting women's cricket. The first, of what became an annual women's tournament, involving the three affiliated states, was organised in Sydney in 1931. It also invited England to tour Australia in 1934–35.

There appear to be several reasons why the two other state associations, Western Australia and South Australia, did not immediately affiliate. Money — the cost of sending teams and delegates to inter-state tournaments and meetings on the east coast was probably the principal reason. There are suggestions that the WAWCA wanted to maintain its own cricketing traditions; however, the tour of the English team in 1934 provided the incentive for these two states to join the AWCC in 1934.

Tasmanian women's cricket, oddly, ran parallel to the men's game. Tasmania played in the first interstate game (as did the men in the first intercolonial) and there was a lot of cricket activity on the north-west coast in the first decade of the 20th century. But from the time of World War I until 1980 there was no women's cricket authority in the state and Tasmania was absent from the annual tournaments in the same way that the men were not part of the Sheffield Shield until the late 1970s.

In Victoria, Agnes McDonnell was the moving spirit behind another important institution, the Pioneer Victorian Ladies' Cricket Association (PVLCA), set up in 1930 with the main object of holding an annual reunion for former players and with the more general objective of assisting the women's game. The PVLCA was set up after a press report belittled women's cricket before the war claiming that it was played in a 'picnic fashion'. Over seventy attended the first meeting when it was decided to found the Association. It was reported in 1958 that membership of the Pioneers had grown to over 500 with members in other states of Australia and from England and New Zealand. The continuing strength of the Pioneers — which continues to draw over 100 women to the reunions — suggests that women cricket players have always taken their play rather more seriously than their critics. The Pioneers have even organised cricket tours of their own such as one to Tasmania in 1933. Although their primary objective was to support women's cricket, many charitable institutions have also benefited from their activities.

Conclusion

Although there were many peaks and troughs in the development of women's cricket from 1900–1931 and while the growth of the game was uneven from state to state, in this era the game was transformed from one with an uncertain status to a well organised sport with state and national bureaucracies and regular competition. In 1931 the future of the game must have looked rosy. There appeared the beginning of a wider social acceptance, there was an expanding number of players and clubs, and the AWCC had talented and committed administrators.

Miss L Brocklebank, who had joined the Hopetoun Club in 1904 and was one of the founders of the VWCA in 1923, expressed what must have been a widely-held confidence in the future of the sport:

[Women's] cricket has come to stay this time [in 1934] and it is the best of all games for young girls. It is to these earlier pioneers that we owe much for the great success of the game amongst women today.[29]

Those running the game were now poised to take the bold initiative of inviting England to tour Australia — a move which was calculated to put women's cricket on the map in Australia.

CHAPTER THREE
THE EVOLUTION OF THE UNIFORM

Sport and costume

The issue of women's sporting costume was a controversial one at the turn of the century. Newspaper reports of women's sport at this time frequently contained more copy on the clothing and appearance of athletes than on their sporting performance. This occurred primarily because women's sport was not taken seriously, and their participation was regarded more in social rather than competitive terms.

There were other reasons, however, why women's sporting costume figured so frequently in the press. In the late 19th century dress played a very important role in defining the character of women's sport and in limiting the extent of physical activity. The uniform of women playing cricket, tennis, croquet and golf — neck-to-ankle full length skirts and broad-brimmed hats — greatly restricted mobility and made it impossible for women to engage in sport in a vigorous and competitive manner. The dresses worn by some women cyclists in the 1890s also inhibited their performance. Due to their voluminous character, it required extra effort when cycling into the wind. When it rained there was a problem because the dress got 'heavy' and clung to the machine and impeded the free action of the lower limbs. There was also the additional possibility of the dress catching in the spokes of the wheel despite net guards.[1]

Costume was in fact one of the principal ways in which women's sport was circumscribed and controlled politically. The fashion pages and the media in general, pointed out Helen King, 'went to great lengths to emphasise the need to remain feminine in appearance while indulging in sports'.[2] Women had to perform in uniforms which were rather more tailored to satisfy the moral scruples of the majority than to assist in physical performance.

It is interesting and significant to note that there have been far more debates about women's sporting attire than of men's costumes. While there have been occasional controversies about what men should wear — such as appropriate swimming costumes in the first decade of the 20th century — an acceptable uniform for women has been a continuing area of often heated disagreement.

From the time Australian women participated in organised sport, dress reform has been close to the top of the agenda. There was widespread discussion in the 1890s as to whether women who cycled should be permitted to wear more 'rational' uniform — bloomers or knickers — rather than more cumbersome dresses. The bloomer costume was widely criticised, and was not totally accepted in the 1890s, but it pointed the way in terms of dress reform, doing away with hoops, whale bone, voluminous skirts and other uncomfortable garments.

Sports associations went to great length in the 1890s to define what women cyclists should wear. The NSW Cyclists' Touring Union specified precisely what uniform it thought would be appropriate recommending:

[a] gown of perfectly plain make, reaching only to the ankle, and cut much narrower than the ordinary walking costume [about 2½ yards wide] . . . It should button on the hips on each side, and must be held down by elastics attached to the top of the hem, about eight inches to each centre of front, or secured to the shoe. No underskirts should be worn, but loose woollen knickerbockers.[3]

The purpose of the elastic loops was to prevent the skirt blowing out. Another way to achieve the same result was to place lead weights at an equal distance around the skirt.

Most of the controversies relating to the next boom sport for women — competitive swimming — centred on the costume. Fanny Durack, who won a gold medal in the first ever women's swimming Olympic event in Stockholm in 1912, almost did not

Cycling costumes in the 1890s.

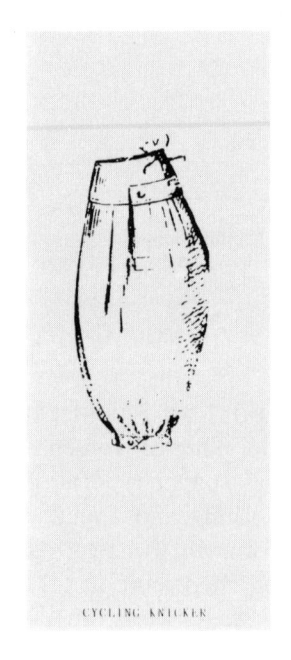

The Sydney cycling costume in the 1890s—not the most practical sporting gear.

get to the Games because the NSW Ladies' Amateur Swimming Association (NSWLASA) did not believe that women should swim in front of men — the costumes worn by female competitors revealed more than it was deemed desirable for men to see. Founded in 1906, the NSWLASA dictated that women should swim away from the prying eyes of men.

Annette Kellermann (1886–1975), one of Australia's early swimming stars who became a long-distance swimmer and a star of aquatic exhibitions, staged her own campaign to promote a more rational one-piece costume. For her efforts she was arrested on a Boston (USA) beach in 1907 when wearing a one-piece swimsuit. Kellermann regarded her part in emancipating women from the neck-to-knee costume as her greatest achievement.

The costume in other sports, such as tennis, was equally cumbersome and restrictive in the late 19th century. Women playing in long dresses and with large hats had far less freedom of movement than men who played in shirts and long trousers.

First cricket uniforms

The attire adopted by women for cricket since the first recorded match in the 1700s to the present has always inspired comment, often tinged with ridicule or sexism. A 1778 painting by John Collett entitled 'Miss Wicket' depicted her dressed in the long, tight-sleeved, softly falling gown favoured by ladies of the day. On her head was a large hat furnished with feathers, flowers and fruit! It was not a particularly practical costume: 'Miss Wicket,' David Frith noted, could hardly have expected to keep her elaborate hat on when 'going for a quick single.'[4]

Another picture from this era — a painting of the Countess of Derby and friends at The Oaks, Surrey, 1779 — is a more sympathetic and graceful portrayal of women involved in a cricket match. While there is some movement by the woman at bat, the keeper and a fielder, most of the others appear rather static fashionably-attired watchers of the game in progress.

Women continued to play in similar uniforms well into the 19th century. When an XI of married women met an XI of single women in Kent in September 1835 the former wore 'light dresses, their waists and heads being decorated with ribbons of the same colour' while the latter were attired in 'close white dresses with pink sashes and cap bows'.[5] Women players in village cricket of the 18th century, however, wore far more practical outfits. Skirts were sometimes hitched up while some reports described women wearing 'trowsers' with light flannel waistcoats and sashes. Coloured ribbons often identified teams.

Commentators on women's cricket over the years have often

devoted more prose to the attire adopted by women cricketers than their ability in the game. On the occasion of the first fully recorded match in Australia at Bendigo, during the April Easter Fair of 1874, the local newspapers outdid themselves with attention to minute detail. A rumour that the women would play in the bloomer costume added to the anticipation but the players appeared in everyday dress.[6]

The *Bendigo Independent* of 7 April 1874 reported the details of the costume worn by cricketers in the procession prior to the game:

Then came three buggies containing the lady cricketers and so pretty did they look in their dresses that we feel certain that, after such an advertisement, their match to take place today will be a grand success. Some of the ladies were dressed in white, trimmed with red and the others in white trimmed with blue. Their dresses, though plain, were pretty, and like true cricketers, they carried with them their cricketing materials, bats, balls etc.

The *Bendigo Evening News* of the same date allowed its imagination to run wild, reporting at length on the costumes and appearances of the cricketers:

This [procession] started from the Town Hall headed by the grand marshall who looked remarkably 'grand' in his scarlet uniform on his grey charger, followed by the Volunteer Band playing martial music and looking very neat and soldier like ushering on the scene a bevy of beauteous damsels, the sight of which for the moment fairly turned the heads of the onlookers. These were the fair cricketers who so nobly had come forward in aid of charity. Many cheers greeted the fair willow wielders 'en route' . . . These ladies were most becomingly attired in calico dresses, with print and blue zouavex [Garibaldi] jacket and they certainly were the principal attraction of the procession as they drove past in 3 carriages.

Although the scorecard of the match was reproduced, the details of the batting, bowling and fielding seem to have aroused far less media comment than the appearances of the women cricketers and their outfits. Two weeks after the event the *Argus* (Melbourne) ran a short article on what it described as a cricket match of a novel description and the players' appearance was applauded as being 'pretty and picturesque'.

When cricket began in Sydney in 1886 there was equal attention to the appearance of the women cricketers. When the Siroccos first met the Fernleas in 1886 they were outfitted in cardinal and blue while their opposition was resplendent in black and gold. The following season when the sides met, the Fernleas wore white hats while the Siroccos were attired in jockey caps and 'with cardinal and blue dresses, and blue bodices — Nancy Lee costumes'.[7] 'Felix', alias Tom Horan, provided more detail of the

The ladies seem more intent on displaying their costume than their cricket. Countess of Derby and friends at The Oaks, Surrey, 1779

Costume was sometimes detrimental to fielding. Pads, when they were worn by keepers, were underneath long dresses — which could be useful in stopping balls

costumes worn, media attitudes toward women cricketers and the extent to which costume constrained the players:

An excellent report of the match in the *Sydney Evening News* says that some of the 'sweet girl cricketers' displayed a knowledge of the game and a proficiency that could only have been acquired by long and regular practice. The report adds that the costumes worn were pretty indeed and appropriate, close-fitting bodices, with loose skirts, and small peakless cricketing caps. The dresses of the 'batsmen' appeared to be less 'in the way' of the ball than might have been supposed, and the gentlemen who acted as umpires were never once in the delicate position of having to give a leg before decision.[8]

There was obviously a great variety in the headwear of women cricketers in the late 19th and early 20th century. When NSW met Victoria in Melbourne in 1910 one press reporter noted the hats and colours of the visitors: 'over their hat, the New South Wales ladies wore pale blue gossamers, tied sensibly beneath the chin, and not flying abroad like the vagrant pennants of the sweet girl on the tram car'.[9]

In England at this time, well-to-do lady cricketers were enjoying country house cricket clad in three piece tailored costumes, discarding the jacket for play. Underneath the skirts were several petticoats and pads fitted over their stockings. This outfit was adopted as the official uniform of the first British club for women, the White Heather Club. Women playing for this club wore a white flannel skirt of walking length, a well cut white shirt, a girth belt, a white sailor hat, tie and hat ribbons in the club colours of pink, white and green. A sprig of heather was also worn by senior players.

Some of the aristocratic women who played with the White

Heather Club were aware of the importance of dress reform. Lady Milner commented:

> Let us not spoil our freedom of movement by encasing ourselves in steel armour, more commonly called 'the correct corset'. So much of our success depends on quickness of movement and suppleness of body that I may be pardoned for pointing out that if we are steel-bound and whalebone-lined throughout, the free use of our limbs which the game demands is rendered impossible. Women are undoubtedly advancing towards freedom of the limbs.[10]

Although cumbersome costumes restricted the mobility of women cricketers of the Victorian era, they were often put to mischievous use when fielding. Lady Milner criticised the custom of 'stopping balls with their petticoats' which was 'a favourite form of fielding with some lady cricketers' pointing out that it was 'bad form' and unworthy of 'real cricket'. However, long skirts and cumbersome costumes, on balance, restricted rather than enhanced cricketing performance. The pros and cons of playing in skirts was weighed up by an Australian newspaper, the *Courier* of 31 March 1906:

> As a rule the skirts were too long to make sprinting easy, but their length came in useful for fielding the ball. When the wind was boisterous the skirts had a habit of obscuring the wicket from the bowler, of preventing smart running and of getting tangled up with the bat.

It also must have been difficult for umpires to adjudicate lbw decisions when pads were worn underneath long dresses.

Agnes McDonnell, prominent in Victorian cricket from the first decade, made a similar point:

> Our costumes certainly hampered us, but at the time we really didn't think so. Just imagine, we certainly wore white or cream blouses, but our skirts were quite full and touched the ground. Certainly the long skirts were very handy when we mis-fielded a ball.[11]

Costume in this era was far from standardised and Australian women cricketers appeared in a variety of uniforms. Women of the Victorian goldfields in the 1890s chose a costume of ankle length skirts, layers of petticoats, blouses with leg-of-mutton sleeves, straw boaters, men's ties and black boots.

When an 'English' team, captained by Miss May McDonnell, met 'Australia' in 1895, in the first major game in Melbourne, the local press had a great deal to say on the appearance of the women cricketers and their costume. The *Weekly Times* of 16 March commented on the uniforms: 'Both sides were very tastefully attired in the orthodox flannel, though not of the rational style of architecture. The ladies wore short skirts and loose blouses and gem hats, one side with red ties and the other with blue'.

A club uniform of Auburn (Sydney) 1930s. (From left: Elsie Devlin, Edith Brown, Mavis Brown) (Courtesy Vann Cremer)

The correspondent of the *Australian*, who reported on the match at great length on 23 March, was far more scathing of the players' costume:

Those who went down to the East Melbourne Ground did not expect much play, and they were not disappointed: but they did hope for and had a right to expect grace in garments. Surely it was the golden opportunity for the wearing of rational dress . . . .

The new and advanced woman we have been confidently assured, has for years been clamouring for 'cloth cylinders' and round these — the Hougomont of the position — the conflict has raged furiously. That the ladies have won all along the line is but an old story. Yet on the grandest field for airing the well-won fruits of victory they utterly discarded them, preferring to envelop themselves in a species of white flannel swaddling clothes. More, they referred to pantaloons in terms of contempt. . . .

Having warmed to the subject the correspondent launched into a direct assault on the costume of women cricketers:

Anything more cumbersome, uncricketlike, and ungraceful than the costume the women players chose is difficult to imagine. They looked for all the world like gigantic white butterflies flapping over the grass, too heavy to rise and too massive to move quickly. . . . How could any human being expect to bowl round arm in a sleeve big enough for a flour bag, or bat with yards of useless flannel blowing about after the manner of a sail adrift, or run with a huge sack dangling from the waist and impaling every movement of the legs? One might direct the attention of women — if they are going to take their cricket seriously — to the clothes mere men find best adapted for free play of the body when engaged in the national game . . . trousers of thin flannel and a white shirt with the sleeves carefully rolled up in order to give the utmost play to the arm.

The correspondent pointed to the more rational attire donned by Miss Nettie Honeyball, the captain of the British Ladies' Football Club, who wore divided skirts, 'a kind of blue serge knickerbockers'.

Australian females played cricket in some unusual garb in this era. When rain interrupted play and created a sodden pitch the girls of Presbyterian Ladies' College, Melbourne, playing against Merton Hall, Church of England Grammar, donned galoshes over their cricket shoes and continued the game despite the damp. In mixed social games, which were frequently played in country areas, it was not uncommon for the men and women to exchange cricket clothing to heighten the fun for all who played and watched.

More rational dress

In the early 20th century, there was a change from restrictive dress to more fluid costume, with fewer petticoats and less constricting corseting and one-piece gowns. Greater freedom of fashion was first achieved in swimming and surf bathing — which became popular in the first decade of the century — and then carried over into other sports. Skirts became shorter, as did sleeves, and the exposure of female flesh became a little less threatening or shocking. However, there was as yet little uniformity in the mode of cricket dress. In Australia, some women such as the Toowoomba team, preferred trousers when playing cricket. Captained by Laura Christie, these players looked smart and comfortable in their trousers with their long-sleeved, v-necked white tops emblazoned with a star and ribbons. A team from Glebe in Sydney in the 1920s wore trousers, and they were equally common among teams in other states.

There was considerable controversy about women wearing trousers in Sydney in the late 1920s and early 1930s. A number of the players, such as Edna Pritchard and Nell Burke, preferred the 'longs' — as they called them — but they were widely criticised. Nell Burke, a former state cricketer, elaborated on this point in the *Glebe* of 14 July 1982:

Though Sydney no longer gapes at the beach girl donning an exact replica of her brother's shorts or 'long-uns', it has been left to the Sans Souci Women's Cricket Club to attempt to carry the fashion into other sport.

After the long trousers were allowed one newspaper captioned a picture of a woman cricketer in 'longs' with "Is it a girl or boy?'

The Preston team in the early 1920s in Melbourne played in skirts which reached just below the knees. Their dress contained a small slit of a few inches to allow room for the pads. Their headwear was also far more practical — they wore 'molly-o' hats and the club colours of red and white were worn on the hatband. Team members also sported a red sash on their blouse.

By the 1920s dress was beginning to become more standardised. The Women's Cricket Association (WCA), which was formed in England in 1926, stipulated a dress standard: 'WCA teams must play in white or cream. Hats and knickers must be white. Dresses and tunics must not be shorter than touching the ground when kneeling. Sleeveless dresses and transparent stockings are not permitted.' Until this decree there had been concern about a lack of an identifiable outfit suitable for women. All sorts of odd attire had been worn, ranging from tennis dresses and long white skirts to sleeveless silk dresses with striped coats or coloured jumpers. By 1931 the length of the dress had shortened to 'not more than three inches from the ground when kneeling' and gym tunics were also acceptable. Underneath it all were white stockings held up by suspenders.

Several issues dominated the agenda of dress reform and standardisation. Women cricketers suffered from a great deal of ridicule over their attire. There was a widespread belief that participating in a strenuous sport, usually associated with men, was not a feminine thing to do. It was considered unnatural by some and likely to induce bulging muscles and other masculine traits which would make them unattractive. The WCA stressed that women players must remain 'feminine looking' and convey the message that they were not copying men.[12] It was for this reason that the wearing of slacks and caps was forbidden. It was not until the more relaxed era of the 1980s that women in the Australian Test team began to wear the famous 'baggy green' cap.

By the time the Australian Women's Cricket Council (AWCC) was formed in 1931, sensible attire was increasingly being adopted in many women's sports. In 1900 women hockey players, for instance, had been burdened with long serge skirts, stiff collars and cuffs and straw boaters. Collars and cuffs were changed at half time. By the 1930s women hockey players took to the field wearing a trim tunic with a shirt and short bloomers and, as a result, there was an improvement in the standard of play.

Similar changes had taken place in tennis. The Queensland Ladies' Interstate Tennis Team of 1908 competed in an outfit

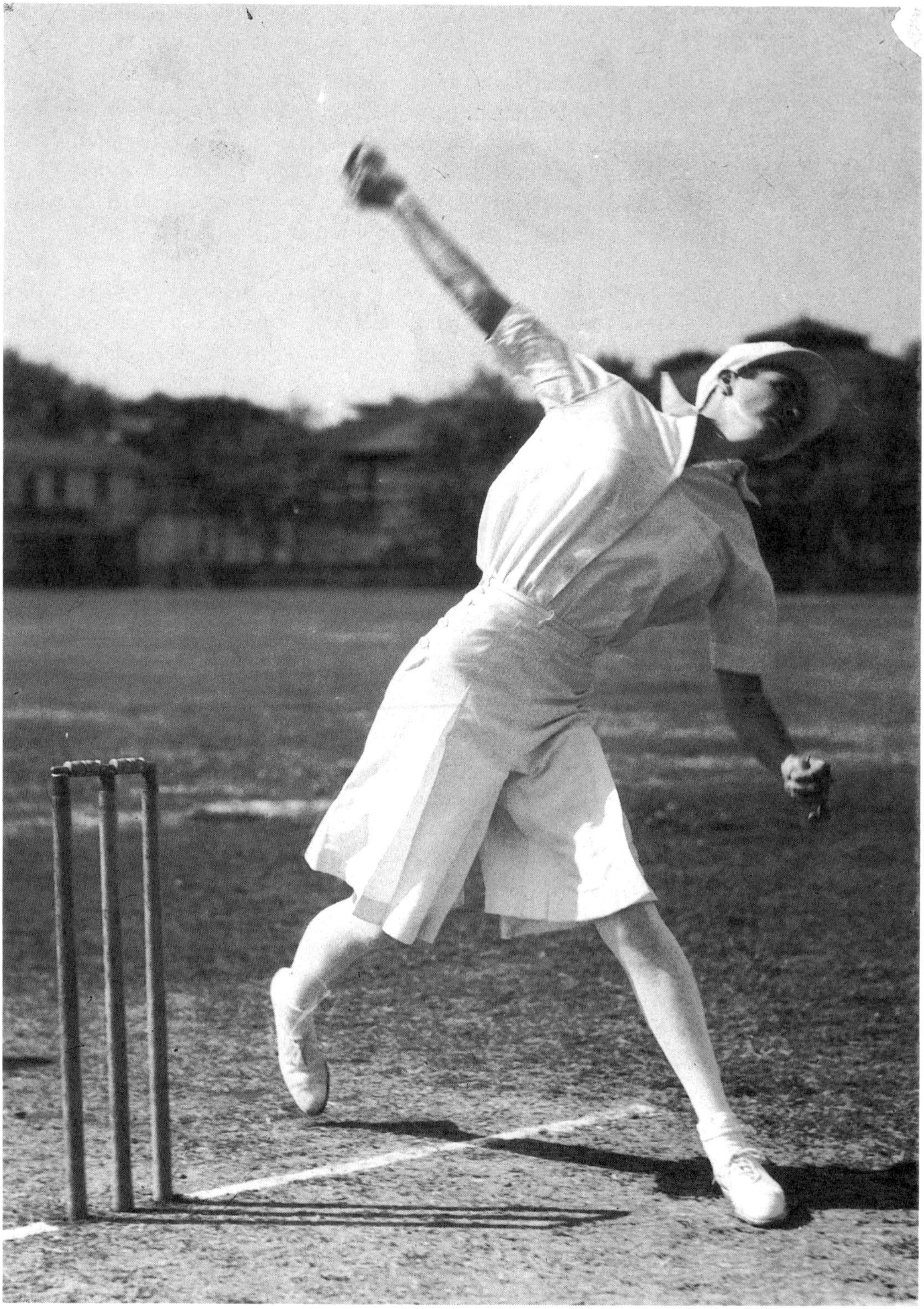

The Australian team for the Third Test, Melbourne, 1935. The captain wore a hat, three others wore jockey caps — at a rakish angle. Back L to R: Umpire, Nell McLarty, Lorna Kettels, Margaret Peden (capt.), Amy Hudson, Barbara Peden, Umpire. Seated: Hazel Pritchard, Esther Shevill, Kath Smith, Rene Shevill, Joyce Brewer, Ann Palmer; Absent: Peggy Antonio. (Courtesy AWCC)

Facing page: When bowler Molly Flaherty operated in the 1930s, the culotte was a much longer garment. (Courtesy Ann Mitchell)

consisting of high-collared, long-sleeve shirts with long skirts, ties and white frilly hats. By 1917, skirts were at mid-calf length but the legs were swaddled in heavy brown stockings with tennis shoes and, by the twenties, there had been a remarkable improvement to knee length dresses and shorter sleeves. Female basketballers in Toowoomba at this time were considerably more daring, adopting a uniform of a bandana, stockings, ties, short-sleeved shirts and knee-length bloomers. Women's rowing, a relatively new sport in the 1930s, was the cause of great concern to some in society who fretted it was far too taxing a pursuit for women to take up. Their attire may have also raised some eyebrows in 1931 as it gave considerable freedom in their limbs — shorts, a sleeveless top, short socks and sandshoes, topped with a fitted cap.

The standardisation of the uniform

By 1933 the AWCC had adopted a fairly standard uniform, a description of which appeared in the *Brisbane Courier* of 8 March 1933 when NSW played Queensland in the opening match of the inter-state women's cricket tournament:

They all wear the prescribed white dresses, white stockings, white sandshoes, and white hats. Two of the New South Wales players fielded wearing white caps. But hush! Even the women have a Board of Control, and according to Mrs E. Feige (president [sic Chairman] of the Queensland Women's Cricket Association and also an all-Australian president) the Board of Control forbids the wearing of such caps . . . The batswomen wore batting pads but no gloves and the expert wicket-keepers wore regulation pads and gloves.

Despite the regulations against caps they remained popular with players throughout the 1930s. Only captain Margaret Peden appeared in a white hat in a formal photograph of the Australian team at Melbourne in 1935; three other players preferred white jockey caps sitting on their heads at a somewhat rakish angle. It appears that the issue of caps was still considered a problem in terms of the image of women's cricket. The AWCC recommended the following to all states for consideration:

'That no caps shall be worn for matches by any member of any State Association.'

The Council members feel that while some players continue to wear caps for play, women's cricket must receive a certain amount of criticism.[13]

When England was invited to tour Australia and New Zealand in 1934, it brought the issue of the uniform to a head for the WCA. It was agreed that a divided box-pleated skirt — an amalgamation of a skirt and short trousers, known as a culotte — was the most appropriate garment for the first touring team and international series. The culotte was selected as a functional uniform which would project a desirable and feminine image for the sport. It was also a practical garment as Betty Archdale, captain of the English side, later pointed out. It had the advantage, unlike a short skirt, of not revealing underclothes when a woman might bend over to field a ball. The culottes were much acclaimed but they were a disaster after the first wash, losing shape and looking very much like a baby's nappy.[14] Apparently a Western Australian reporter described the outfit, which was topped with a white blazer, as a 'hybrid kind of one piece garment which could not be classified as frock, suit, skirt, shorts or divided skirt, yet appears to embody the features of all — a kind of white romper suit'.[15] However, the idea was embraced by Australian authorities and divided white linen skirts were adopted, though they were a little longer than the British uniforms.

Not all women in Australia were keen to abandon trousers, however. In Western Australia, where an Association was formed in 1930, there was much resistance to dress reform. Initially the

---

MOLLY FLAHERTY

(1914–89) was of medium stature and slender build but was a strong and dedicated individual who became a fiery fast bowler — known as the 'Demon Bowler' — and was the quickest around in the 1930s and 1940s. She was the second youngest in a large working class family of ten and the only one to become keenly interested in sport. Hailing from Dulwich Hill NSW, she attended St Paul of the Cross School but learnt her cricket on the streets playing with the local boys. She played first for the Cheerio Club and later Vice Regals and Kuring-gai. She took 59 wickets for 297 in 1937–38, at an average of just 5, to lead the Cheerio Club to a premiership. She later played for the Vice Regal Club and in one match demolished Kuring-gai returning 5–1. She was also a useful bat and an excellent fielder. During World War II she worked in an AWA munitions factory.

When she toured England in 1937 she surprised many of the opposition with her pace and lift and Nell McLarty took a number of catches off her at short leg. Flaherty also played in the 1948–49 series against England.

Flaherty was a determined cricketer and when she was dropped from the NSW side in 1950, she played for 'The Rest' and secured her revenge by taking 7–49 against the state side. The first ball she bowled spreadeagled the wicket of June Rabey and the force of the delivery snapped the bail in two.

Flaherty injured her back playing cricket and she had to undergo numerous operations. She also represented Australia at baseball and played golf.

She was a keen collector of clippings on sport (both men's and women's) and her scrapbooks were later donated to the National Museum.

The glamorous outfits worn by W A (Bert) Oldfield's Ladies' Cricket Team in 1931. Back L to R: Dot Edwards, Paula Krumback, D Adair, D McMahon, F Adair, S Carlton. Middle: Katie Lang, Norma Saunders, Vacey Turner. Front: Maisie Mudie (now Lupton), Evie Carpenter. (Courtesy Maisie Mudie)

only requirement in that state was that players should wear something white. A variety of often ill-fitting trousers were most popular and the Association eventually narrowed down the requirement to tailored white slacks; this continued for a number of years despite opposition from the AWCC. In November 1934, when Western Australia played host to the touring English team, the state team took to the field in cream slacks and shirts, and black and gold caps with matching state blazers.

When the Geraldton (Western Australia) Women's Cricket Association was formed in 1934 thirty-five members agreed upon a white uniform in pinafore style which was similar to a hockey uniform. During the same season, the women of Northampton (WA) organised teams which enabled them to meet socially and for companionship during the Depression. With equipment borrowed from men whom they often played with and against, the women dressed in men's cricket pants, shirts, caps and sandshoes. Players without similar sized brothers and boyfriends sewed their pants from white headcloth. After Western Australia became a member of the AWCC in 1934, the State Association conformed to the established dress regulations — a divided box-pleated skirt and white stockings — when they participated in the interstate competition in 1936.

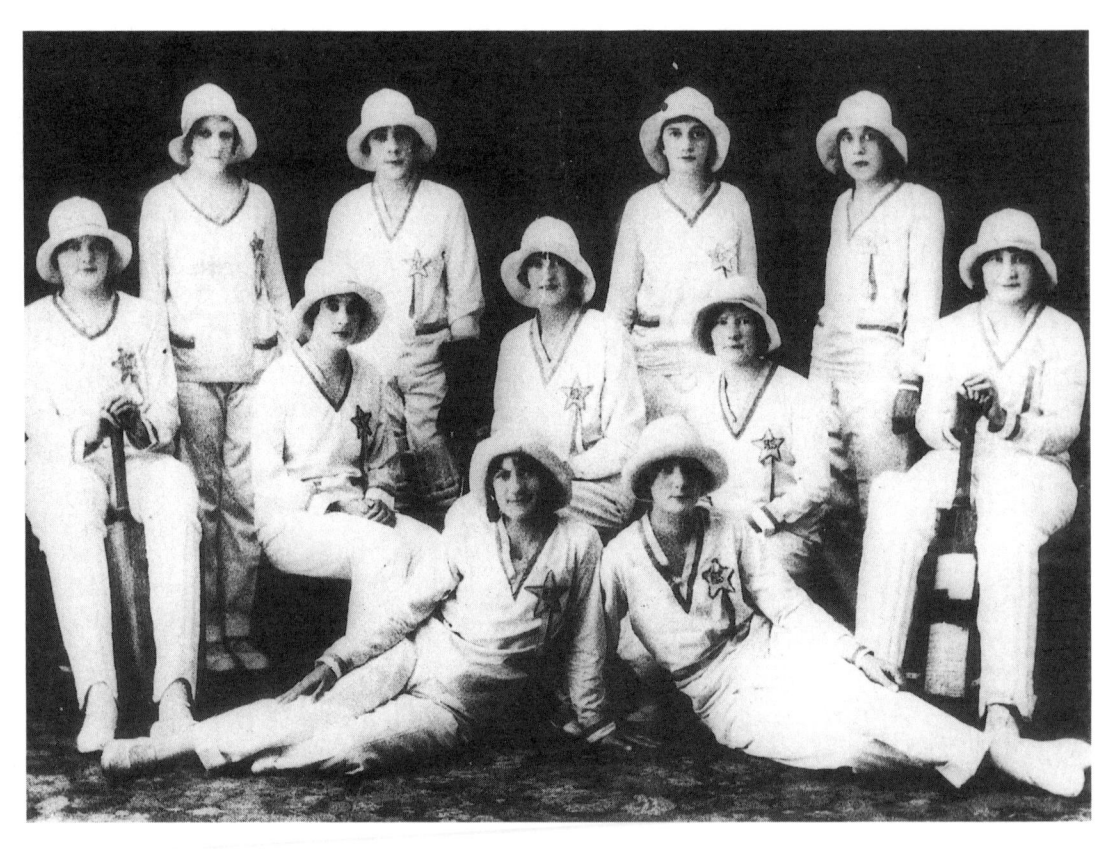

The contemporary uniform

By the 1940s women were freed of long stockings and suspender belts and played in long socks. The official uniform which was established then is the one still in force. It consists of culottes (a divided box-pleated skirt), white shirt, long white socks and caps or hats. Over the years, culottes have become progressively shorter, no doubt in keeping with fashion trends. It is only in the last few years that manufacturers have been producing culottes commercially as previously there had never been a perceived market for them. Initially players made their own, using a standard pattern which was passed around; later a Melbourne tailor was able to accommodate the Australian team. In recent times some of the larger manufacturers, such as Symonds and Gray Nicolls, have tested the market and now it has become much easier to purchase culottes through retailers. The Kingsgrove Sports Centre in Sydney, for example, made a marketing decision from 1981 to target women cricketers by supplying culottes along

Trousers were popular in a number of states in the 1920s and 1930s. Toowoomba Ladies' Cricket team (1928), Laura Christie (captain). (Courtesy John Oxley Library)

Kuring-gai Club team, Central Park, Willoughby in the 1950s. Some of the younger players wore shorter culottes and one player appears to be wearing a dress. Back L to R: Pat Press, Pat Weston, Norma Stanfield, Lilias (Bill) Henderson, Joan Rae, Front: Hazel Perty, Jean Sutton, Pearl Cottle, Thelma Hodges. (Courtesy Jean Sutton)

with other cricketing accessories and has even designed bats especially for women.

According to Ann Mitchell, president of the AWCC and former manager of the Australian Women's Cricket team, some of the first culottes presented problems because they were often cut wrongly and they did not always sit well on some figures. Sylvia Faram reported that there was often a problem with the longer culottes of the 1930s and 1940s, which could catch over the top of the pad. This problem has been alleviated with the shortening of the length of the culotte.

The contemporary uniform of women cricketers still attracts a degree of comment, often both unfair and unflattering, from the media and even players. There are those who still argue in favour of trousers, which is the uniform worn by women cricketers in India, the West Indies and Holland. Yet others advocate knickerbockers and a dash of colour. Culottes attract criticism for the lack of protection they provide against sun, wind, rain, and for exposed knees. Until the recent introduction of velcrum straps, there was also a problem, noted Betty Butcher, in the tendency of the buckles on the pad straps to scratch the back of the legs. Women in Melbourne were encouraged 'to have the buckles outside' which was the opposite practice to men's cricket: they wore pads 'with buckles inside to prevent the ball hitting the buckle and being mistaken for a snick'.[16] It is also extremely difficult to wear a thigh pad with comfort underneath a pair of culottes yet the rules clearly stipulate that this is the only acceptable position. But, on the positive side, they do provide great freedom of movement and are cool on a hot day.

In India and the West Indies, where women's cricket really began to get off the ground in the 1960s, long pants were and still are worn, following the tradition of men. Probably because of strong cultural taboos in India against the exposure of flesh (in terms of legs), there was never any question of women playing in culottes. It is ironic that while Indian culture has dictated that women play in trousers, Australian culture has determined the opposite. In Holland women traditionally preferred trousers to culottes. Ann Mitchell believes that the majority of Australian women prefer culottes though she can appreciate the arguments in favour of trousers. The future of culottes, Mitchell argued, is very much associated with the creation of an acceptable image for the sport. 'We have an image problem in Australia,' she pointed out, and 'as a result there have been times when women felt uncomfortable about saying that they played cricket.' Since cricket has always been defined as a man's sport, many in the media and the general public have stereotyped all those women who play cricket as 'mannish'. The Australian preference for the culotte rather than trousers has been an attempt to correct this image by clothing women in a more feminine uniform. Ann Mitchell has no doubts about the consequence of changing from culottes to trousers: 'if we take to wearing trousers, we may well be accused of being butch.' The issue of acceptable women's costume is both a delicate and a sensitive one for women administrators, as Mitchell commented further:

If we are sensitive, it's because of some of the ridiculous things that have been written or suggested by the men involved in sports journalism. We tread a thin line. Some people do feel very strongly about changing the uniform and it is the same in other sports like tennis where women continue to wear skirts rather than shorts.

In 1951 the Australian team arrived in London and created a new trend in fashions off the field. Their stylish walking out uniforms of grey skirts, white blouses, grey felt hats and green blazers with name badges impressed other countries such as England and New Zealand which soon followed suit. During the 1968–69 tour of Australia, it was England that created a stir with a very smart and colourful range of 'stepping out' clothing which had a revolutionary effect on Australian players. The image of the Australian team

---

ANN MITCHELL OAM (b 1945) did not get a chance to play cricket until 1962 when she was a student at the University of Sydney. Before that her cricket was restricted to backyard rousabouts with her brothers. By 1964–65 she was picked for the NSW juniors before playing for her state from 1967 to 1983. She toured New Zealand as a member of the Australian team in 1975.

It is administration that is Mitchell's forte. She began as Secretary of the Sydney University Club in 1963, became President of the NSWWCA from 1974–1988 and was delegate to the AWCC from 1968–1988. She was President of the IWCC from 1982–88 and has been President of the AWCC since 1988.

Ann Mitchell has managed many cricket teams including NSW Juniors, Under 25s and Seniors in the 1970s and was Australian team manager from 1977 to 1988 — a period in which the national side lost only one international series. She resigned her position as Manager of the Australian team when she took on the job as Director of the University of Sydney Women's Sports Association.

One of Mitchell's greatest achievements has been the creation of an increased public awareness of women's cricket through extended media coverage. She has also been instrumental in creating greater sponsorship, initiating development schemes, and enhancing training and coaching schemes.

Ann Mitchell reflected in the *Sydney Morning Herald* of 6 July 1988.

'I always say that I could have been a millionaire. Every year for a very long time I have spent thousands of dollars on travelling and accommodation during tours. Now I don't own a house. And maybe my health has suffered . . . and I'm getting too old for a loan now, but I do have friends in every State, and I'd like to think I have stimulated interest [in women's cricket] in Australia.'

Ann Mitchell was awarded an OAM in 1991 for her services to women's cricket.

The shorter culottes of the 1980s. Australians appealing exuberantly in England 1987. From left: Denise Annetts, Lindsay Reeler, Chris Matthews, Sally Griffiths and Lyn Larsen (captain). (Courtesy Lindsay Reeler)

today is a positive one and for the last three years they have stepped out of their whites and into the vibrant Desert Designs range, an Aboriginal label. They set an example for teams such as the NSW State side which, in 1989, were fitted with white dresses adorned with hand-painted Waratahs.

Colour in the playing uniform may now not be a far-fetched idea as, according to Ann Mitchell, coloured uniforms are being considered for the 1993 World Cup in England. If colour is introduced into international cricket for women, it could eventually filter down to the club level; currently in grade cricket, colour is permitted only in caps or on jumpers. Colourful State emblems appeared on representatives' shirts by the mid 1980s: approval was granted for NSW to sew a Waratah on the shirt pocket and Victoria was allowed a big V. South Australia, however, was refused its first application to the AWCC for a whole red pocket. At the same time, State colours were allowed on sleeves and for edging on jumpers.

During the 1988 World Cup, the Australian team received socks from sponsors Interknit which were trimmed with the national colours. This style had already been introduced at PLC

> **WOMEN'S CRICKET IN NEW SOUTH WALES QUEENSLAND & VICTORIA**
>
> **INTER-STATE MATCHES**
>
> This year, for the first time in the history of women's cricket in Australia, a series of matches has been arranged in which teams from three States, Queensland, Victoria and New South Wales, are playing.
>
> The first Interstate match arranged by the New South Wales Women's Cricket Association were two matches played on the Sydney Cricket Ground No. 2 in April, 1930, when a Victorian Eleven played a match against the First Eleven of New South Wales and also a match against the Second Eleven of New South Wales. New South Wales won the First Eleven match and Victoria the Second Eleven match.
>
> **AUSTRALIAN WOMEN'S CRICKET COUNCIL**
>
> A constitution for an Australian Women's Cricket Council has been drafted, and delegates from the Women's Cricket Associations of Queensland, Victoria and New South Wales appointed.
>
> The objects of the Council are, *inter alia*, to arrange, control and regulate visits of teams to and from Australia, representative matches in Australia in which cricketers of more than one State are engaged, and an annual cricket carnival between State Women's Cricket Associations.
>
> DELEGATES TO THE COUNCIL.
> Victoria: Miss D. Hosking, Miss M. Elvins, Miss I. Webster.
> Queensland: Miss M. G. Wood, Mrs. D. Waldron.
> New South Wales: Miss M. Peden, Miss E. Pritchard, Miss E. Preddey.
>
> **Have You Seen the New Cricket Frock?**
> Such a comfortable, sensible one-piece frock, and how smart it is! The shirt type blouse joins to a divided skirt. A skirt that is really shorts with wide legs but with pleats that make them look like the usual sports skirt. Made in your own Club Colours at 25/-.
>
> **DAVID JONES' - SYDNEY**

David Jones recognised the market potential of the culotte in 1931.

Pymble, and some other private schools then copied the look. Ann Mitchell subsequently experimented with a shirt adorned with a very bold green and gold graphic design with the logo 'Shell Bicentennial World Cup'. It was not recognised as an official uniform but was used to effect during warm-up matches against State sides. However, the idea was not well received by the IWCC as some of its members, stated Mitchell, objected to sponsorship on playing uniforms.

Conclusion

Appearance and clothing continue to play a bigger role in women's sport than it does for men's games. While a number of young men have begun to play lawn bowls as the men's uniform does not discourage youthful participants, the costume for women helps to maintain its status as a game for more mature females. The costume of women bowlers — the long dress and white stockings — provides a strong disincentive for younger women to pursue this sport.

Those who run women's sports have the added burden of designing a uniform which will attract the young to the game but at the same time project the appropriate image for the community. It is a burden placed on women's sports by a society which has not yet learnt to fully accept female participation in previously masculine domains. In a sense the culotte is a compromise between what women's cricket authorities would like to have and what they must accept. However, in recent times shorter versions of the 'pragmatic' culotte have made it more fashionable and have increased its popularity amongst players. The culotte even became a fashion item for everyday dress by 1990.

The greater variety in the uniform of the women cricketers from one country to another underlines that it is far more difficult to arrive at a standard costume in a women's sport than in men's. While the men's cricket costume was standardised at a relatively early stage in its development, the standards for women have varied considerably over the past century.

CHAPTER FOUR

EXPANSION AND ACCEPTANCE: THE GOLDEN DECADE OF THE 1930s

The 1930s were the golden years of Australian women's cricket. The bold moves of the administrators to expand the game were more successful than the organisers might have hoped. There was growth in the game at all levels — club, interstate and international — and there was a dramatic rise in the number of women and girls playing cricket on a regular basis. Equally impressive was the fact that women's cricket was no longer the exclusive preserve of middle-class 'ladies' or private school girls; it was now played right across the social spectrum with state schools, working class suburbs, factories and major chain stores all entering teams in competitions. There was expansion in all states in both the city and the country.

Women's cricket, really for the first time, drew substantial crowds which continued to support the game at all levels throughout this decade. Daily crowds of around 5 000 were not uncommon at the women's Test matches of this era and provided the hope that the women's game could be established on a more secure financial basis. There were also crowds of up to 3 000 at some suburban club matches indicating that the local community was both supportive and interested in their team.

Even more important was the media support and public acceptance of the women's game. Full page spreads on women's cricket appeared in some of the major city newspapers, and popular magazines, such as the *Women's Weekly*, had a regular report on the game. The AWCC itself started a magazine of its own, *Australian Women's Cricket*, which appeared for the first time in March 1938. Edited by Dot Debnam, this sixteen page magazine retailed at 3d.

Women cricketers also had the opportunity to play in what the *Sydney Morning Herald* of 10 November 1930 claimed was the first ever 'night' game at the Sydney Sports Ground, although the 'lighting of the ground was not altogether satisfactory'. The match, which attracted a large crowd, was organised by the City Girls' Amateur Sports Association to honour the recently-returned Australian men cricketers who were pitted against some of the leading women players. Prior to the match there was a lantern parade of 800 female cricketers from some forty-three clubs.

Before 1930 women's cricket was a fringe activity existing on the sporting margins but during this decade the game started to become part of the sporting mainstream and its leading exponents began to enjoy some of the adulation hitherto reserved for the men's game. Test player Peggy Antonio (b 1917), who played cricket with boys in the street in the 1920s, recalled that she had no idea that 'girls' teams' existed. Nell McLarty (b 1912) was equally surprised to come across a group of women playing cricket at Albert Park (Melbourne) because she too had no idea that women played this game. Soon after she was roped in to play club cricket when the Clarendon Club was one short. Although she had only ever bowled with a tennis ball, McLarty achieved the remarkable figures of 7–2 in her first club game. Her experience of cricket had previously been limited to informal street games because all that was offered to girls at her school was basketball and rounders — cricket was unheard of.[1]

Reminiscing on women's cricket in the 1930s Nell McLarty and Peggy Antonio stated:

Yes, we were taken seriously [as cricketers], I think much more than now . . . . We got heaps of publicity in 1934. The Melbourne *Herald* sometimes ran a whole page feature (including photographs) on women's cricket. . . . It was quite common for people, unknown to either of us, to come up to us on the street and say: 'Hello Nell' or 'Hello Peg'. . . Although women's cricket gets far more promotion to-day, they seem to have less acceptance than we had.

Women's cricket in the 1930s appeared ready for 'take off', to change its status from a minor sport to a more popular and widely-accepted game approaching perhaps the status of the men's game.

Club cricket was sufficiently prominent to attract the attention of cartoonists. (Courtesy Eileen Smith, nee Milham)

Club cricket

When 10-year-old Betty Wilson went to watch a women's club game at Mayor's Park, Clifton Hill, in the 1932–33 season, she was part of a crowd of over 1 000 which was three to four deep all around the perimeter of the playing field. Nell McLarty recalls playing club games in front of 3 000 at the home of Collingwood at Clifton Hill. The crowd took an active interest in the proceedings: there was plenty of barracking and even betting — 3d bets were popular — on the game.

While the size of this crowd may have been partly due to the Depression — local entertainment which was free was well supported — it also reflected a remarkable shift in the movement of women's cricket. In the early 1930s the women's game had spread from the middle class suburbs, such as Brighton and Kew, to more working class suburbs such as Collingwood.

Collingwood was in fact one of the stronger clubs around in the 1930s, playing the district final against Clarendon in

> **PEGGY ANTONIO**
> (b 1917), a diminutive — just over 5 ft, (c 153 cm) —right-arm leg-spin and googly bowler is generally regarded as one of the finest spinners to have ever represented Australia.
>
> Born into a Spanish-Australian working class family she developed an interest in cricket by playing the game with boys in back streets before joining the Collingwood Club. She was fortunate to work at Raymond's Box Factory — a supporter of women's cricket — where she made cardboard boxes. She represented Victoria at the age of fifteen and just two years later played in the first ever Test series taking 12 wickets at a cost of 18.25. She was even more successful on the tour of England taking 19 wickets at a cost of 11.20. Although she had an easy and natural action, she worked hard at her game — sometimes bowling all day Sunday under the watchful eye of her coach, club cricketer Eddie Conlon. She had some good scores with the bat on the 1937 tour including 103 not out against Lancashire.
>
> Peggy Antonio married shortly after the tour and reared a family of four, retiring from cricket when she was only twenty.
>
> Her skill as a bowler and her unassuming personality made her a popular figure with cricket crowds. In recognition of her talent she was referred to as the 'girl Grimmett'.

1932–33, and boasting prominent cricketers such as Peggy Antonio and Nell McLarty, who were both from working class backgrounds. Many of the women who played and watched cricket no longer came from private schools such as Merton Hall or PLC. Betty Wilson herself was the daughter of a boot maker who attended Victoria Park State School. Antonio, McLarty and Wilson all left school at age fourteen to work. Some of the players in other states, such as Amy Hudson in NSW, also came from working class backgrounds.

There was a dramatic growth in the number of club teams in Melbourne in the 1930s: there were four in 1923, five or six by 1930 and thirty-nine by 1939, which meant that there must have been about 400 to 500 women involved in regular club cricket. The range of teams also underlines the widening appeal of the women's game, which attracted players from a broad social spectrum. The Semco factory team of 1923 was followed by two other factory teams: Pelaco (shirt manufacturers) fielded a team from 1931, and at one time supported two teams, and Raymond's shoe factory joined in the same year. The Labor Social Club had enough players to enter two teams and the YWCA also joined the competition. Factory and retail teams, such as Pelaco, David Jones and Oldfield's, also emerged in NSW.

The factory teams could boast some of the best players in the state. Peggy Antonio, who made cardboard boxes at Raymond's, found employers who were sympathetic to her sporting interests and she never had trouble getting time off to play the game. Elsie Deane, who played for the Brunswick Club from 1925 to 1929, was invited to join Semco at the age of twenty as a supervisor in the roller department, and also to double as a 'sports mistress' coaching the women's cricket and basketball teams. Deane was a prominent cricketer who became Captain of Victoria and Vice Captain of the 1937 Australian team.

Factories supported women's cricket in many ways providing time off for practice and play, equipment and coaching, and the use of suitable grounds often near to the factory itself. There were also smaller and more subtle means of support such as providing afternoon tea for the players. Semco provided refreshments in the work room at their picturesque Black Rock Oval.

Women's cricket also received support from other businesses which may not have entered a club team. Nell McLarty, who was a machinist in Henry Buck's, reported that the management was thrilled when she was selected to play for Australia in 1934. The factory at Henry Buck's helped McLarty by making eight shirts for her after she provided the material.

The popularity of Sunday charity games in this time provides a measure both of the acceptance and support of women's cricket teams. Games, played in a 'picnic atmosphere', were organised against various men's teams including the fire brigade, air force, navy and various radio stations. Those who played in the games recall that they were both interesting and enjoyable.

During the 1930s women's cricket in Melbourne also made some inroads into the public school system. An article in *Australian Women's Cricket* in March 1938 stated that 'every high school, with the exception of Coburg, has taken up cricket, and that the game has met with the approval of the girls is evidenced in the large numbers that turn out for the practice'. Women's cricket was played at the following schools: high schools at Dandenong, Frankston, Mac Roberston, University, Williamstown; Sunshine Technical School and Preston and Richmond Girls' Schools. The growth of school cricket provided a good nursery for club cricket. Two former captains of the cricket team at Mac Roberston, Margaret Frey and Billie Hargraves, had graduated to the ranks of the Clarendon Club by 1938. Another club, Ramblers, secured the services of Nancy Kinneburgh, who was both a fine athlete and dux of Hampton High School.

In previous decades women's cricket appears to have been based more on a small number of elite private schools. School teams represent a vital cog in the chain of recruitment between

Some prominent male cricketers, including Bert Oldfield, supported women playing cricket in the 1930s. This advertisement appeared in Australian Women's Cricket.

LADY CRICKETERS!

SEE and USE

BERT OLDFIELD'S SPECIAL EQUIPMENT

TWO BAT SPECIALS!

THE FAMOUS GUNN AND MOORE "AUSSIE" 27/6
THE LATEST GRADIDGE LADIES' MODEL 21/-

BATTING PADS, Canvas, 12/6, 15/-, 17/6; Buckskin, 15/-, 17/6, 25/-.
BATTING GLOVES, Pull-on Type, 8/6, 9/6 pr.; Wrap-round, 8/6, 9/6 pr.
CRICKET SHOES, Canvas, Leather or Rubber Soles, 14/11 pr.
WHITE HATS, 3/11.
CRICKET BALLS, fully guaranteed, Crown 7/6, Peerless 8/6.

LADIES! AVAIL YOURSELVES OF
OUR EASY REPAYMENT SYSTEM

BERT OLDFIELD'S SPORTS STORE
54 HUNTER STREET, SYDNEY, N.S.W.   Phones BW4257-8

informal backyard and street games and club cricket, and without that link many potential club cricketers must have been lost to the game. As well as providing the first real introduction to more serious team cricket, school teams also represent a form of legitimacy and community support for the women's game.

There was a similar expansion of club cricket in the other states, particularly in NSW. After the NSWWCA was formed in 1927 the *Sydney Morning Herald* reported on 6 January 1928 that there were already nine or ten affiliated teams, representing a broad cross section of society including the City Girls' Amateur Sports Association, Hazelbank School, women employees of the Public Trustee, the Registrar-General, and the Agricultural Departments, along with Sydney University undergraduates and students at the Teachers' College. There was rapid growth by 1930 as reported by Ruth Preddey in the *Coaching Magazine* of the NSWCA on 1 November 1930:

> The women's cricket season opened with 10 first grade teams, 23 second grade teams, and 4 teams in the late-comers' division. Vice-Regals are running a weekly competition, and there are also five teams playing in the morning division. This brings the number of teams playing in the metropolitan district to 48.
>
> The Association is expecting the following country teams to affiliate: Goulburn (19 teams), Canberra, Thirroul and Northern Rivers.

Indicative of the strength of cricket in NSW was the formation of two new associations in 1931–32. Four clubs — Fernleigh, Forest Lodge, South Sydney and Whoopee — banded together to form a new association which competed as a division of the second grade competition. No less than eleven teams were affiliated to the Illawarra Women's Cricket Association when it was established: Bellambi, Catholic, Coniston, Corrimal, Helensburgh, Mt Keira, Mt Kembla, Port Kembla, Thirroul, Waratahs, Wollongong. If these additional clubs are added to the sixty-seven mentioned by Preddey in 1930, there were a total of eighty-one clubs involved in women's cricket in NSW and possibly around one hundred teams if school cricket was as widespread as in Victoria.

The formation of an association on the south coast was a result of a 'missionary' tour organised by Margaret Peden consisting of members of her Kuring-gai Club augmented by the Shevill sisters of the Sans Souci Club. With the aim of 'spreading the word about women's cricket' Peden's team camped in tents and were referred to as the 'horse and cart team'. Although the Illawarra Association did not last beyond the 1930s it did produce Ruby Monaghan, who played for Australia in 1934.

The affiliation of so many teams suggests that there must have been informal competition in the Wollongong area before 1931. The strength of women's cricket in the more working-class city of Wollongong also suggests that the game in New South Wales was spreading beyond the confines of the middle class, as in Victoria. The existence of a Catholic team also provides the hint that the game was reaching out from its initial Anglican and Protestant support base.

There was similar growth in club cricket in other states. Clare Papasergio and Janice Moy, in their history of the game in Western Australia, noted that the tour of the English women in 1934–35 was a great stimulus and there were nine teams playing in Perth on Saturday afternoons, representing possibly about 150 women, who were affiliated to the state association. The teams were: Fremantle Suburban, Fremantle Rovers, Cambridge, Western Girls, Trotting Girls, Claremont Mental Hospital, Maylands, City, and Ideal Kookaburras. By World War II a few more teams had been added including Coles and Foys — suggesting that retail establishments in addition to factories were supportive of the women's game. Although there was much support for women's cricket in the west, the Perth City Council turned down a request for a turf wicket to be laid down on Birdwood Square. The women had to be content with a matting-covered concrete strip at the Esplanade.[2]

By the end of the 1930s club cricket was established in the major cities on a firm footing. Some of the clubs formed in the 1920s and 1930s, such as Sydney University (1926), Kuring-gai (1927) and Hawthorn (1933), have continued to operate ever since (with an occasional break of a year), unlike many other clubs in Melbourne formed after 1905 which all folded after a few years. Women's cricket also appeared to have had greater social depth in Australia than in England. Whereas the English team of 1934 consisted almost entirely of well-educated middle-class women, Australia had a more mixed team with university-educated alongside working-class women.[3]

Although the figures are rather scanty, it is possible to arrive at an educated guess as to the number of women and girls playing cricket in the 1930s. It is probable that NSW and Victoria both had more than one hundred teams consisting of clubs in the city and country and school teams. If one allows for a figure of fifteen players per team, both states would have had approximately 1 500 players involved in the game on a regular basis. A conservative estimate for the other three cricket-playing states — which were less strong in women's cricket — would be that each had a total of 150 players, giving a grand total of about 3 450 regular players. For every regular player there may have been other women who played irregularly, in a scratch or social match, or

NSW schoolgirls' team, Launceston Wharf, 1936, carry their own equipment. Pat Benn (2nd from L), Miss Dettmann (concealed), Margaret Dive (3rd from L), Erica Way (5th from L), Gwen Thompson (7th from L). Others in the team included Sheila Bell, Shirley Arnot, Beryl Somerville, Jill Makinson and Nellie Shute. (Courtesy Mollie Dive)

played simply for fun, or dabbled with the game as an alternative to basketball or hockey.

The above exercise suggests a rough estimate of approximately 4 000 players (regular and irregular) in the 1930s. Women's cricket did not better this figure until the 1970s and 1980s as during the 1950s and 1960s there was a decline in the number of women playing. It is only in recent years that the sport has enjoyed growth: there were 8 992 registered players by 1990 and 12,281 in 1991.

Country cricket

Few records other than photographs survive of some of the earlier country matches. Photographs of women's cricket in Queensland, assembled by Max and Reet Howell and David Brown, convey the variety and atmosphere of the game in that state.[4] Mixed cricket was a frequent occurrence. A game between men and women at the Cooroy Show Grounds in the first decade of the 20th century conveys a sense of social cricket. None of the players are dressed in cricket costume — the men have dark trousers and even dark vests — and the game appears to be an

"Marry me and do the teas for the club on Saturdays."

adjunct to a picnic. Cricket was played more seriously in other country areas: Croydon Villa's 'mixed team' in 1909 were dressed in cricket attire. The Howells note that mixed teams were not uncommon in country areas as 'often there were insufficient numbers to make up single-sex teams'.[5] There were clearly sufficient numbers in some country towns as was indicated by pictures of women's cricket teams at Bundaberg in 1908, Memerambi (south west of Maryborough) about 1911 and Toowoomba in the 1920s.

During the 1930s the enthusiasm of city women for cricket was replicated in a number of country areas where concerted efforts were made to establish clubs and regular competition. Papasergio and Moy provide an insight into what turned out to be a brief burst of enthusiasm for the game in two country towns in Western Australia — Geraldton and Northampton.[6]

Men's cricket had long been strong in Geraldton, a town 424 kilometres north of Perth, which boasted two associations by the

Cricket in the bush. Ladies and gentlemen play a picnic game at the Cooroy Showgrounds, Queensland. (Courtesy John Oxley Library)

Mixed teams were common in the bush. The Croydon Villa (Queensland) team. (Courtesy John Oxley Library)

1930s. The inspiration for a women's cricket association came from two male cricketers, Jack Shea and Noel Gugeri, who placed an advertisement in the local newspaper on 25 October 1934. A public meeting, chaired by the President of the men's Geraldton

Cartoons drawn by Test cricketer Arthur Mailey.

Cricket Association, attracted forty women who 'enthusiastically agreed' to the formation of an association. Women's cricket was very much in the air at the time as the visiting English women's cricket team played their first match in Perth in November 1934.

Three cricket clubs were established in Geraldton — the Cardinals, Imperials and Royals — and a premiership competition started with the Cardinals proving successful in 1934–35 and 1935–36. A number of men who were prominent in cricket threw their weight behind the new association. Percy Elliott, an ex-South Australian player, assisted with coaching, umpiring and even scoring. Jack Shea and Noel Gugeri helped with match arrangements and took responsibility for the storage and safety of the equipment. The local Town Council was also sympathetic to the new association, providing them with a ground, storage facilities, a shelter shed and a rainwater tank. During the first season

The NSW team in Melbourne for the 1932 tournament enjoyed themselves off the field as well as on. Amy Hudson is in the front row, fourth from right. (Courtesy E Jenkins)

games were also organised with a neighbouring country town. A combined team travelled to Northampton, a farming region fifty kilometres north of Geraldton, in March 1935 and then entertained the Northampton team when they visited Geraldton.

Despite this initial burst of enthusiasm the Geraldton Women's Cricket Association lasted only two seasons and was then disbanded; an Association did not reemerge until 1972. Papasergio and Moy list four main reasons for the demise of women's cricket in this country town: the poor condition of the ground allocated, Maitland Park, and the lack of any other ground; the loss of the main administrative personnel to run the Association — Jack Shea moved to Perth to further his promising career and played eight games for Western Australia and two for an Australian XI; the reported loss of interest in cricket of some women who took up alternative summer sports such as tennis, swimming and yachting; the relocation of several women following marriage.

The story of women's cricket in Geraldton was repeated in neighbouring Northampton. The Northampton Ladies' Cricket Club was formed in 1935 by Mrs Connie Johnson (nee Patterson), who had played cricket for the Fremantle Rovers earlier in the decade. The local male cricketers assisted the women's club, providing equipment and coaching. Northampton differed from Geraldton in that there appears to have been only one team so the women played games against the men and there were even games with mixed sides.

The women's cricket club functioned for only one season before it was disbanded. Papasergio and Moy provide an even longer list of reasons why this club folded after such a short life. They include: marriage; shortage of transport — some members lived more than thirty kilometres away; lack of money; the problems in obtaining cricket equipment when not used by the men; the lack of cricket pitches after the first season; and the loss of cricket players who were enticed away to hockey and tennis.[7]

What happened with the women's game at Geraldton and Northampton must have been repeated in many other country towns. Cricket in the 1930s was something of a passing fad, an occasional alternative to the more enduring women's sports of tennis and hockey. Without a strong base women's cricket suffered rather more from the problems of women's team sport in country areas: the problem of travel and the lack of established competitions and opposition teams.

Distance was less of a problem in Victoria where the teams formed had the added incentive of participating in a Country Week Carnival in Melbourne. Victoria could boast of no less than four country asociations by 1939. The first overseas tour of the Australian women's team in 1937 played a role in the expansion of country clubs in Victoria. 'The interest of the girls' at Emerald, a small town forty-eight kilometres from Melbourne, was 'first seriously aroused' by this tour and a club was formed. A team was also formed in the same year at Belgrave, a mountain district of Victoria, and they were hopeful of entering a team in the Melbourne Carnival in 1938. Teams from the metropolitan areas also travelled to country areas and other towns. A city team met the Belgrave team at Belgrave in 1938 and a team from Hawthorn LCC made the trip to Geelong to play the YWCA there.

NSW, too, had its country tournaments by the late 1930s. Goulburn was one of the more successful country teams and defeated Clarence River at the University Oval in 1938 to retain its premiership.

Interstate tournaments

Whereas interstate matches had been few and far between prior to 1930, the AWCC organised them on a regular basis from 1931. Given the expense of organising interstate matches by associations which operated on a very limited budget, tournaments were confined to one period of the year, when all the teams travelled to one venue. January was the most convenient month for the players to combine cricket with recreational leave since special leave for cricket was problematical for most at other times of the year. Women's cricket has never been able to afford — and still cannot — individual interstate matches spread throughout the cricket season. The annual tournament week provided a once a year event when women's cricket could do its annual business: play the interstate games, select national teams, and have meetings of the AWCC.

The first tournament, involving Queensland, Victoria and

NSW, was held in Sydney in March 1931. Persistent rain threatened to wash out competition. In the deciding match NSW defeated Victoria on a difficult and spiteful wicket in an afternoon.

Attempts were made to involve other states and Western Australia was invited to take part in the tournament in 1935. Western Australia had to turn down that invitation because 'its players had had very little experience of turf wickets and their money and time could be more profitably spent on gaining experience at home and concentrating on improving playing conditions here'.[8] The cost of, and the time involved in, travel made it very difficult for the West to compete and the state was not usually represented at the annual tournament because of these problems. A Western Australian side did not appear in the tournament until the 1936–37 season at Adelaide when they did not win a game. They were not any more successful when the first post-war touring side, captained by Olive Leslie, travelled to Melbourne in the 1947–48 season. The tournament was first held in Perth in the 1951–52 season.

Getting to the annual tournament was often a problem for another smaller association, Queensland, which sent a team each year 'even though it was a severe financial strain on the private members of the Association'. The extent of the determination of the Queensland side to field a team in the 1938 tournament was acknowledged in *Australian Women's Cricket* in March 1938:

> Rather than disappoint the SAWCA Queensland decided to send those girls available, and on the first day of their match against SA had only nine players. The following day Rose Bouel arrived to make the 10th player for the team, and those girls represented their State through the remainder of the matches. . . .
>
> It takes a lot of keenness and courage for any State to compete in the Interstate matches without a full team, and when one realises that the Queenslanders travelled 1 686 miles, with three consecutive nights in those hot, uncomfortable trains, no praise can be too great for their plucky efforts.

International tours

Given that women's cricket was operating on a shoestring budget in the early 1930s, it was a bold and imaginative gamble to invite an English team to visit Australia in the summer of 1934–35. An extended series of matches including three Test matches, games against most of the states, and a number of matches in several country towns and districts was proposed. When the invitation was made the AWCC had just 14s 8d in the bank, but the far-sighted administrators who were running the women's game recognised that the tour had the potential to put women's cricket

"My bloke reckons cricket's a woman's game because they field in slips and have so many draws."

on the Australian sporting map. Ruth Preddey, in an article in *Women's Weekly* of 24 November 1934, dwelt on the importance of the tour:

> To the Australian players this tour also means a great deal . . . To occupy the leading pages in the newspapers, to be photographed, and to know that their names are being broadcast throughout the Commonwealth and England adds glamour to the scene.

Although the precise details of the funding of this tour are not known, it is clear, as Netta Rheinberg later wrote, that the financing of this and subsequent tours was 'difficult'. Each of the English tourists to Australia in 1934–35 had to pay their own passages of £80 and purchase their own equipment for the six month tour. The fare represented a very large sum: it amounted to forty-three weeks' salary of an Australian female on the basic wage.[9] The fund raising was the responsibility of the individual cricketer, her club, family and friends, but once the tourists reached Australia their expenses were the responsibility of the Australian cricket authorities. The host country 'bore all expenses of hospitality, entertainment, and travelling on home grounds, but retained all match profits'.[10] Most of the day-to-day expenses were covered voluntarily by local associations who billeted the tourists. The major bills for the AWCC were for the interstate travel of the tourists, hiring of grounds and publicity. In 1934–35 the AWCC gambled on a sufficient public response to

---

JUNE COLE (nee Porter) (1918–77) started playing cricket when recruited to make up the numbers in a side and from that point she was hooked on the game. She began playing, at the age of fourteen, with her sister Mae with Raymond's Club and subsequently with Pelaco. She became player and coach of the YWCA in 1944.

When June Cole and her family, which included two children, moved to England in 1948 she continued her involvement with cricket, becoming an administrator with a club known as 'The Redoubtables'. Returning to Australia in 1951 she expanded the YWCA club into four teams — an unheard of number at this time — which she achieved by attracting back retired players.

June Cole occasionally played in the same side as her daughter Jill Crowther in the 1950s, although mostly they played in different sides with June captaining the 2nds and Jill playing in the 4ths. Jill Crowther followed her mother's footsteps into cricket administration: she has been VWCA registration/match results secretary since 1965 and also became a life member of this association. June played with the YWCA until the age of forty when illness restricted her cricket. A year later she returned to club cricket when some former YWCA members asked her to help form, and coach, a new club — the Melbourne Ladies' Cricket Club. She occasionally played a game for this club and also helped to form another, the Brighton Beach Ladies' Cricket Club.

June Cole played an important role in promoting cricket in Victoria and in Australia generally: she was a long term member of the VWCA and its President for a number of years. She was also Secretary of the AWCC and was honoured with life membership.

During the 1950s she hosted a Saturday morning radio program on 3DB. The program focussed initially on women's cricket but developed into a more general program on women's sport. She played a role in reporting the 1956 Olympic Games.

June Cole died while scoring for the Melbourne Ladies' Cricket Club.

the tour — gate money revenue — to make ends meet.

It was clear from the very first match that the tour would be an outstanding success. A crowd of some 3 500 turned up at the WACA on the first day of a two-day match between Western Australia and the tourists — which is still a record for the largest attendance for a women's match in Perth. Press reports established that England had an articulate and astute captain in Betty Archdale, who was fully aware that this was the first international tour since the infamous Bodyline series in which the practice of leg theory was regarded by many as unfair. Archdale recognised that women's cricket could advance its cause by stressing that it could help to heal the wounds of Bodyline. At Perth she urged the reporters to 'please tell Australia that we are not here for any Ashes but merely to play Test cricket'.[11]

From that point on the Englishwomen made a triumphal progression across the country. Although there was not time for a match in Adelaide — their ship was berthed there for just a matter of hours — civic dignitaries, the press and the general public almost tripped over each other to provide a big welcome. *Women's Weekly* of 8 December 1934 reported that:

Seldom in the history of South Australia has a reception to a sports team caused more commotion than that tendered by the Lord Mayor of Adelaide to the English girls. They were followed into the vestibule by a great crowd of spectators all craning their necks to catch a glimpse of the young women . . . The gathering was held in the Lady Mayoress' parlor. The visiting cricketers almost had to fight their way through . . . the seething mass of people there.

The tourists must have been impressed and even touched by their star status. Tour manager, Miss Betty Green, commented that 'the programme of entertainment seems almost too good to be true. . . You are indeed treating us like royalty'.[12]

The pattern was repeated when the tourists arrived in Melbourne on 3 December. They had a hectic round of engagements on the day of arrival which included an official reception at the Victorian Cricket Association, a civic reception at the Melbourne Town Hall, an official luncheon at the MCC, and afternoon tea at Parliament House as the guest of the Speaker. Not to be outdone by the cities, two country towns in NSW (Deniliquin and Junee) declared a public holiday when the tour caravan visited them.

Matches between the tourists and Victoria (7 and 8 December) and NSW (14 and 15 December) drew very respectable crowds of about 4 000 per day with 5 428 attending the Saturday of the Sydney match.[13] The two-day match aggregate of about 8 000 was roughly equivalent to the attendance of an average men's

Shield match of this era, although the blue ribbon event of the season — NSW versus Victoria — could draw a total of over 20 000 and even 30 000 spectators.

The majority of the crowd, rather surprisingly, were men. Some obviously came out of curiosity: one male spectator expressed surprise that the women bowled overarm, as he thought that they would be bowling underarm. There were many other press reports that others came to scoff but were impressed with the quality of the cricket and remained to applaud. Ruth Preddey noted in *Women's Weekly* of 22 December that one elderly member at the SCG paid the players the highest compliment in that he stated that 'I keep forgetting that they are women I am watching'.

The presence of a good crowd on the Sydney Hill (mainly men and youths) for the NSW versus England match was another indication of acceptance by the cricket fraternity. There was even some good-natured barracking to add to the entertainment. When the players were rather tardy to take the field one

Margaret Peden (left) loses the toss to Betty Archdale in the very first women's Test at Brisbane in 1934. (Courtesy Betty Butcher)

Expansion and Acceptance: The Golden Decade of the 1930s

The famous barracker, Yabba, attended women's matches in the 1930s.

barracker called out: 'Shake it up with the powder puff in there, girls!' Another replied: 'Don't get impatient, old chap. Women are never on time these days. Anyway it's a woman's privilege to keep a gentleman waiting.' During the game yet another barracker called out to Yabba — the Hill's most famous identity — 'Hey, Yabba, why ain't yer yowling?' Yabba's reply indicated his acceptance of women's cricket: 'Why should I, the ladies are playing all right for me. This is cricket, this is ... Leave the girls alone.'[14]

The crowds which attended the lead-up games to the Tests were enthusiastic. Ruth Preddey reported in *Women's Weekly* of 22 December that the general public swarmed around the dressing rooms of the players and formed human lanes, as much as six

Sydney Morning Herald 5 January 1935.

deep, as the players went on and off the field. Crowds even gathered outside the gates at the end of matches and 'cheered lustily as each English or Australian player made her way to the waiting car'.

Perhaps the Australian women were rather overawed by the publicity and suffered from nerves when they batted in the very first women's Test at the Brisbane Exhibition Ground before a Friday crowd of around 3 000. They were routed for just 47 runs in under two hours with only Kath Smith — the Vice Captain

Women's Cricket 769

FIRST WOMEN'S TEST MATCH
AUSTRALIA v. ENGLAND

At Brisbane, December 28, 29, 31, 1934. England won by nine wickets. The importance of the occasion, the first Women's Test Match, proved too much for the Australians who never recovered from a disastrous start. They lost five wickets for 13 runs and were out in under two hours. Maclagan, the English fast bowler, took full advantage of her opponents' uncertainty and was almost unplayable. By her batting, Maclagan saved England when they went in, for few others showed confidence against the slow bowling of Palmer who spun the ball appreciably. Australia, 107 in arrear did better in their second innings, thanks to a splendid knock by Shevill, but England were left only 32 to get for victory.

Australia

H. Pritchard hit wkt b Maclagan	4	— c Snowball b Spear	20
R. Monaghan c and b Maclagan	4	— run out	4
N. McLarty c and b Maclagan	0	— c Snowball b Spear	8
E. Shevill b Maclagan	0	— not out	63
K. Smith c Spear b Maclagan	25	— b Valentine	12
H. Hills retired hurt	2	— absent ill	0
M. Peden b Taylor	1	— c Partridge b Spear	11
L. Kettels c Partridge b Maclagan	9	— b Spear	0
A. Palmer c Partridge b Maclagan	1	— b Partridge	4
P. Antonio c Partridge b Taylor	0	— b Spear	5
F. Blade not out	0	— c Child b Hide	4
Extra	1	Extras	7
	47		**138**

England

M. Maclagan b Palmer	72	— b Antonio	9
B. Snowball c Shevill b Antonio	15	— not out	18
M. Hide c Kettels b Palmer	9	— not out	6
M. Child c McLarty b Palmer	5		
J. Partridge b Palmer	0		
B. Archdale not out	32		
D. M. Turner c McLarty b Palmer	2		
J. Liebert b McLarty	1		
M. I. Taylor c McLarty b Smith	0		
M. Spear b Palmer	9		
C. Valentine b Palmer	0		
Extras	9	Extra	1
	154	One wkt.	**34**

England Bowling

	Overs	Mdns.	Runs	Wkts.	Overs	Mdns.	Runs	Wkts.
Maclagan	17	11	10	7	28	12	31	0
Taylor	14.3	8	9	2	19	6	30	0
Spear	8	7	2	0	34	24	15	5
Hide	4	0	6	0	21	7	26	1
Turner	4	1	7	0	13	7	14	0
Partridge	2	0	12	0	5.3	2	6	1
Valentine					5	1	9	1

Australia Bowling

	Overs	Mdns.	Runs	Wkts.	Overs	Mdns.	Runs	Wkts.
Blade	10	2	24	0				
Smith	13	2	32	1				
McLarty	10	4	12	1	2	0	4	0
Antonio	15	1	41	1	5	1	20	1
Palmer	13.2	4	18	7	6	1	9	0
Kettels	8	2	8	0				
Shevill	4	1	10	0				

BB

This report of the first ever women's Test match in 1934 did not appear in Wisden until 1938 by which time a second women's series had enhanced the status of women's cricket.

and the one Queenslander in the side — providing any resistance with 25. Smith was a tall player with as 'stately a walk as a naval man' and at the wickets was known for her 'full-blooded hooking'.[15] English slow bowler Myrtle Maclagan took 7–10 off seventeen overs. England were 5–116 at stumps.

A Saturday crowd of over 5 000 saw an improved showing from the local side. They dismissed the visitors for 154 and had replied with 5–99 with Essie Shevill 46 not out. Although Shevill remained unconquered on the third day at 63, Australia were dismissed for 138, before a crowd of about 1 000, and England hit off the runs required with the loss of just one wicket.

Women's cricket authorities must have been well pleased with

Today's Peterson

The English Women Cricketers meet N.S.W. tomorrow.

TWELFTH MAN

Courtesy John Fairfax Group Pty Ltd.

the public response to the First Test. The three day crowd of about 9 000 was approximately the same number which attended the three men's Shield matches in Brisbane in that season.[16]

Margaret Peden must have had a busy first week in January 1935 as she was again Captain of the national side for the Second Test at Sydney beginning on 4 January. But, as Secretary of the NSWWCA, she was also responsible for the Test arrangements and the match advertisements in the local press, which announced special trams to the ground, and were published

AMY HUDSON
(b 1916), an all-rounder from NSW, attended South Annandale Public School and Petersham High School before leaving school at the age of fourteen to help her family survive in the Depression years. She worked for most of four decades at McKenzie's Food warehouse, which during World War II packed food for Australian troops overseas. Subsequently she was a matron with the police, looking after prisoners. Because she had to work long hours in the 1930s and 1940s — forty-eight hours a week — there was no time to practice her cricket.

Being the only girl in a street with some twenty boys, Amy joined in street cricket. After seeing a photograph in a 1930 newspaper of a Sans Souci team she told her mother that she would love to play in a cricket team. Her mother helped Amy found the Annandale Cricket Club which thrived from that time until Hudson's retirement in 1953. Amy Hudson's mother had an ingenious idea to recruit players: she persuaded the owner of the Annandale Picture Theatre to include slides in the cinema program advertising the need for players. Within a week Annandale had a side and within a month the club launched a second side. Her mother became Secretary of the Annandale Club and was later Secretary of the NSWWCA.

When Hudson made her state debut she was only sixteen and was a fast bowler. She made her Test debut while still a teenager in the Third Test of the 1934–35 series at Melbourne. She toured with the 1937 Australians but played only in the final Test.

Amy Hudson's career blossomed after World War II. She became a permanent fixture in the Australian side during the series against England in 1948–49, and finished with a series average of 46.25. Her well-flighted spinners — she had changed from a medium pace to a leg break bowler in 1948 — were effective at Melbourne (where she took 5–46) and at Sydney (3–28).

She was the veteran of the side during the 1951 tour and the first woman cricketer to tour England twice.

under her name. Another unusual feature of this game was that the Australian side included two pairs of sisters: Margaret Peden was joined by her sister Barbara, and Essie Shevill played alongside sister Rene.

After a poor start (3–22) Australia recovered to a good total of 9–147 with Kath Smith scoring a fine 47 with six fours before a sizeable Friday crowd of 4 641. After play was washed out on Saturday, England took control of the game on Monday in front of 4 963 spectators. They dismissed Australia for 162 and then Myrtle Maclagan recorded the first century (119) in women's Tests and put on a record opening stand of 145 with Betty Snowball (71). England declared their innings closed at the end of the second day's play at 5–301. Watched by a crowd of 2 593 England dismissed Australia for 148 and hit off the ten runs required for the loss of two wickets.

Considering that there was no play on Saturday, the three-day total crowd of 12 197 and a gate of £524 3s 6d must have been very encouraging. Gate entry of 1s (ground) and 2s (stand) was half the cost of male Test cricket. Patrons appear to have watched only two (as distinct from three) sessions of play as women's Tests began at 1.15 p.m. Cricket was competing with many other forms of popular entertainment: it cost from 1s to attend one of the many popular dance halls or city and suburban cinemas.[17]

Australia saved its best performance for the final Test at the Melbourne Cricket Ground when diminutive leg spinner Peggy Antonio, who was admired for her smooth action, returned her best Test performance of 6–49 and England were dismissed for 162. Myrtle Maclagan recorded her third consecutive half century. The largest crowd of the series — 7 029 — turned up on Saturday to see Australia reply with a respectable total of 150, thanks to some lower order resistance from Anne Palmer (39), Joyce Brewer (26) and Barbara Peden (24 not out). A final day crowd of 2 641 witnessed Australia hold out for a draw (8–104) after England had declared at 7–153. The crowd aggregate for the match was approximately 13 000 and gate takings were £485 5s 6d.

While the series was comfortably won by England, two Tests to nil, the younger Australian side — with teenagers such as Peggy Antonio and Amy Hudson — was clearly improving and becoming more of a match for the tourists.

Favourable and extensive media coverage

Not much research is needed to verify the recollection of Peggy Antonio and Nell McLarty that 'we received heaps of publicity' in the 1930s. There was extensive material in all the major dailies

Kath Smith, Australian Vice Captain, takes block in 1934.

> **KATHLEEN (KATH) SMITH**
> (b 1915) was a strongly-built all-rounder from Queensland: a left-hand opening bowler and a right-hand punishing middle-order bat with a fierce hook. She attended three different primary schools in Brisbane — St Joan of Arc, St Stephen's Cathedral and St Patrick's — but did not continue on to high school. She learnt cricket on the street, playing with the local boys, and first joined a club at age eleven. She spent most of her playing years with the Victoria Cross Club.
>
> Smith, who was appointed Australian Vice-Captain in the first ever women's Test at Brisbane, scored more than half her side's total (25 out of 47) in this game. Her innings included three out of the five boundaries scored in the match. She finished second in the Australian batting averages for the series (scoring 121 runs at an average of 20.16).
>
> Selected for the 1937 tour — the only Queenslander in the side — she improved on her batting record, scoring 214 in six innings including 88 in the First Test.
>
> During World War II Kath Smith worked as a forewoman in Dalgetty's factory in Brisbane and then later worked at Treadways Store in Melbourne.

— match reports, background articles and a large number of photographs. The *Sydney Morning Herald*, for instance, had a collage of illustrations from the first day of the Sydney Test and followed this up with another set of photographs of play from the second day. The leading sporting weekly of the country, the *Referee*, also provided extensive coverage of the tour. 'The Ranger' provided a lengthy article on the English tourists on 22 November with short profiles of each of the fifteen players.

Some journalists were even quite carried away by the phenomenon of women playing Test cricket. One journalist of the *Courier Mail* of 29 December 1934 waxed lyrical and even romantically about females tripping across the cricket sward:

The two umpires seemed quite lonely among so many bright young ladies, who tripped like sylphs across the brilliantly green oval . . . If the girls lacked the strength of men players, the spectators found compensation in their graceful bearing and willowy movements. Figures flying across the green after the ball, as if swept by a stiff breeze, denoted great resilience, and the upright poses of the fair ones knocked out all the unpleasant arguments associated with 'bodyline' . . . the English girls . . . resembled Grecian statues . . . The girls were intent only on playing the game. Sceptical fellows who went out expecting to see a better display of powder puffs and legs than batting found no such silliness in evidence, and some of them growled because the girls had left high heels, mirrors, lipsticks 'and all that' in the dressing room.

Women's cricket was fortunate that Ruth Preddey was Sports Editor of *Women's Weekly* and the tour gained a large amount of publicity from this magazine, which devoted a page or a half page to the tour week by week. Preddey served up an interesting and varied diet of features covering the matches played, the atmosphere of the games, crowd responses and interesting sidelights of the tour — such as the reaction of the tourists to Australia. *Women's Weekly* also went further to actively promote the game. An article in the issue of 22 September 1934 was headed 'Cricket *Should* Be Taught in Girls' Schools'. The same issue included a series of illustrations, under the title of 'Improve your game', featuring some of the shots played in cricket.

Most of the media coverage of cricket was sympathetic and favourable. It was, as the *Women's Weekly* of 15 December described the England versus Victoria game, 'serious, dignified cricket . . . as it should be played'. The praise heaped on the women's game by J C Davis, the leading male cricket writer of the country and the Editor of the *Referee*, seemed to indicate that women's cricket was winning the battle for acceptance. The lengthy article, printed on 20 December, was headlined 'THE WOMEN ARE REAL CRICKETERS' followed by 'Men Who Turned Out to Scoff Remained to Applaud and to Praise'. In this article Davis argued that women proved to all the sceptics that they could play cricket in just as enterprising and spirited a manner as men.

Davis went on to claim that the women's game included 'sparkle, skill, enthusiasm, freshness' — some of the qualities which were less evident in the men's game. The last day of the match in question included a generous (though risky) declaration in the interests of the spectators. 'It was sporting and kindly. It was risky, but the actual result of the match mattered little.' No doubt such comments were partly a criticism of men's cricket — which was still recovering from the far from kindly Bodyline series — but there is no question that Davis was a generous supporter of the women's game. Betty Archdale commented, many years later, that 'Bodyline did us a lot of good . . . People were so relieved to find that we could play cricket without trying to kill the other side'.[18]

There were some occasional discordant notes in the media from time to time. The tourists were sometimes referred to as 'girl' cricketers and at other times 'women' cricketers. (Adult male cricketers were always referred to as men.) The term 'girl' cricketer was not perhaps quite so derogatory as it might first appear as the term 'girls' was used by the women's cricketers themselves. Betty Archdale referred to her team, before the tour, as 'a gallant group of very jolly girls, keen and business-like'.[19]

There were occasional debates about the question of whether women should be involved in cricket. The *Referee* of 22 November 1934 hinted that Betty Archdale was mannish in appearance: she was described as 'sturdy, tweed-clad, with hair cropped as close as a boy's, and even J C Davis felt obliged to ask whether 'proficiency at games, as we are now seeing it, [will] de-womanise women?' which Davis thought would not be the case.

The dress of the women cricketers, not surprisingly, featured rather more prominently than it did in the reports of men's cricket. 'Our Perth Representative' provided very detailed information for the *Women's Weekly* of 1 December 1934 of what the tourists wore:

Already their cricket uniform has created interest. They played in the match wearing divided skirts, and shirts made of linen which open at the neck, and have short sleeves.

Their hats are of a light fabric, with tropical gauze lining. They wear thick white stockings, and spiked shoes are favored for batting and in the field occasionally. They have rubber soled shoes, but are doubtful if these will be utilised in the very hot weather.

The general tenor of media treatment of women's cricket was, however, extremely favourable and this continued throughout the 1930s. Peggy Antonio and Nell McLarty recalled that Pat Jarrett of

---

BARBARA PEDEN
(1907–1984) attended Abbotsleigh where she was Head Prefect and a member of the school cricket team. She then attended the University of Sydney where she was one of the first women graduates in architecture in 1924. She later became a member of the Royal Institute of British Architects. While at University she was a member of the Student Representative Council and won a University 'blue' for cricket.

A medium paced bowler and a specialist slip fielder, she represented Australia in the first Test series against England in 1934–35. Although she had moved to London, she again represented her country when Australia toured England in 1937.

When her Scottish husband, Colin Munro, became a prisoner of war during World War II, she became active in setting up a support group. She founded, along with her uncle, the POW Relatives Association in Sydney and made regular broadcasts on the ABC on the subject. She and her husband were reunited in 1946.

Barbara Peden was considered a pioneer of women's affairs in Australia. She was Patron of the University of Sydney's Women's Sports Association from 1955 to 1982 and was also a member of the Board of the Royal Alexandra Hospital for Children in Sydney.

> HAZEL PRITCHARD
> (1913–67) attended Newtown High School and then worked with her father, a Newtown jeweller. Hazel was born into a cricketing family: her father was keen on the game, her brother played for the St George Club and her elder sister, Edna, who played for the Cheerio Club recruited Hazel to the team.
>
> Edna later represented NSW at cricket, and Hazel Pritchard followed her sister into the state side. Edna described Hazel as 'a pretty girl with a lovely figure, about 5ft 3 ins (159 cm) and very neat'. She had 'timing and ability with a bat' and 'real bat sense'. She was one of the most stylish and graceful players of the 1930s with a fluent batting style featuring delicate drives, cuts and glances. She also hit the ball very hard and was referred to as 'hard-hitting Hazel'. Her Test debut series in 1934–35 was not very auspicious as she returned scores of 4, 20, 0, 0, 5 and 5. She made her pair at Sydney. Myrtle Maclagan was her nemesis, dismissing Pritchard on four occasions.
>
> Pritchard got her revenge on the 1937 tour scoring 306 runs and three half centuries in the three Tests at an average of 51. She scored 87 in the First Test at Northampton and figured in a record second wicket partnership of 127 with Betty Wilson — a record which stood until 1991.
>
> During the final Test at The Oval, Pritchard scored 66 runs in just 70 minutes with ten fours and earned the plaudits of Major C H B Pridham, who in the *Cricketer* of July 1937, wrote that she took 'obvious pleasure in her cricket and bats with joyous abandon'.
>
> After marriage to Les Scanlon, Pritchard moved to remote Mount Isa, Queensland, and raised two children under harsh conditions. She retained a keen interest in cricket and when the family later lived at Kyogle, NSW, she persuaded her former city coach, Fred Griffith, to travel to Kyogle to coach country teams.
>
> Hazel Pritchard also represented NSW at basketball (now netball) and was a keen golfer.

the Melbourne *Herald* was given carte blanche to send back as much material as she wanted during the 1937 tour and the newspaper frequently featured a full page spread on the tour.

The first overseas tour in 1937

The success of the English tour of Australia of 1934–35 encouraged administrators to organise a tour to England in 1937. They were establishing a rate of tour exchange on par with the men's game — with a tour and a return tour approximately every four years.

The selection of the Australian touring team reflected the geography of Australian women's cricket which was strong in NSW and Victoria and relatively weak elsewhere. Eight players, including the Captain, Margaret Peden, were from NSW, five from Victoria and one each from Queensland, South Australia and Western Australia. The team may have been even more lopsided, in favour of the bigger two states, but for AWCC policy to take at least one player from the minor cricket states in order to encourage the development of the game there.

Australian players who toured England recall that the ship voyage was enjoyable and a valuable opportunity to get to know each other despite the rather spartan tour rules, framed by the tour manager, which included the following:

No member shall drink, smoke or gamble while on tour.
No girl may be accompanied by her husband, a relation or a friend.
Writing articles on cricket during a tour is strictly forbidden.
While on board ship, no girl shall visit the top deck of the liner after dinner.
Members of the team must retire to bed by 10 p.m. during the voyage.
Members will do physical drill on deck at 7.15 a.m. daily except Sundays.
The team will participate in all deck games

Because of the Coronation and the difficulty of obtaining a later passage, the Australians arrived at Southampton on 3 May, almost a month before their first game. They were billeted privately and enjoyed the hospitality of individuals, clubs and schools.

The first game against Kent on 1 June established that the tour was going to be a successful one. In front of a crowd of 1 500 the Australians demonstrated that they had a strong batting side. Solid opener Margaret Peden (45) put on a fine opening partnership with Peggy Antonio (53), who scored heavily on the tour, paving the way for Hazel Pritchard — a rather small and fragile looking player — who played some lovely cuts and drives in her 74 not out, while Kath Smith hit hard for 68 not out. Patricia Holmes, who failed in this match, got some big scores later in the

BUT IS IT CRICKET?

"They shall not drink, smoke or gamble, bring husbands, relatives or friends, write for the Press, visit the top deck after dinner or be out of bed by 10 p.m."
—*Commandments issued in respect of the Australian girl cricketers to tour England.*

Source: Bulletin
September 1936.

THE GIRL WHO VISITED THE TOP DECK!

Australian Women Cricketers to tour England next year have to sign an agreement which rigorously insists, amongst many other restrictions, that the players shall not visit the top deck of the ship after dinner and that they shall be in bed by 10 p.m.

tour including a double century against West and a century against Lancashire. Fast bowler Molly Flaherty, who generated good pace off a run of fifteen yards, was in good form taking 7–32. Australia 3–257 declared easily beat Kent 173.

The Australians continued on their winning ways up to the First Test which was played at Northampton before a crowd of 5 000 starting on June 12. Two contrasting innings by Hazel Pritchard (87) and Kath Smith (88) helped Australia amass a fine total of 300: Pritchard cut and glanced fluently and delicately while the powerful Smith bludgeoned the ball to the boundary. Australia restricted England to just 204, thanks to another six wicket haul (6–51) from Peggy Antonio 'with that lovely easy action of hers'. Australia managed only 102 in the second innings but they had enough runs in hand to win the Test by 31 runs when they dismissed England in the second innings for 167.

The Second Test began a fortnight later at the Stanley Cricket Park Ground, Blackpool. The public response was again similar to that in Australia. There was a good crowd of 4 000; they were mostly men and they were somewhat surprised by the quality of the play. Marjorie Pollard reported that one man stated: 'I thought they'd bowl lobs — but by jove, they can play.'[20] The one difference between women's cricket in the two countries was that these Tests were played on the minor cricket grounds — which did not even have county status — whereas the Australian Tests were on some of the major grounds of the country.

England batted first and scored 222 which was largely due to yet another century by Myrtle Maclagan (115). Australia again headed the English side (302) with Pritchard (67), Smith (63) and George (62 not out) the leading rungetters. England again batted soundly in the second innings to accumulate 231. Peggy Antonio (5–31) achieved her third five-wicket haul in three successive Tests and had the outstanding match figures of 8–65. Set just 152 runs to win, Australia reached 3–68 before Molly Hide bowled an inspired spell to rout the middle order. England, dismissing Australia for 126, won the Second Test by 25 runs.

Hopes of the Side

For the final Test of the series, begun on 10 July, the women cricketers achieved access to one of the Test grounds — The Oval — though they were not admitted on the turf of Lord's until the 1970s. The game was again watched by a good crowd of 6 123. The match could have ended in another close finish but the loss of some time due to rain helped end it in a draw. Australia scored 9–207 declared and 224 and in reply England were 9–308 declared and 3 wickets for 9.

Indicative of the success of the tour was the large crowd of 10 000 which turned up to see the Australians play in their last game against Surrey. Marjorie Pollard captured some of the atmosphere of the occasion:

Mitcham Green surrounded by 10,000 spectators — and more prams, dogs, small children, ice-cream men, and bikes than I have ever seen before, anywhere! As the crowd increased, so the boundaries decreased. Trams, buses, cars crashed [sic] by on three sides of the ground. There was tremendous enthusiasm everywhere.[21]

Women's cricket was clearly gaining acceptance in England similar to that in Australia, with recognition coming not only from the general public but also from some of the male cricket establishment. Through the efforts of E W Swanton and 'Plum' Warner the first contributions on the women's game appeared in *The Cricketer*, and in 1938 the august and authoritative cricket annual, *Wisden*, published its first feature on women's cricket, reproducing the Test scorecards of the 1937 series and a belated publication of the results of the 1934–35 series.

In the following season of 1937–38 a team from New Zealand visited New South Wales as part of the NSW 150th anniversary celebrations. The five games played in twelve days did not include a Test match.

> **NELL MCLARTY BEM**
> (b 1912) was born in Western Australia but was brought up (along with her elder sister) by an aunt in Melbourne after her mother died when she was a baby.
>
> Although Nell McLarty had a secure childhood, her aunt was not keen on sport and she had to sneak out to play cricket with the boys in her street. She did not play women's club cricket until the age of eighteen when she was commandeered at the very last moment by the Clarendon Club to make up their numbers. Although she had only ever bowled with a tennis ball, she took 7-2 in her first club outing. She was selected for the Victorian team in her first season and it was only after lengthy discussion between her aunt and other family members that they agreed for her to tour interstate.
>
> Nell McLarty left school to work in a clothing factory, Henry Bucks, at the age of fourteen and remained there for thirteen years until World War II when she worked in a munitions factory and then became a bus conductress. Later she worked in a store and then in the laundry of Bethesda Hospital.
>
> McLarty was a member of the Australian team in the 1934-35 home series and the 1937 English tour. By the time of the tour she was a member of the Collingwood Club and they held functions, including a ball at the Town Hall, to raise funds for the tour.
>
> From the age of eighteen, McLarty's sporting career was plagued by ill health — first it was a fractured wrist, then a broken jaw and finally a spinal problem which led her to give up sport. Despite these setbacks she is remembered as a short leg fielder whose fine reflexes earnt her many good catches.
>
> In spite of poor health and frequent pain she coached four Melbourne club teams to premierships and coached many prominent Australian players including Betty Wilson, Miriam Knee, Sharon Tredrea and Ruth Buckstein. She was awarded a BEM in 1980 for her services to women's cricket.

Arrangements for another English tour of Australia in 1939-40 were well advanced and the team selected when the outbreak of World War II was declared and caused its postponement. This would have been the third exchange between Australia and England in just six years.

Conclusion:

The gamble taken by the women's cricket authorities in inviting the English women to Australia, and establishing international women's cricket was more successful than the authorities could have ever hoped for. Australian women's cricket was put on the map really for the very first time. The flood of publicity created a considerable public awareness and acceptance of the women's game and provided rewards and incentives for girls and women to play cricket.

The immediate rewards for women's cricket were larger crowds and gates, which brought the necessary finance to promote the game. The coffers of the AWCC were in a far healthier state when they embarked on the 1937 tour than they had been in 1934: they had swelled from 14s 8d to £422[22] and the AWCC was even able to allocate £300 towards the tour. The longer term results were a greater number of women's clubs and players and the expansion of women's cricket in both private and public schools.

Cricket authorities must have been aware that this was just a beginning of recognition of the women's game. It was noted that the majority in the crowd at the major women's matches were men, many of whom came simply out of curiosity, and the authorities must have realised that the future of the game depended rather more on women and girls: both as players and spectators.

The boom in women's cricket was undoubtedly related to a golden decade for cricket as a whole, when there was more public interest in the game than perhaps there has ever been. The first women's Test series occurred immediately after the much-discussed Bodyline series, the introduction of ball-to-ball national radio broadcasts and the Bradman phenomenon. Australia was a nation which was 'cricket mad' in the 1930s and the obsession affected men and women alike. Nell McLarty recalled that she was so enthralled by the Bodyline series that 'I didn't miss a ball'.

As a result there was a sizeable audience in the 1930s for all forms of cricket. Men's Test cricket attracted larger and larger crowds and the biggest Shield crowds ever date from this decade. Large crowds, in the thousands, even turned up to watch men's grade and pennant matches as they did for all levels of the women's game.

Hazel Pritchard (left) and Peggy Antonio, two of the most successful tourists, going out to bat in England in 1937. (Courtesy Ann Mitchell)

The novelty of women playing Test cricket must also have been a factor in the success of the 1934–35 and 1937 tours. There was even surprise that women's cricket — which had been virtually hidden from the public since its beginning — was of a reasonable standard and an enjoyable variation of the men's game. The question which hung over the women's game, when it was suspended at the time of World War II, was whether the crowds in particular and the public in general would continue to take an interest in the game once the novelty wore off.

CHAPTER FIVE

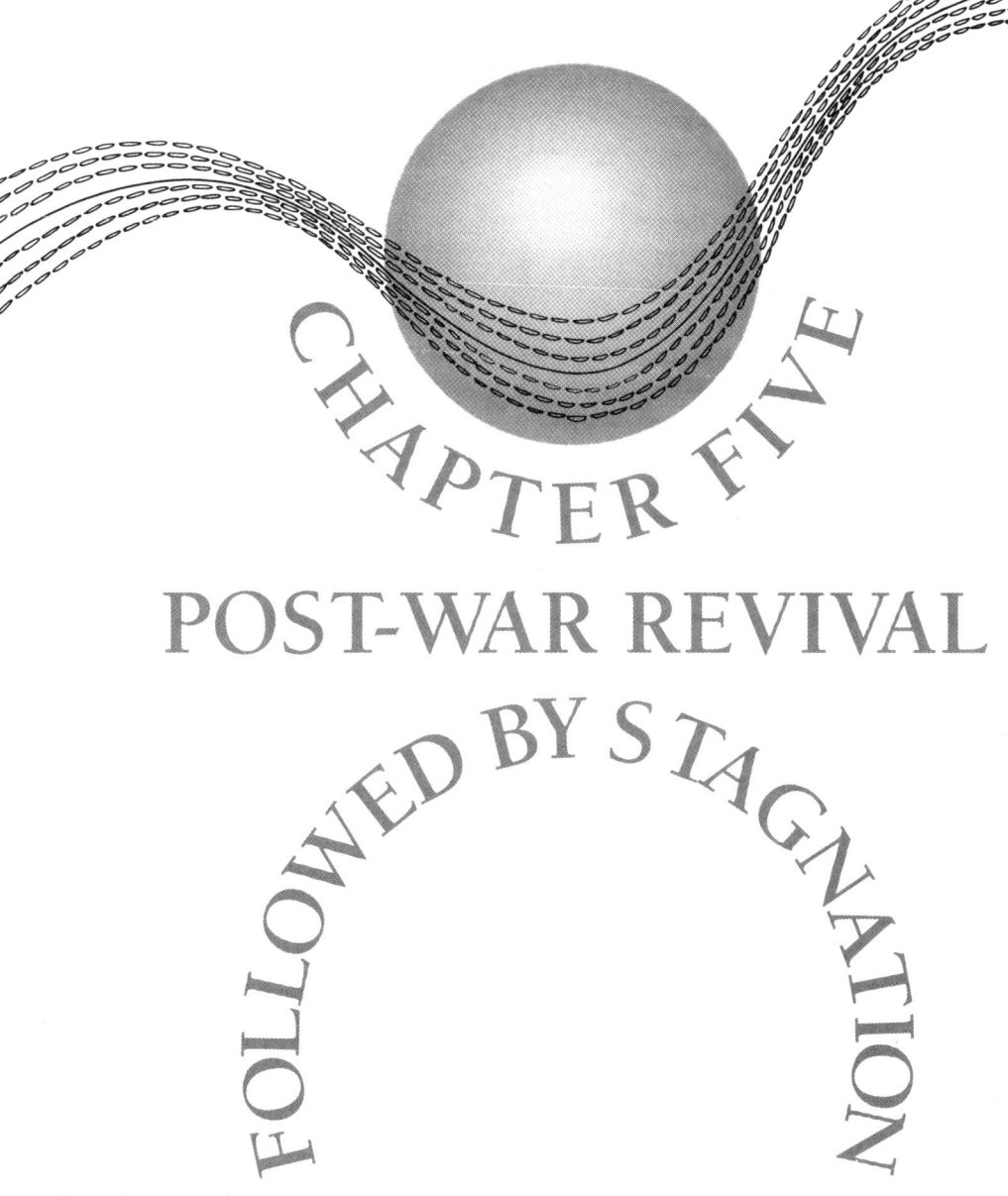

POST-WAR REVIVAL FOLLOWED BY STAGNATION

Starting again

War disrupted both men's and women's cricket — the latter almost virtually having to start all over again in 1945 as they had had to do in the 1920s. Several of the clubs which had flourished in the 1930s were disbanded in war-time and did not reemerge in peacetime and some of the players who toured in 1937 had retired by the time of the first Australian tour to New Zealand in 1948.

However, women's cricket emerged in far better shape after World War II than it had from World War I as the boom in this sport in the 1930s provided a better basis for revival in the late 1940s and 1950s. There were also a number of teenagers from the 1930s — Amy Hudson, Betty Wilson, Mollie Dive and Una Paisley — who were reaching their cricketing maturity in the late 1940s.

Women cricketers were very much in demand after World War II and a team captained by Mollie Dive, and including Betty Archdale and Amy Hudson, was recruited to play

Betty Wilson (left) and Una Paisley at Adelaide where they saved Australia with a century stand. Betty Wilson's preparations, including her well-starched hat, were meticulous. (Courtesy Hilda Thompson)

against the male Colgate-Palmolive team, which included the radio stars and comedians Jack Davey, Hal Lashwood and Roy 'Mo' Rene in 1946. The match raised £110 for Legacy. Played on a Sunday, this match was criticised by the President of the NSWWCA, Mrs A E Thomas, who threatened to resign if there were any more Sunday matches. The women players argued that they had not breached the Association rules — which forbade Sunday play — as they had played as 'Mrs Hazelton's team' rather than as an Association XI.[1]

Given the long lean years of the war, immediately afterwards there was a great public thirst for leisure and a rise in support for all manner of spectator sports. Women's cricket was no exception. Although there were not as many clubs and players in the immediate post-war years, there were some record crowds at women's international matches in the late 1940s and early 1950s — numbers which have never been equalled.

Australia, captained by Mollie Dive, embarked on a brief tour to New Zealand in March 1948 playing eight matches including one Test. The visitors had an impressive record winning seven games and drawing the eighth. The one Test at Wellington was easily won by the Australians who scored 6–338 declared and dismissed the New Zealanders for 149 and 87. The batting star was Una Paisley (1922–1977) who scored 108 — a century on her Test debut and the first Test century by an Australian. She was a steady bat who loved playing the cut and had an excellent temperament. Paisley had been a schoolgirl prodigy in the 1930s, making her club debut at the age of eleven and playing for Victoria in 1937 at the age of fifteen. She went on to become Victorian captain and captained Australia in the 1958 series. Mollie Dive certainly pulled her weight on the tour scoring 123 in one provincial match and ending with a fine average of 78.7.

The New Zealand tour proved a good warm-up for one of the most successful tours ever when the Englishwomen visited Australia in 1948–49. Adelaide Oval was the site of the First Test — the first for this city — and it proved an inspired move as the largest crowd recorded to date turned up to watch a day's play in a women's Test in Australia : 9 159 spectators and a gate of £656. The three day crowd totalled 17 025 with a gate of £1 172. The Test could have been called 'Betty Wilson's Test' as the talented all-rounder made a brilliant international debut on home soil. Coming in when Australia had lost 3–19 she and Una Paisley attacked the bowling and put on a century partnership in only 111 minutes. Wilson reached 111 by tea-time. She then wrecked the England innings taking 6–23 with her off spinners. After England scored only 72, Australia declared at 5–173 with Amy Hudson scoring 81 not out. England were again bundled out for 128 with Wilson taking 3–39.

The second and third Tests at the MCG and SCG respectively, although not as well supported as Adelaide, attracted good crowds: there were 5 272 spectators, for instance, on the first day of the Sydney Test. England improved its performance in these Tests in that they achieved two draws, but they never looked like winning. They were unable to dismiss Australia cheaply in any innings (Australia scored 265, 4–158 decl. and 272) with all the Australian women contributing good scores — particularly Betty

Wilson, Una Paisley and Amy Hudson. Mollie Dive, who led the Australians, had the distinction of wresting the Ashes from the English team for the first time.

During the 1948–49 series women's cricket seemed to have become popular. Large crowds also turned up to watch the visitors play the state teams. Lorna Thomas recalls that 5000 turned up on one day to watch the English team play NSW at the SCG. During the Third Test at the SCG the women Test players were permitted to change in the men's dressing rooms for the first time. On the final day the hallowed dressing rooms were adorned with evening dresses hung on hooks on the walls as the players had to attend a reception immediately after the game.

During the earlier match between NSW and the tourists both sides had changed in rooms underneath the Sheridan Stand (which was subsequently pulled down and replaced by the Churchill Stand). When the players met the Governor, Sir John Northcote, they lined up beside the 'men's' gate, which was adjacent to the men's change room in the Ladies' Stand. After they had met the Governor the women cricketers were about to head back to their own gate and change rooms when the Governor ushered them in from the field via the 'men's' gate.

Bill O'Reilly, who had just begun his long career as a cricket journalist, attended the first day of the Sydney Test and was agreeably surprised by the quality of the cricket played. He wrote a thoughtful and sympathetic appraisal of the play in the *Sunday Herald* of 20 February 1949:

I found that the game suffered not at all by the manner in which the girls handled it.

All the time-honoured precepts of batting, bowling, and fielding were well and truly observed,

Molly Flaherty, Australia's pacy bowler, began to bowl well-directed outswingers at a speed which would be called medium pace in men's cricket.

When Betty Wilson and Una Paisley were entrusted with the spin attack I realised that, if we men have any laurels, we had better set about their defence immediately.

Each of these spinners turns the ball either way and maintains a standard of accuracy which would be highly commendable in any class of cricket. . . .

From this time onward I shall steadfastly refrain from saying that 'so and so' batted or bowled 'like an old woman'.

Regrettably for the women's game, for every fair-minded male commentator there has always been another totally indifferent to women's cricket and yet another (usually far less informed than O'Reilly) who has been totally hostile.

The majority of the spectators in the outer at the SCG were men, as they had been in the 1930s. It is also probable that there

---

UNA PAISLEY (1922–77) was the only child of working class parents. She attended Westgarth Central School in Northcote, Victoria, before she went to Melbourne Royal Institute of Technology where she completed a commercial course in office work. She was employed in Foy and Gibsons, a large retail firm in Collingwood, for her working life.

Her father, Thomas, assisted Una's cricket career taking her down the road to nearby Smith's paddock, where the Northcote Ladies' Cricket Club played, and encouraged her to join the club when she was ten. She had an association with this club of some thirty years as a player, captain and administrator; her father also served as its President for a time.

Una Paisley represented Australia in twelve Tests from 1948 to 1961. She was a solid bat, with a penchant for the square cut, and a useful off and leg spin bowler.

She had the distinction of scoring a Test century on her debut (108 against New Zealand in 1948) which was the first century scored by an Australian in women's Test matches. When she captained Australia for the first time against New Zealand in 1957, she repeated this feat scoring a memorable 101. She also captained the Australian side against England in 1957–58. Although a shy individual, she was a determined captain who gained the respect of her team.

Una Paisley featured in two large stands with Betty Wilson. In the 1948–49 series they put on 115 for the fourth wicket against England, and in the Test against New Zealand in the previous year they put on 163, a world record fourth wicket partnership against any team.

As an off spin bowler, she flighted the ball well and was often responsible for breaking up stubborn partnerships. Although short and stocky, she was an agile fielder with an accurate throw.

Una Paisley captained Victoria for several years and later became a state and Australian selector. She served on the VWCA Executive and was Victorian delegate to the AWCC.

were more men than women in the Members' stands. The same issue of the *Herald* reported that women were attempting to secure the right of membership to the SCG which at the time had no provision at all for female membership: a Lady's ticket represented an associate membership in that it was only issued to male members. The SCG Trust was reported as unsympathetic to the concept of female membership in 1949 and women were not granted independent membership (in their own right) at the SCG until about 1978.[2] It took even longer for women to achieve the same status at the Melbourne Cricket Ground (1984) and at the Gabba (c 1987). Women have yet to gain access to the hallowed Long Room at Lord's as the members did not support Rachael Heyhoe Flint's attempt to join the MCC in 1991.

It is ironic that in two of the states which were slower to take up women's cricket, South Australia and Western Australia, women enjoyed greater rights and privileges at the major cricket grounds. Kingsley Preston, Secretary at the WACA, reported that women had always been entitled to full membership at the WACA. The very first life membership of the Association, awarded in 1893, had been to Sylvia Forrest, daughter of Alexander Forrest, Mayor of Perth. In South Australia, where women were first granted the right to vote, women had been entitled to full membership status at Adelaide Oval as far back as could be remembered and certainly prior to 1939.

With the success of the English women's tour Australia organised a return visit to England in 1951 with the team again captained by Mollie Dive. The success of the 1948–49 tour was replicated in England. A closely-fought match against Yorkshire, for instance, which Australia won on the last ball of the day, was watched by a Headingley crowd of 5 000. The final Test at The Oval created a record aggregate of around 15,000 and there was a substantial tour profit of £3 169 achieved through gate money and the sale of the souvenir program which sold well at all the matches.

The Australian women achieved plenty of publicity. Various members of the team appeared on television which had not yet been introduced to Australia. They also participated in a number of radio programs including 'In Town Tonight', 'Women's Hour' and the Overseas Service of the BBC. Even the male cricket

Sydney Morning Herald
19 February 1949

WOMEN'S INTERNATIONAL CRICKET
THIRD TEST —— ENGLAND v AUSTRALIA
SYDNEY CRICKET GROUND, FEBRUARY 19, 21, 22.
Admission: Ground, Adults 1/11, Children 9d; Grand Stand, Adults 3/-, Children 1/3.
Schoolgirls in Uniform admitted Free on Saturday afternoon.
Play commences each day at 11 a.m.; stumps at 6 p.m.

NORMA JOHNSTON (nee Whiteman) (b 1927) from Bathurst, NSW, attended Bathurst Primary and High schools. All her family were keen on sport and she joined her brother, Ted, in many cricket games at home or in the park. It seemed, she recalled, the natural thing to do: 'balls were there to be thrown, caught or hit.' She joined a girls' cricket team, the Boomerangs, at age eleven.

She made her debut as an eighteen-year-old fast bowler for NSW and was recognised as the fastest bowler in the 1948–51 era. She generated considerable pace from an easy action. Her best bowling performance was 5–50 in two innings off 31 overs against England in 1949.

She was also a useful bat achieving an average of 37 during the 1948–49 series, and as a fielder she proved outstanding taking twelve catches in only seven Tests.

She toured New Zealand in 1948 and England in 1951.

Before she was fifteen she found an ideal job — working in a Bathurst sports store. After marriage, she and her husband, John Johnston, later managed motels.

The First Test played against New Zealand. (Courtesy of Mollie Dive)

establishment seemed to be softening its attitude towards women's cricket in that they were permitted to practise at Lord's. Although it was to take more than two decades for women to actually play on the sacred turf at Lord's, the Women's Cricket Association of England (WCA) was suitably deferential (if not obsequious) in its acknowledgement of having got its toe in the door of Lord's. The WCA report of the tour stated:

The Australian side at Adelaide Oval, 1948 — the first ever women's Test there. Back L to R: Lorna Larter, Myrtle Craddock, Amy Hudson, Joan Schmidt, June Ingham, Joyce Christ; Front Flo McLintock, Betty Wilson, Mollie Dive (captain), Una Paisley (vice captain), Norma Whiteman, Alma Vogt. (Courtesy Mollie Dive)

During the first few days in London after their arrival, the Australians were greatly honoured by being the first women cricketers to be permitted to practice at Lord's, a privilege much appreciated by the Women's Cricket Association.

The doors of the male establishment were being opened ever so

Courtesy Mollie Dive

slowly. Two years previously the WCA had been invited by the MCC — the first invitation ever — to send two delegates to present women's attitude to the game to an inquiry committee.

England proved tougher opposition for the Mollie Dive-led Australians in 1951 than they had in the previous tour. In the First Test at Scarborough the English opener Cecilia Robinson scored a patient 105 in almost five hours to help the home side to a good total of 283. Australia replied with 248 which included a powerful 70 by Amy Hudson and a fluent 81 in 87 minutes by Betty Wilson. Time did not allow for a result in the Test: after England declared at 8–178, Australia were 2–111.

Australia retained the Ashes in a very close and low-scoring Test at Worcester. After England were dismissed for 158 Australia could manage only 120 with only Joan Schmidt (42) and Betty Wilson (41 not out) offering resistance. Australia, spearheaded by Betty Wilson (4–42), then fought back to dismiss the home side for 120 but then required 159, the largest score of the match, to win. Captain Mollie Dive (33) and Betty Wilson (35) worked hard to set up a win but at 8–131 it was anyone's game. Norma Whiteman (25 not out) and Myrtle Craddock put on a priceless and undefeated partnership to secure an Australian win.

It was England's turn at The Oval when they won the last Test

Southern Districts XI (NSW), 12 February 1949, being introduced to the Governor General, Sir William McKell. There is a good crowd to see the locals take on the touring English side. (Courtesy June Williams)

> **MOLLIE DIVE**
> OAM (b 1913) was born at Fivedock, NSW, on 26 June. She was the daughter of Percy and Mary Dive — her father was a slow bowler who played one match for NSW in the 1924–25 season. Backyard cricket involving her father, brothers, neighbours and Mollie herself occurred frequently. She was educated at Roseville Girls' College from 1921–27 and PLC Pymble from 1928–31. At school she played hockey, netball and tennis. She was Head Prefect in her final year and was a member of the school council from 1951 to 1978.
>
> It was not until Mollie Dive attended the University of Sydney — where she took a Bachelor of Science degree — that she joined her first cricket team and subsequently she achieved Blues in both cricket and hockey. She was also associated with the Sydney University Women's Sports Association for fifty years and became an Honorary Life Member. After her studies she became a technical librarian at AWA from 1936 to 1941 and then worked as a scientific officer in the Length Section of the National Standards Laboratory.
>
> Mollie Dive played with the Sydney University Women's Cricket Club from 1932–52 and represented NSW almost continuously from 1933–51, becoming captain of the side in 1938. She captained Australia in her very first Test and led the side in three Test series from 1948–51. Later she became a NSW and Australian selector and was President (and held various other executive positions) in the NSWWCA and the AWCC. A versatile sportswoman, Mollie Dive enjoyed many other games including hockey, tennis, squash, golf and lawn bowls. Dive represented NSW in hockey in 1933 and 1946–49 and then managed the state hockey side for several years. She was a NSW and Australian selector, a top grade umpire and a life member of the NSWWHA.
>
> In 1987 Mollie Dive was awarded the Order of Australia Medal, for her services to women's cricket and hockey. She was further honoured when a stand was named after her at North Sydney Oval in 1987.

and squared the series. After England secured a lead on the first innings of 238 to 192 they declared at 7–174 at 2.20 p.m. on the final day setting Australia 221 to win. Mollie Dive accepted the challenge and totally recast the batting in the interest of quick runs. As so often happens in such situations the Australian top order fell apart due to an inspired spell by Mary Duggan who had the figures of 5–5 at one stage. Australia then shifted to defence and looked like saving the game due to imperturbable Amy Hudson (17 not out in two hours) and Mavis Jones (17) but the last wicket fell with just fifteen minutes remaining.

The four tours between Australia and England from 1934 to 1951 had all proved remarkably successful for women's cricket. Good crowds at all the major matches had resulted in profits which provided the necessary capital to run the game and could be ploughed back into its development. Tours also provided the women's game with much-needed publicity of a positive kind which was extremely beneficial and undoubtedly was the reason why more women and girls were playing cricket in this era.

The doldrums: the later 1950s and 1960s

It is puzzling that after so much growth and such a positive public response in the 1930s and shortly after the war that women's cricket seemed to go backwards over the next two decades. It did not happen immediately; rather it was something of a gentle slide into what seemed like possible oblivion.

The evidence for such a decline is overwhelming in that it affected every aspect of the women's game. The most obvious indicator of malaise was the increasing infrequency of international tours, which had been the cornerstone of the game. Whereas the pattern of exchange tours between 1934 and 1951 looked set to occur almost as frequently as with the men's game — a tour and a return tour every four years — there were fewer and fewer exchanges between Australia and England after 1951. The next tour to England did not take place till more than a decade later (1963) and then there was a gap of ten years before the next English tour (1973). There was a similar pattern in English tours of Australia, which occurred at gaps of roughly ten years: in 1948–49, 1957–58, 1968–69.

The reason for the sharp decline in the frequency of tours is a relatively simple one — the crowds which had flocked to women's games in the 1930s and early 1950s had dwindled by the late 1950s and almost disappeared in the 1960s. Along with reduced crowds women's cricket seemed to disappear from the media, becoming a forgotten sport with the public now showing a monumental disinterest in the game.

All of these factors totally changed the economy of international tours. In 1951 and in the previous years tours had generated funds for the AWCC and created a much-needed and enormous amount of free publicity. Without public interest, media coverage and crowds, tours became a substantial drain on AWCC resources. During the 1960s it became more and more difficult to mount tours to England which made the shorter and cheaper exchanges with New Zealand a feasible alternative.

Cost was undoubtedly the main reason why women's cricket disappeared from the major Test centres during the 1960s. During the 1957–58 series women moved off the SCG and MCG, though two Tests were played at the Adelaide Oval and the WACA. However, by 1968–69 all the Tests had been moved to suburban grounds at North Sydney, St Kilda and Thebarton. The move off the most famous cricketing ovals was a visible symbol of the marginalisation of women's cricket. By the late 1960s English women began to be provided with some government support — the British Government provided a grant of £1 000 to defray touring expenses in 1968–69 — but women's cricket authorities in Australia had to battle on in the 1960s with virtually no government assistance or sponsorship.

Mollie Dive, at the end of the 1968–69 tour to Australia, argued in the *North Shore Times* of 12 February 1969 that there should be more regular tours and reflected on the problems of long gaps between tours:

> Of the necessity to sustain interest in women's cricket by having a Test tour every six years, perhaps instead of the present 10 years. . . .
>
> Again, with 10 years separating each Test tour, we are faced each time with having to start out on a re-education programme; to say nothing of players who have moved out of cricket in the intervening period and the necessity to find others to fill their place.

From the 1960s women's cricket received diminished media attention in most states. Victoria was a possible exception to the rule in that even in this era it had well-placed supporters of the women's game such as Dot Mummery, whose program 'Calling all Sportswomen' was broadcast on the ABC each Saturday morning at 10 a.m., and Steve Hayward, June Cole, and Danny Webb on 3DB. The crowd attendance at women's Tests was no longer recorded in the newspapers as the numbers had declined to those which have attended ever since — a few hundred, composed of players, their friends and relatives and a scattering of club cricketers. The general public, which once attended Tests, no longer bothered to come.

It was a case of out of sight, out of mind. Without the necessary publicity fewer were recruited to the game and there was a decline in the 1960s in the number of players and teams, school and club. The extent of the malaise was worst felt in Queensland, one of the founding states of the AWCC, which ceased to exist as an Association from 1963. The records of the AWCC include a letter from the Executive of the QWCA of 25 October 1963 which outlined the sad state of affairs in Queensland:

> Over the last five seasons, interest has been steadily declining and no persons are now able or willing to make an effort to revitalize the Association. The University club, which virtually maintained the Association for several seasons, no longer exists.
>
> After payment of debts to the AWCC, the cash remaining in hand is now less than £3. It is therefore clearly impossible to continue paying affiliation fees and delegates' fares to the AWCC.
>
> Under these circumstances, of lack of membership, lack of interest and enthusiasm, and financial insolvency, the QWCA has ceased to exist, and we therefore request: 'That the Queensland Women's Cricket Association be declared an inactive member of the Australian Women's Cricket Council, under the terms of the Constitution as currently adopted.'

Some other states, such as Western Australia, battled hard to survive. The cost and time involved in sending a team to the interstate tournaments meant that Western Australia did not appear in any tournament from 1956 to 1962, and without the possibility of representing the state (and country) there was far less incentive for club cricket to continue there.

At the end of the 1960s the question was even raised in some quarters as to whether the game had a future given its decline from its peak popularity in the 1930s. One unidentified commentator wrote that 'the big question for women's cricket in Australia (in the 1970s) is — will it survive?'[3]

There are a number of possible explanations for the era of the doldrums. The fate of women's cricket again ran parallel to the men's game. Men's cricket enjoyed a brief boom after World War II but after the retirement of Bradman the men's game failed to sustain the popularity of the 1930s. Apart from a brief interlude between 1958 and 1961 when the Benaud-led Australians and the West Indians helped to rekindle interest in the game, cricket administrators were worried by declining crowds and a lack of 'brighter' cricket. Attendances declined at all levels of the game: Test, Shield and grade. The hundreds and even thousands who attended district games in the 1930s have never been seen since,

The decline in men's and women's cricket was partly due to the emergence of more individualistic alternative sports. Tennis, which produced a succession of young stars, was fast overtaking

---

MIRIAM 'MIM' KNEE (b 1938) played cricket at Yarra Road Primary School — where her teacher, George Collis, interested her in the game — and at Lilydale High School. She had no trouble practising cricket as a girl as she had four brothers, all of whom played in the Ringwood district competition. She began playing cricket for YWCA in Melbourne before co-founding the Mitcham Club in 1965. A talented all-rounder she was first selected for Australia against New Zealand in 1961. After touring England in 1963 she stood down in 1966 for personal reasons but was persuaded to return to the national team and became Australian Vice Captain in the 1968–69 series against England. She had a fine series scoring 55 and taking 8 wickets in the First Test and reaching 96 runs in the Second. It was the second occasion on which she had taken 8 wickets in a Test, the first occasion being the Second Test of the 1963 series. Miriam Knee captained Australia in the first ever World Cup in 1973 and captained the Rest of the World versus England in the same year.

At a state level, Miriam Knee represented Victoria for more than sixteen years as a player and captain. When she moved to Sydney, Knee continued to play an active role in the development of women's cricket, acting as a coach for the NSW team and selecting the state squad for many years. She was an Australian selector from 1971–79 and again from 1985–89. Her contribution as an administrator at club, state, national and international levels over twenty-five years was recognised in 1988 when she was awarded a life membership of the AWCC. The then President, Sylvia Faram, described her as a person of integrity who had been a great ambassador for Australia and for women's cricket.

cricket as one of the more glamorous sports and the successes of the Olympic swimmers and athletes in 1956 were rather more inspiring to Australians than the demolition of the 1956 Australians by Jim Laker who took 19 wickets for only 90 runs in the Test at Old Trafford, Manchester.

Team sports, such as cricket, were casualties of greater post-war affluence, due to which an increasing number of Australians had access to alternative forms of leisure. More families owned cars in the 1950s and 1960s and many could afford to travel in Australia and overseas. There was a post-war boom first in home tennis courts and later in swimming pools, and surfing also became a more popular pastime.

There were also some specific reasons for the decline in women's cricket, one of which was the adverse effect caused by the rise of softball as an alternative sport. The game had first been played in Victoria in 1941, according to one source, when it was introduced by a group of American Army nurses.[4] Another version credits its start to Sgt W B Duvernet of the US Special Services who introduced the game to Victoria in 1942 to provide recreation for troops and nurses.

Whatever the precise origins of the game in Australia it became extremely popular in a very short time. Softball, which was far easier and cheaper to play and took much less time than cricket, became the summer game at many schools. Ken Knox reported in 1961 that in Victoria alone there were 8 500 senior players and probably about four times that many playing the game in schools, making an estimated total of players of 40,000 in this one state.[5] If the same proportions of women and girls were playing softball in other states, there must have been approximately 143,000 playing softball in the 1960s (the Victorian population was 27.9 per cent of the Australian total at the time). There were many more playing softball than have ever played women's cricket. Softball continued to grow in the 1970s when NSW could boast of 15,000 registered players and there were more than 200,000 players in the country including teams in educational institutions from primary to tertiary levels. Papasergio and Moy noted that there were many defections from cricket to softball in Western Australia, including former Australian player Flo Ireland.[6] Softball, hockey, tennis and netball were the most popular schoolgirl sports in South Australia in the two decades after World War II.[7]

It is extremely paradoxical that an imported bat and ball game from America should take root and grow at a much faster rate than an inherited British game with a long history in Australia. It is also ironic that this North American game was the fastest growing sport in the country in the 1960s and 1970s. There are a number of possible explanations. Softball was regarded as a suitable 'women's game' because it was a modified form of the men's game of baseball. While it was played by men and women in the USA, it was entirely a women's game in Australia and did not intrude in any way into the territory of men. The instant success of this game suggests that women and girls were just as keen to become involved in a team sport as men and boys were.

Although softball was often a social game, interstate and international competitions were set up in a comparatively short period. Australia defeated New Zealand by two Tests to one in Melbourne in 1949 and became the first world champions of softball by winning the world series in 1965, defeating the United States in the final.

Despite the very large numbers of registered and social players and the success of the national team, softball, along with netball — which was the next women's team sport to boom — has not become a mass spectator sport with a sound commercial basis, nor has it attracted wide media attention. In fact a newspaper report of 19 October 1975 noted that the NSW Softball Association 'shares the financial strains that all amateur sports endure'.[8] It is likely that softball has suffered because it has been viewed more as a social sport than as a serious competitive one — which has been the lot of many women's games.

It is also likely that team games involving women suffered in the conservative climate of the 1950s when women seem to have been regarded rather more prominently as home-makers or, in the case of Hollywood stars such as Marilyn Monroe, as sex objects. However, the correlation between growth in women's cricket and eras of strong movements for female rights is far from perfect. Certainly there seems to be a link in the first decade of the 20th century and in the 1970s and 1980s, but there were clearly other factors involved in the 1930s which was not an era noted for its strength in women's movements.

The decline of women's cricket in the late 1950s and 1960s suggests that, despite the great gains in the 1930s, the game was not established as yet on a permanent and continuing basis. Many of the crowds which had enjoyed the game in the 1930s did not stay with the game in the 1950s. The most likely explanation was that continuing prejudices against women playing this team sport were maintained well into the 1970s by large sections of Australian society.

Club, school and interstate cricket

Women's club cricket had to start all over again in 1945. Six years was a long gap in a woman's career and during this period many had retired, had a family, were too old or had drifted into other sports or leisure activities. Many of the administrators, too, had moved away from cricket or were no longer committed to the game. It was only a minority of the stronger clubs — such as Collingwood and Hawthorn in Victoria and Kuring-gai and Sydney University in NSW — that continued after 1945.

Most states had much smaller competitions after 1945. Whereas Perth had boasted nine teams in the 1930s, only three reformed after the War: Subiaco (Cambridge), YWCA 1 and 2. There was a gradual increase in the number of teams in Perth over the next decade: Willows and Maccabeans were established by 1948 and South Perth by 1952. Not all the teams survived however and the Willows folded after a few years. Although there were other clubs around in the 1950s — Midland, Cygnets, Fremantle and Bassendean/Bayswater — the number of clubs was well below the halcyon years of the 1930s and the teams which did exist in Perth in the early 1950s often battled to fill their numbers week by week.

A similar picture emerges from club cricket in Victoria though

The Sydney University side, photographed on Adelaide Railway Station, took four days—sitting up in a 2nd class compartment—to reach Adelaide for the Intervarsity. From left: Gwen Stone, Moira Whiteside, Ruth Jones, Helen Brolly, Marie Burns, Joan Shaw, Jill Worrall, Joan Handsman, Marion Castle, Kath McCredie, Jean Coriskin, Enid Shaw (captain). (Courtesy Helen Brolly)

this state did more to nurture women's cricket through its difficult decades. During the 1960s Victoria dominated the interstate tournament — winning it six times in a row from 1965–70 — largely because it was able to maintain an effective network of club cricket. Although there were never as many as the thirty-nine clubs of 1939, there were still some twenty-eight teams playing in the state in 1969. Victoria, according to one commentator, at this stage fielded as many teams as all the other states put together.[9] If this was the case, it is likely that there was less than half the number of clubs in the country (approximately sixty) than there had been in 1939 (with a known total of ninety-six clubs in the states of NSW, Victoria and Western Australia).[10]

Women's cricket survived through the 1950s and 1960s because the core who remained in the game, as players and administrators, were deeply committed to the game. Some of the obstacles to playing top level cricket were formidable. Western Australia managed to attend two interstate tournaments in Melbourne and Sydney even though the cost and time involved in travel was very substantial. It took six days of train travel to get to Sydney (and another six to return) and by the time the players reached the eastern states for a ten-day tournament there they were often too tired and unfit to give a good account of themselves on the field.

Coralie Towers who, at the age of thirteen (the youngest player ever to represent her state) made her debut for Western Australia at the Melbourne tournament in the season of 1952–53, recalled the problems of getting to Melbourne and, in the following year, Sydney. First there was the problem of persuading her father to allow her to travel such a long distance and stay away for such a considerable period. Since her father had previously allowed her sixteen-year-old brother to participate in inter-state football, he felt he could not deny his daughter a similar experience. Towers recalled that travelling to the eastern states included several nights of sitting up on the Adelaide to Melbourne and Melbourne to Sydney legs. On her first trip to Melbourne she curled up on the luggage rack, sleeping on a bed of blazers and skirts, but during the next night she was informed that she had had her sleep and would have to sit up the next night like the rest of the team.

Towers had only started playing club cricket for Subiaco 2nds two months before making the state team. She had always enjoyed playing cricket with the boys in her street but was surprised to discover (like so many other women in this era) that women actually played cricket. Her father had heard of women playing cricket but thought this occurred only in Victoria and not in Western Australia.

Selected for the 1961 and 1963 tours to New Zealand and England respectively, Towers recounted that there were similar sacrifices to be made simply to be part of an international tour. The 1963 team was in fact announced thirteen months before the tour so that the women could raise the large amount needed to cover their fare. The sum she had to raise was £500 which represented about a year's salary. For the privilege of representing her country she had to sell her car, obtain leave without pay from the Department of Education and help organise and be part of a round of fund-raising activities such as fashion parades and club barbeques. All the players of this era had to work very hard to tour.

Dawn Rae (nee Adams) of Victoria actually missed out on the tour to New Zealand in 1961 because of a quaint custom (which she had overlooked) that each player who wanted to be considered for selection had to pay a deposit of £20. Rae was selected in the side but her selection was overturned because of her failure to pay the deposit. She was unlucky enough to miss two more international series: in 1963 she married and in 1968–69 she gave birth to one of her two children. She finally made the World Cup tour in 1973 but required great support from her mother — who minded her two children — her husband (a club cricketer) and her club, Olympic, which raised an enormous amount towards the airfare of $800–900.[11]

Raising the fare was only one part of the preparations. Betty Wilson recalled that travelling to England for a long tour required a substantial wardrobe. In her case it included two evening frocks, three after dinner frocks for meeting dignitaries, three or four walking out sets, a travelling uniform, a practice uniform and a playing uniform.

It is quite obvious that Towers, Rae and Wilson and the other players of this era were very dedicated to the game of cricket, for the rewards and recognition were minimal. When Western Australia was unable to be part of the interstate tournament from 1956–62 Coralie Towers and another top player, Maureen Brigatti, were still keen to play in the tournament with whomever would give them a game. They joined a composite side and even played for another state, such as Queensland.

It is interesting to explore why players such Towers, Rae and Wilson dedicated so much of their sporting life, and made so many sacrifices, to play cricket. In each case there was obviously a great love of the game and in Dawn Rae's case her family played an important role in her cricket career. She claimed that she had 'no choice' but to play cricket as her grandfather, 'Pop' Anderson, who was the organiser of Collingwood Women's Cricket dances for years, had mapped out her sporting career

---

MAY MILLS OBE MACE (1890–1984) was born at Millbrae on her family's South Australian property, the first Merino stud farm in the state. She was the middle child of nine and attended Black Hill Valley School and MLC Melbourne. Her father, William George James Mills, was an MLC. The family property 'Sturtbrae' is now a National Trust classified building.

May Mills was a teacher from 1914–52 and taught at Unley High School for thirty years. She became the first female President — after serving four year as Vice-President — of the SA Institute of Teachers in 1943.

May Mills played a prominent role in the development of women's cricket and women's sport in South Australia. She was President of the SAWCA and the AWCC in the 1960s and became a life member of both. She became President of the SA Women's Amateur Sports Council and lobbied the then Premier, Sir Thomas Playford, to secure greater playing fields for women's sport. She succeeded in gaining tenure of twenty-six acres which became the Women's Memorial Playing Fields — honouring women who fought in the war — on which were constructed three ovals, eight tennis courts, and the well appointed Mills Pavilion. She enticed major corporations, such as ISAS, to test their heavy machinery on the ovals by clearing and levelling the grounds, thus saving thousands of dollars in developing the ovals for sporting pursuits. The Fields are the de facto headquarters of the SAWCA, which has been unable to secure tenure because of some legal ambiguities in the trust left by Mills.

May Mills took a keen practical interest in all aspects of the playing fields, clambering around embankments in her often muddy rubber boots, planting, watering and tending ground cover and young trees and organising armies of young cricketers, with military efficiency, to harvest the almond crop which provided a source of additional funds.

A notable woman in her time, May Mills was active in many spheres of public life. She became the first President of the SA Film and Television Council in 1957, was a founding member of the Australian College of Education, a life Vice-President of the National Council of Women and a life member of the Royal Commonwealth Society. When she stood as an LCL candidate in 1958 she failed by just 502 votes to emulate her father and win a seat in the Legislative Council.

May Mills was the first woman to secure a driver's license in South Australia. She was also an ardent royalist.

Her contribution to women's cricket was recognised by the creation of the May Mills Trophy for the Under 18 national Championship.

---

before she had even thought of it. When the crowds dwindled at club games in the 1950s Dawn Rae could always count on a good number of her family, both parents and grandparents, attending matches on a week-by-week basis.

Coralie Towers was fortunate to secure great support from some of the leading men cricketers of Western Australia including coach Ken Meuleman and leading players Graham McKenzie and Des Hoare. She benefited greatly by training with the men's team at the WACA. When her teaching career took her to the country she opened the bowling for the men's team at Quairading.

Player after player of this era attested to the lack of any alternative team sports for women and girls. Dawn Rae, who played street cricket with lots of boys in her street, stated that if you didn't play cricket 'you stayed home and sucked your thumb'. She would have loved to have played football but that was not an option open to girls. School team sports for girls in the 1950s were limited: there was no cricket at Westgarth High, the school Dawn Rae attended.

Sylvia Faram was fortunate to attend Abbotsleigh, one of the private schools in Sydney with a long cricketing tradition. The school has produced many top cricketers including the Peden sisters and Denise Annetts and had two cricketing headmistresses, Betty Archdale and Kath McCredie. Sylvia Faram, who captained the First XI, recalled that cricket was not particularly strong at Abbotsleigh — there was much greater interest in other sports such as tennis and softball. The school boasted of just one team and the competition roster was a limited one with a match against PLC Pymble and a game against the local boy's college, Barker, 'which was a bit of a joke'. The experience was sufficient, however, to whet Faram's appetite to play more cricket as an adult. After representing Australia in hockey in 1954 she joined the Melbourne YWCA club in 1955 and represented Victoria in 1962–63.

Cricket also survived in the 1950s and 1960s because it had a core of dedicated administrators determined to sustain the game. Despite the declining numbers supporting the game, administrators took a number of initiatives to further its development. The first Junior (Under 21) Interstate Cricket Tournament was held from 13–19 January 1960 in the NSW country town of Deniliquin. It involved teams from NSW, South Australia and Victoria along with a side from New Zealand and a local team representing the host town. The age of players in the NSW side — the only one with listed ages — ranged from fourteen to eighteen. In Western Australia another initiative was the instigation of the Secondary Schoolgirls' Competition in 1964. At the initiative of Coralie Towers a competition was begun and was

Ian McBain's — — — — — — — — — Sportoon

One of the silent, impressed male spectators at the women's cricket match at Adelaide Oval on Saturday was sports cartoonist Ian McBain. His healthy respect for the cricket ability of these Amazons he shows in his cartoon of the day's play.

"The Advertiser"

Courtesy Mollie Dive

administered by the State Schools' Sports Association.

Leonie Randall, in her study of sport at the secondary and tertiary level in South Australia from 1945–65, has suggested that the occasional school cricket game in the 1950s was replaced by more regular competition in the 1960s and 1970s. At Woodville High School there was an inter-house competition in 1946 but there was no further activity until 1957 when the school entered an inter-school competition. Adelaide High School joined the same competition in 1961 but others, such as Walford and MLC, did not participate in cricket competitions until 1975.[12]

There was rather more activity at the University of Adelaide when a women's cricket side was formed in 1948 and two players, Lurline Barlow and Ruth Dow, were selected for the state side, and in the case of Dow, the national side. There was also an active team at Adelaide Teachers' College from 1948 but by 1962 and 1963 interest in the game began to dwindle and the team was disbanded temporarily due to insufficient players.[13]

Victorian administrators did much to nurture interest in the game. Although the state was not able to produce a magazine of the quality and size of the *Australian Women's Cricket* in the late 1930s, the VWCA published a magazine for much of the 1960s — a simpler format and a cheaper gestetner-produced publication — which provided details of club news and events.

> **SYLVIA FARAM**
> (b 1929) developed an interest in cricket while watching her brother play in school matches. She played cricket at Abbotsleigh, and became captain of the school cricket and hockey teams.
>
> When Faram attended Melbourne University she played hockey rather than cricket. After playing right half in the University A team, she won a place in the Victorian team in 1951 and made the Australian team in 1954 when she played in an international tournament in Sydney. She later coached the Melbourne University and Nunawading teams. When the Victorian Women's Hockey Association divided into a state and a Melbourne association, she became the first President of the Melbourne Women's Hockey Association. She managed the Australian Women's Hockey Team on its first tour of Malaysia in 1962.
>
> A right-arm off break bowler, Faram joined the YWCA Cricket Club in 1955 and represented Victoria in 1962. She was prominent in cricket administration from the 1960s: she was on the executive of the VWCA — and its President for two periods in the 1960s and early 1970s — its delegate to the AWCC and President of the AWCC from 1978-88. After resigning from this post she took on the role of Archivist. She became a life Member of the AWCC in 1988.
>
> Sylvia Faram also made her mark as a pennant golfer with the Metropolitan Golf Club and was elected Associate Captain in 1984 and 1985. She came from a sporting family — her brother, Brian, represented Victoria in rugby.

Faced with limited resources, administrators did their best to provide the most innovative program of cricket possible. New Zealand was invited to Australia for a short tour in January 1957 in which they participated in the interstate tournament and then played a Test at King's College Oval, Adelaide. The Australians, thanks to a Una Paisley century (101), hit up a big score of 9-354 declared which was sufficient to beat New Zealand (98 and 168) by an innings and 88 runs. It is interesting to note that women's cricket authorities were doing far more to encourage the development of the game in New Zealand than their male equivalents. After the New Zealand men offered little resistance in one Test in the 1945-46 season they did not secure the privilege of a Test until the 1972-73 season.

Papasergio and Moy have suggested that the 1960s was in fact the 'starting point for the great upsurge in women's cricket in the 1970s'.[14] While there was not much evidence of revival on the surface, the groundwork was being laid for the more receptive 1970s and 1980s. It seems quite clear that some of the leading players of the 1950s and 1960s were determined to assure the future of women's cricket.

International cricket 1958-68

A decade elapsed between the 1948-49 English tour to Australia and the next in 1957-58. The First Test from 7-10 February proved a dismal event. By 1958 the women cricketers had moved from the grandeur of the SCG to the unimproved North Sydney Oval with one tiny grandstand and primitive facilities. To make matters worse it rained heavily and the match was abandoned without a ball being bowled.

Rain also saturated the St Kilda Oval and there was no play on the first day of the Second Test but a damp and treacherous wicket set up a very intriguing second day. Sent in to bat, Australia could only manage 38 runs with Betty Wilson top scoring with 12 and leg spinner Mary Duggan taking 7-6 off 14.5 overs. One Australian barracker at least had a good sense of humour. When Australia subsided to 5-17 and the name J Christ went up on the board the loud comment was heard around the ground: 'Thank God, we've got a chance. J Christ is out there now.' The first name of the Australian Christ was actually Joyce.

The wicket which suited Duggan was tailor-made for off spinner Betty Wilson who outstaged Duggan in that her 7-7 off sixty-three balls also included a hat-trick — the first in women's Tests. England were bundled out for only 35 runs. It was always difficult to keep Betty Wilson out of the game and she scored a fine century on an improving wicket enabling Australia to declare

The easy and balanced bowling action of Betty Wilson. (Courtesy AWCC)

at 9–202. Australia had England on the ropes at 8–76 — with Wilson in the action again with 4–9 and Ruth Dow taking 4–21 — but some determined stonewalling by English bat Wilkie, who scored only 5 runs in eighty-six minutes, saved the tourists.

It is hard to imagine a more commanding Test performance in the history of men's and women's Tests than that of Betty Wilson. She took 11 wickets for just 16 runs including a hat-trick and followed that up with a century in a low scoring match. She top-scored in both innings. She was the first Test cricketer, male or female, to complete the match double of 100 runs and 10 wickets in a Test match. (Alan Davidson achieved this double two years later in the historic tied Test at Brisbane.)

The Third Test at Adelaide from 8–11 March was played on a much better batting wicket but Australia again looked to Betty Wilson to rebuild its innings after losing 4–66 and the star player obliged with her second successive century, 127 out of a total of 292 — Wilson's score at the time was the highest made in Anglo-Australian Tests. England made a good response of 325 but Cecilia Robinson's 102 took up too much time (365 minutes) and the match petered out to a draw. Betty Wilson, who took 6–71, showed that she was an effective bowler both on the difficult St Kilda pitch and the truer Adelaide wicket.

The location of the final Test at the WACA ground, Perth, two weeks later speaks volumes for the initiative and enterprise of those who ran women's cricket. Despite the decline in women's cricket in the late 1950s the authorities had seen fit to add a fourth Test to the program and to take the game to Perth. They were far more imaginative than the men who did not play a Test at the WACA for another twelve years.

The Test was played under the most promising circumstances. Apart from being the first ever cricket Test in Perth it was billed as Betty Wilson's last. The fate of the series and the Ashes was also at stake. In the circumstances there were reasonable crowds — Coralie Towers recalls that there were about 500 a day. The days when women's Tests drew crowds in the thousands, as had come to the WACA in the 1930s, had long gone.

The wicket in Perth, as had been the case in Adelaide, proved too good for a decision to be reached in three days even though both sides made sporting declarations in the interest of a result: England declared its first innings closed at 6–253 and Australia replied with 7–280. After England were dismissed for 188 Australia had the impossible task of scoring 162 runs in 51 minutes. By her own high standards, Betty Wilson had a moderate game, scoring 43 runs and taking 2–83 and 2–34. Australia's captain Una Paisley would have preferred to have retained the Ashes with a better result than 0–0 in four Tests.

The Australian women cricketers did not have an opportunity to tour anywhere during the decade from 1951 until there was a short tour of New Zealand in 1961 which included one Test. New Zealand cricket had obviously improved during the 1950s — by the late 1950s they had six associations and about 1 000 players. They had the better of Australia in the rain-affected Test at Dunedin played on 17–20 March. New Zealand declared at 8–241 and 193 while Australia replied with 138 and 8–100.

In 1963 Australia took a largely new team to England from that of 1958, though captain Mary Allitt was one of the survivors of two previous series. There were no other players from the previous tour which had occurred twelve long years before. England also had a number of new players, including the talented Rachael Heyhoe, and in fact had a good blend of young players and seasoned campaigners such as Mary Duggan and Ruth Westbrook.

The First Test was played at Edgbaston on 15–18 June before what must have been an encouraging first-day crowd of 2 000. After Australia totalled 173, thanks to an aggressive and hard-hitting 47 by Hazel Buck, England replied with 196 with off break exponent Miriam Knee (4–39), the pick of the bowlers. A conservative declaration by Mary Allitt at 5–223 left England only 105 minutes to get 200 runs and a draw resulted.

Dismal weather — rain on the first day and thick fog on the final day — robbed Australia of victory in the Second Test at Scarborough a fortnight later. On the first day Miriam Knee (5–35) combined with left arm pace bowler Helen Lee (3–24) to dismiss England for 167. Skipper Mary Allitt (76) and Miriam Knee (82) put on a record sixth wicket partnership of 125 to build up a total of 276. Mary Allitt batted more than four hours for her runs and was the subject of some ribald barracking from some building workers perched on the scaffolding.[15] England were on the verge of an innings defeat but were saved by thick swirling fog which resulted in the loss of two-and-a-half hours play. Miriam Knee, who was fielding in slips, recalled that there were times when all she could see of the fielder at square leg, Elizabeth Amos, was her socks and shoes.

England won the series and recovered the Ashes in the final Test of the series at The Oval — winning the game with only three minutes to spare. On a firm and true batting strip England's captain Mary Duggan scored a fine 101 not out enabling England to declare at 8–254. Hard-hitting Elizabeth Amos (55) and Hazel Buck (47) were then the top-scorers in the Australian reply of 205. England hit up some quick runs on the final day and, after declaring at 7–160, set Australia a reasonable run chase of 210 in 225 minutes. Although Australia were in trouble at the last interval at 5–98, the match was in doubt until the final wicket fell and Australia were all out for 160.

The verdict of some of the Australian players on this tour was that while standards of cricket in the two countries were comparable, women's cricket 'has taken a stronger hold over there [in England]'.[16] Certainly a measure of financial support, in terms of government grants, occurred earlier in England than Australia, as did sponsorship. When the 1968–69 English team visited Australia they looked 'smart' and 'cool', according to a local newspaper, in their patterned blue Courtelle mini dresses which were supplied as part of a £500 grant from Marks and Spencer. The well-known chain store had helped to defray individual touring

---

BETTY WILSON
(b 1921) was the daughter of a boot maker who worked in Hoddle Street, Collingwood, and made special lightweight boots for his daughter. A talented and natural athlete who could 'run like a hare', Betty Wilson developed a fine throw when still at primary, Victoria Park State School. She learnt her cricket playing against the lamp post with neighbouring children.

While watching a game of the Collingwood Women's Cricket Club at Mayor's Park, Clifton Hill, she impressed when she returned several balls from the boundary and was recruited to play for the club side although she was still only ten. She played out the season with this adult club scoring 25 not out in the final and being voted the 'most improved player'. Wilson was extremely keen on cricket and used to work on her footwork at home, using a ball in a stocking attached to the clothes line.

When she was hit by a ball while batting in her first season with Collingwood, questions were raised in the local council as to whether a child should play an adult game. Her father, along with her mother, who were keen supporters of her cricket career and who had great confidence in her natural ability stated that 'she has been hit once ... she won't be hit again'. Her parents always attended games when she played.

Betty Wilson was one of four children in a not very well-off family, and at the age of fourteen she left school to attend Business College which enabled her to get a job as a clerk in an office. By that age she had already been selected for the Victorian 2nds and travelled to Adelaide to play in a match against South Australia. Two years later she had made the senior state side. Because of the war she did not have the opportunity to play Test cricket until 1948.

During the time she played Test cricket, Wilson established a reputation as an outstanding all-rounder — an attacking bat and a fine off spin bowler — the leading woman cricketer of her day and the greatest female cricketer ever to represent her country. She created over a dozen Test records and played in an attractive and confident manner which was much admired. Photographs establish her natural and fluent style of both batting and bowling.

Although Wilson played only eleven Tests, she scored 862 runs at an average of 57.47 including three centuries and three half centuries. She took, in addition, a record number of 68 wickets at an average of just 11.81. Included in this was one astonishing innings return of 7 wickets for 7, which included a hat trick. During this match (the First Test against England in 1958) she created a record for the number of wickets in an innings (seven) and the number of wickets in a match (eleven).

Her achievement as a cricketer was a combination both of her great natural ability and her keenness to harness her talent. Such was the meticulous way that she prepared for her game that she even starched her hat so that it would not flap while she batted. She was very much ahead of her time in that she practised every day whereas most of her peers were satisfied with practice once a week. With her talent and confident outgoing personality she became a celebrity in her day.

After her retirement she moved to Western Australia. She was honoured in the 1980s when she was the first woman cricketer admitted to the Australian Sporting Hall of Fame. Under 21s compete for the Betty Wilson Shield at the Australian Championship.

WOMEN'S CRICKET

AUSTRALIA
v
WANGANUI

COOK'S GARDENS

Saturday, 25th February, 1961
11 a.m. to 6 p.m.

Souvenir Programme and Score Sheet - Price 1/-

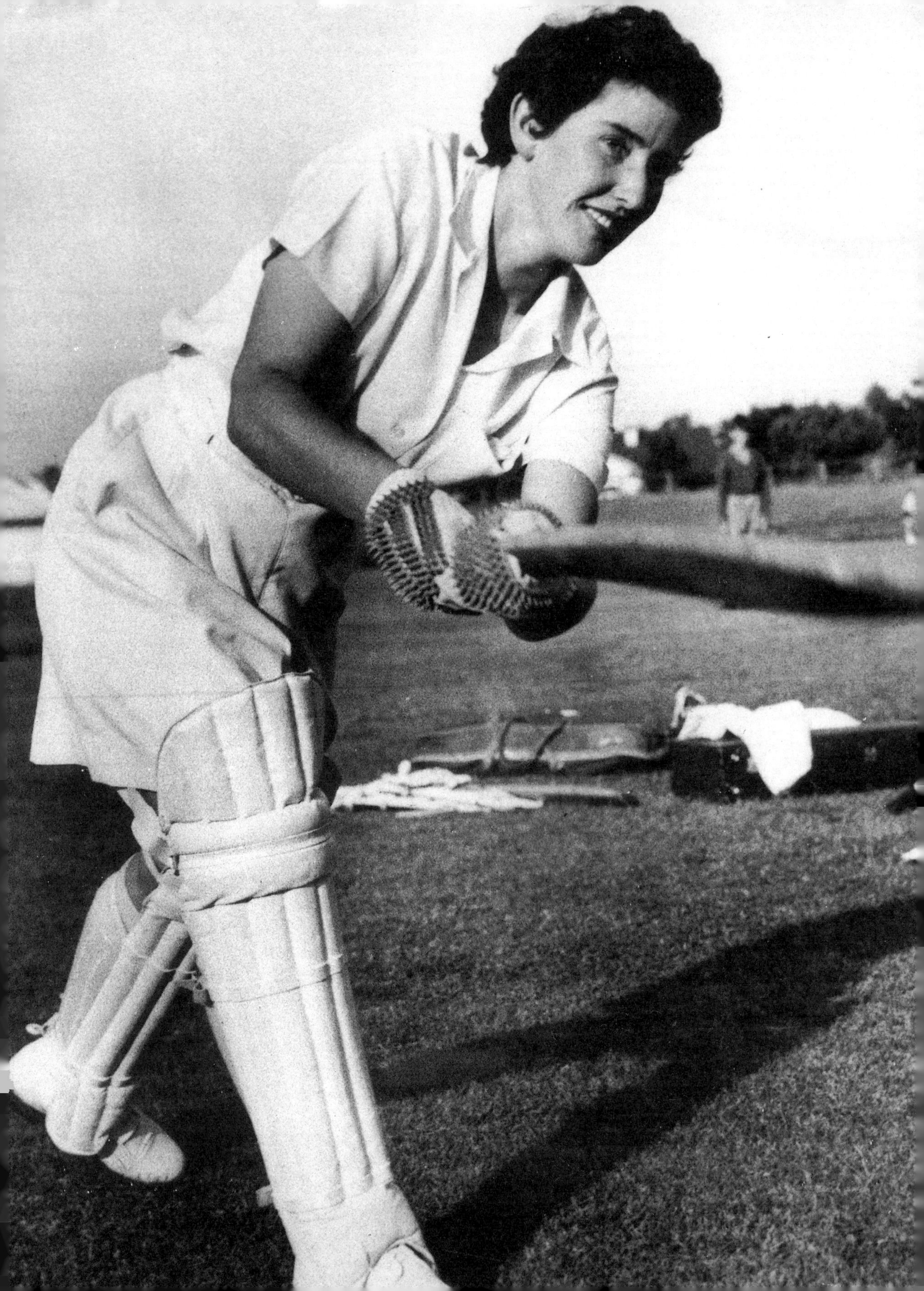

MARY ALLITT (nee Loy) (b 1925) was born in Deniliquin, NSW, and worked on the family farm prior to her marriage. Her first experience of cricket was at a small one-teacher school, Pretty Pines, where all the available children, boys and girls, were recruited to form two teams. She later attended Deniliquin High School. Mary Allitt came from a large family and all 12 children played cricket often and even the dog fielded in family games. There were occasions when the Allitts formed an XI and challenged other sides. She had no formal coaching and as a child played with limited equipment. There were no gloves, a pick handle was used for a bat, a box or tin constituted the stumps and a composite or tennis ball was used for play.

Allitt trained in Deniliquin with the men's team as a women's cricket team, which had functioned before the war, had been disbanded. It took more than twenty-four hours by train to reach Sydney for selection and representative matches and Allitt made this trip two to three times each season.

A solid opening bat, renowned for her powerful back cut, Allitt played eleven Tests for Australia over twelve years. She was a member of the 1951 tour to England and was Vice-Captain in the home series against England in 1957-58 and Captain on the 1963 English tour where she scored two centuries (150 and 118 both not out) in county games. It was during the latter that she achieved her best Test score of 76 in the Second Test and with Miriam Knee put on a world record sixth wicket stand of 125 rescuing Australia from a position of 5-51. Mary Allitt was dismissed by Mary Duggan in both her first and last Test innings.

Facing page:
Miriam Knee, captain of Australia in the first World Cup. (Courtesy Muriel Picton)

expenses by the 'generous kitting-out of "on duty" uniform — to the tune of four separate outfits each'.[17] The NSW team — presumably lacking any form of sponsorship — looked 'dull' by comparison.

Muriel Picton, Vice Captain to Mary Allitt in 1963, was selected Captain for Australia for the First Test played at Thebarton Oval from 27 to 30 December 1968. England, led by Enid Bakewell (113) and Captain Rachael Heyhoe (76), scored at a good rate to reach 270 fifty minutes before stumps. Australia scored an even bigger total, declaring at 7-339, but batted far too slowly and into the third day and the game petered out into a draw. Miriam Knee had an outstanding match with bat and ball — taking 5-49 and 3-19 and scoring 55. Three other Australians batted well: Lyn Denholm (93), Dawn Newman (76) and Joyce Goldsmith (58). The English Captain scored 68 in the English 2nd innings.

Both the Second and Third Tests, at St Kilda and North Sydney ovals respectively, were drawn providing a second 0-0 Test series and assuring again that the Ashes were retained (this time by England) without the satisfaction of a win. It was becoming more and more obvious that it was difficult to achieve a result in three days — even with several sporting declarations — though a four-day Test against England did not eventuate until the 1984-85 series. The number of draws also underlined the improvement in the standard of women's cricket. Gone were the days when a stronger England side could demolish an Australian XI in three days as it did in two of the three Tests in 1934-35.

In the 2nd Test in 1968-69 Captain Heyhoe (54) — her third successive half-century — and Vice Captain Edna Barker (100) laid the basis of another impressive English total of 8-254 declared. Australia were deep in trouble at 5-53 but Miriam Knee was again prominent with a fine 96 runs out of a total of 216. Both sides attempted to make a game of it on the final day: England declared at 7-143 leaving Australia 182 to win in 119 minutes. The task was too difficult and Australia finished at 5-108. Australian pace bowler Anne Gordon had a fine double taking 5-61 and 5-57.

Australia, batting first and scoring 213, set the pace in the final Test. After England replied with 193 Australia produced some of the liveliest batting of the series and declared at 3-210. It was England's turn to chase quick runs in the fourth innings but the target of 231 runs in 165 minutes proved too difficult and the visitors ended at 6-155. Lorraine Kutcher, who had toured in 1963, had a good comeback Test, scoring 52 and taking 5-49 and 1-19.

Conclusion

During the 1960s women's cricket almost disappeared from public notice and from the sporting map. Tests, played on suburban grounds, were lucky to secure a brief paragraph or two in the newspapers, often buried at the bottom of crowded sports pages. There was more media attention in Victoria, where the women's game had a few loyal media supporters, than in any other state.

The general sports public, which had shown some degree of support for women's cricket in the 1930s and again after World War II, now exhibited a massive indifference to the game. Once the novelty of the game had worn off, the crowds which had attended previous matches deserted in droves. It must have been extremely difficult for players and administrators to retain their enthusiasm given that there was so little sympathy for their efforts and virtually no recognition whatsoever. Women's cricket was saved from potential oblivion because there was a sizeable core of persons with a great love for and dedication to the promotion of the game. In an era of general decline new junior and school competitions were established and new initiatives, such as a Test at the WACA and more exchanges with New Zealand, were introduced.

The revival of cricket in England in the late 1960s must have provided much hope for the future. England had an outstanding captain in Rachael Heyhoe who had a flair for promoting the game on and off the field and the beginning of government and business sponsorship pointed the way to a better future.

MURIEL 'PIXIE' PICTON (b 1930) was born in Singleton NSW and grew up on a farm. She attended Maitland High School and Newcastle Teachers' College. There was no women's cricket at school and limited cricket at college and she developed her interest by playing with her brothers at home and practising with the men at Teachers' College.

When she became a primary school teacher she moved to Sydney to take up an appointment at Bankstown East (now Greenacre). She remained a teacher until her retirement in 1985.

Muriel Picton played club cricket for YWCA from 1951 until the 1970s. She was a right arm slow bowler (mainly off breaks) and a useful lower order bat who captained Australia against New Zealand in 1961 and against England in 1968–69. She played in seven Tests of which six were drawn.

A quiet and unassuming individual, she showed a determination to play positive and sensible cricket and to bring out the best in her side. Her best performances included match figures of 3–51 off 23 overs in the First Test against England in 1963 and a ninth wicket partnership of 53 with Helen Lee in the Second Test of the same series.

She represented Australia in hockey at an international tournament in Holland in 1959 and Malaya in 1962. She was President of NSWWCA for a few years.

CHAPTER SIX
REVIVAL IN THE 1970s

Introduction
The context of women's sport changed in the 1970s with the emergence of feminist movements, popularly dubbed 'women's lib'. The impact of feminism on women's sport was gradual and indirect. Many of the leading feminists of the 1970s were not particularly sympathetic to sport and it did not figure on their political agendas. They did not address the problem of female sporting rights, arguing instead that sport was so riddled with male culture that it would be better for the whole culture to be dismantled. Anne Summers devoted one chapter in *Damned Whores and God's Police* to the 'Sporting Wife' who guarded the home front while her spouse disported himself at the pub, club or the sports ground.[1] Academic Lois Bryson argued in 'Sport and the Oppression of Women' that sporting culture was so deeply misogynist that it was almost beyond redemption.[2]

It is also true that while feminist movements were successful in reframing political agendas, society was slow to adjust and to accept some of their central tenets. Many men, in particular, were hostile to feminist movements which were ridiculed as the excesses of what the media defined as a bra-burning minority. Other men accepted the need for some change but their concessions to women were token at best. Long-held prejudices, particularly against women playing team sports, did not disappear overnight.

The important area of change in the 1970s related more to women than to men. Feminism encouraged a widening independence. Women joined the work force in greater numbers than ever before: the number of women in the Australian work force increased by 68 per cent from 1966 to 1982 as compared with an equivalent increase in the male rate of 26 per cent and by 1982 women made up 40 per cent of the work force.[3] Work opportunities provided women with more discretionary income and self sufficiency.

It was during the 1970s that many women, who had long accepted male dominance of sporting culture, became far less willing to accept gender restrictions on sport. It was in this decade that some women began to run and swim marathons, to lift weights, to become involved in bodybuilding, to become jockeys, to sail long distances solo and to participate in sports, such as boxing, which had been largely reserved for men. Pam O'Neill, a Brisbane beauty salon proprietor, had become one of the new breed of 'jockettes' by the mid-1970s. By September 1973 the Queensland Turf Club had introduced the first official race for female jockeys and had benefited from increased gate takings. Many other clubs followed this example. A number of women had the opportunity to enjoy international rowing competition when an Australian team contested the first ever world women's rowing championships at Lausanne, Switzerland, in 1974. Bev Francis was beginning to make her name in the macho world of bodybuilding which would have been unthinkable in previous decades. This was also the time that other women started knocking rather more loudly on the doors of male sporting establishments, such as Lord's, demanding admittance.

In this period women also had a greater participation in team sports. Netball, previously known as women's basketball,[4] was the fastest growing sport in the country in the 1970s and 1980s and its explosion in popularity in this time exceeded that of softball in the 1950s and 1960s. Leonie Randall has suggested that netball, like softball, was another modified game embodying the 'principles of limited movement and non-contact' and 'was ideally suited to the perceived physical deficiencies of women and the current concepts of appropriate feminine behaviour'.[5] National registrations for this sport, which were 2 891 in 1947, jumped to 200,000 by 1977 and to 359,351 persons in 1990, which made netball the fifth largest participant sport.[6] It was estimated that if unregistered and social players were added the total number of netballers would be more than 750,000 at that time.[7]

Slowly a more sympathetic environment to women playing sport emerged. The media, which had ignored for decades most women's sport outside the Olympics and tennis, began to take more interest in a wider range of women's sport. This was in part because of the changing character of women's sport, which was creating many newsworthy items, such as the first female jockey or the first women to play at Lord's. Greater publicity also occurred because of an ongoing shift in the attitudes on the part of the audience. The media, always sensitive to shifts in the orientation of audiences, gradually came to terms with the greater consuming power of women in the 1970s. There were also a minority of more progressive males — politicians, journalists, educators, businessmen — who recognised that the time had come for a fairer go for women in sport.

Adrian McGregor contributed a thoughtful article to the *Bulletin* of 7 February 1974 in which he stated that he believed that male chauvinism in sport was because 'men don't like women to be like men: they equate aggression as a male characteristic and aggression in sport as their inalienable right'. McGregor also contended that males feared any challenge to their dominant sporting position:

Male admiration for sportswomen is often accompanied by a fear of the physical superiority of these women. Several of Australia's best sportswomen never married and complained privately of the awe with which men treated them socially.

At Hawkesbury Agricultural College last year student Emily Cohen confounded male students by winning the sportsman of the year cup. She only competed against the boys in one event, the cross country, but the boys were piqued at her taking the trophy, symbol of male physical dominance in any educational centre.

The changing attitudes towards women and women's sport also encouraged some male journalists to have another look at women's cricket, perhaps their first serious examination since the 1930s. Former Shield player and cricket journalist, Alan Shiell, attended the January 1973 interstate tournament at Scotch College, Adelaide, and filed a frank report on the attitudes of men towards women playing cricket in the *News* of 8 January 1973:

Sadly, or otherwise (depending on whether you're a male chauvinist pig or in sympathy with women's lib.) women cricketers have been subjected to the type of derisive gossip and frowns normally afforded male ballet dancers.

I mean it's a man's game, ain't it, sport?

Yes, a girl's thinking is questioned when she tells friends she is a cricketer...

For those who had reservations Shiell recommended that they watch the tournament. He discovered it to be a 'slightly unnerving experience' as the standard of play was 'amazingly high. The girls' enthusiasm would put many district cricketers to shame.'

It was in the 1970s that women's cricket was thrown the 8lifeline of sponsorship which provided, really for the first time and in a tentative manner, the prospect of long-term continuity and even growth. By the 1970s it was quite clear that no minor sport could hope to flourish without substantial government and private sector backing. Such support was essential to stage more regular international events, which were becoming increasingly costly but were the necessary foundations for a build-up of public interest and media attention.

World Cup of 1973

A casual chat after dinner in June 1971 between Rachael Heyhoe Flint[8] and millionaire, Jack Hayward, who was based in the Bahamas, led to the first ever World Cup with Hayward offering to contribute the huge sum of £40,000 to cover the accommodation expenses of players. It wasn't Hayward's first act of magnanimity towards women's cricket; previously he had underwritten two English tours to the West Indies in 1970 and 1971. Hayward and his daughter, Susan, had flown to the West Indies during the latter stages of the first tour to support the team. The new post of Patron was established by the WCA in 1974 to honour the grand benefactor of women's cricket.

The World Cup was a major boost for women's cricket in the 1970s. It generated much needed publicity for the game, the likes of which had not been seen since the 1930s. This imaginative concept preceded and perhaps inspired an equivalent men's World Cup which followed two years later in 1975.

The first World Cup involved seven teams. The three founding Test nations were represented: England, Australia and New Zealand. They were joined by two West Indian teams: Jamaica, and Trinidad and Tobago. The remaining two were Young England and an International XI.

The inclusion of two sides from the West Indies added to the interest in the series. A Jamaican Women's Cricket Association was formed in 1966 followed by a Trinidad and Tobago Women's Cricket Association in October 1967. English teams toured the West Indies in 1970 and 1971 and an unofficial Test was played between England and Jamaica in February 1971.

An experienced and balanced Australian side, captained by

Miriam Knee, included a short week-long visit to the West Indies to play several warm-up matches before the World Cup. Despite the generosity of Jack Hayward members of the Australian team had had to raise £600 towards their own expenses for the privilege of playing in the World Cup.[9] 'Many of them' were reported to 'have done two jobs, day and evening, for well over a year to raise money for the trip'.[10] After two limited overs games Australia had the better of Jamaica in a two-day match: Australia 5–222 declared led Jamaica 152 and 1–56. Dawn Rae's hard-hitting 95 was the feature of the Australian innings. She had a penchant for large scores. Two seasons after the World Cup Rae scored 228 in a record-breaking partnership of 478 along with Jan Wilkinson (252 not out) in a Melbourne club match. Then in the following season, in 1975–76, she scored 249 not out for her club side Olympic.

During the five weeks of the World Cup, Australia and England emerged as the strongest sides in the tournament with New Zealand and the International XI as the next best. Midway through the tournament Australia stood at the top of the table with four straight wins though the match against New Zealand proved a tight one with Australia winning by 35 runs.

Weather then intervened in two crucial matches. England were desperately unlucky to lose against New Zealand. In a rain-reduced match New Zealand scored 7–105 in 35 overs. The match was called off after England had batted 15 overs and were 1–34. New Zealand won on a superior run rate. Australia, in their second last match, could have achieved a near unassailable position — at worst they would have finished on equal points with England — with a win against the International XI but rain only allowed five overs and the Australians had to settle for one point rather than four points for a win.[11]

The quirk of the weather set up the best possible final between the two best sides at Edgbaston on 28 July. The match was played on a damp and dank day in front of a crowd of 1 500 and in the presence of Princess Anne. The final produced some entertaining cricket. After England won the toss they produced some scintillating batting with opener Enid Bakewell playing a fine knock of 118 and gaining valuable support from Lynne Thomas (41) and Rachael Heyhoe Flint (64). England achieved a record and winning score of 3–279 off their 60 overs. It was a remarkable achievement for Bakewell who had scored 1 031 runs and taken 118 wickets on the 1968 Australian tour — the first woman to achieve this tour double — and who, by 1973, was a mother of three. Australia made a good initial effort at chasing the score but fell away after the dismissal of openers Bev Wilson (41) and Jackie Potter (57) to end the day at 9–187.

It was a popular win for Rachael Heyhoe Flint's side and a fitting climax to weeks of competition. The Australian captain Miriam Knee, who had battled hard to take 2–53 off her eleven overs, was gracious in defeat conceding that while Australia had been unlucky not to win the coveted Cup, England were deserving victors. Knee must have recognised that this popular win for the home side was a great boost for women's cricket in England and throughout the world.

A few weeks after the World Cup win the successful English women took on a team of 'Old Boys' — some of the former male cricket greats including Compton, Evans and Hutton — at the Oval before a crowd of 5 000. The match, organised by the *Evening Standard*, saw Old England squeeze home on their second last ball after the women had scored 6–171 in 45 overs.

Courtesy Ann Mitchell

The impact of the World Cup

Women's cricket authorities must have been delighted by the extent of publicity generated by the World Cup. However, not all the publicity was necessarily favourable and many male sub-editors had a field day devising headlines featuring plenty of puns and sexist language. One article on the Australian team was headed: 'A side full of fine legs', and another 'No longer on cricket's outskirts' and yet another 'Bowling the maidens over'. Other headings were simply 'corny' such as the following: 'What a frill, England win the Cup'. There was no reference to sport whatever in the heading of one story on the World Cup final: 'Bakewell cooks up a mum's special'.

There was also a certain amount of confusion on the political implications of women playing cricket. An article written by Heyhoe Flint to mark the beginning of Cup competition on 20 June was headed 'Milestone for Women's Lib'. However, *The Field*, in a lengthy feature on the Cup, on 14 June, assured its mainly male readership that they had nothing to fear in that the 'women are truly amateur, anything but militant and had been at it, without male uprising, long before suffragettes were invented'.

The Field ended with a rather quaint and diffident final paragraph about the coming World Cup competition:

'Girls,' says the song, 'were made to love and kiss, And who am I to interfere with this?' The next six weeks may show whether girls were made to bowl and bat; but, whatever the answer, who am I to interfere with that? I wish them well and much fun. There seems little doubt that they are intent upon it, and that is a good start.

However, during the World Cup the bulk of the publicity — mostly written by male sports writers — was decidedly favourable. Richard Streeton, who watched the match between Young England and New Zealand, reported that he had 'a far happier day than I had expected' and that the players 'radiated enjoyment and enthusiasm'. Vivian Jenkins took his hat off to the Australians (and other teams) who had sacrificed so much to participate in the World Cup. David Talbot wrote on 28 July that 'it is no longer fashionable to disparage women's cricket; not that anyone who has seen the England team in action is ever likely to do so'.[12] He ended his feature with a positive portrait of Rachael Heyhoe Flint who found cricket tremendously challenging since it was both a team and an individual game. Flint, whom he believed had 'perhaps the liveliest mind in British women's sport' was also 'lucky to have a husband who understands why I have to go dashing off to play'.

Gerry Hand in *The Times* offered a rather more sober assessment and warned against getting carried away with the success of the tournament:

Money is the great problem. The first ever competition was entirely dependent on the generosity of Midland-born businessman Jack Hayward, who contributed £40,000 towards the accommodation costs of the players. It will be hard enough finding again players of the quality of Bakewell, Flint, and Wilson to arouse the public interest. It will be even harder to find another Hayward.[13]

Hand's assessment proved unduly pessimistic. The amount of media coverage and public interest generated by the World Cup assured that other sponsors were likely to queue up behind Hayward in the future.

The success of the Cup confirmed the prospect of future play at Lord's. One of the disappointments of the Cup was that the Final match was not staged at the headquarters of cricket even though every variety of the men's game — including school, village and county cricket — was played there. After the Final the President of the MCC, Aidan Crawley, announced rather condescendingly that women had passed the test and could anticipate future play at Lord's: 'You have done enough to deserve a game at cricket's headquarters, and a date should be reserved there for a Test between England and Australia in 1976.'

When the IWCC met after the World Cup two new members, Barbados and India, joined for the first time. It was reported that 'enthusiasm for women's cricket was growing' in India. In the same year as the World Cup a Women's Cricket Association of India was founded and the first National Women's Championships, involving five provinces, was held in Poona. The new Indian association made a request for an English team to tour there in 1974.

Other international tours

The revival in women's cricket in the 1970s led to a far more extensive and varied program of international exchange. In the previous two decades Australia had toured only three times and participated in six Test series playing fourteen Tests against two countries: England and New Zealand. During the 1970s there were four overseas tours and a fifth for an under-25 team. There were six separate Test series (eleven Tests in all) played against four opponents: India and the West Indies were added to the old rivals of England and New Zealand.

A greater number of tours meant considerably more costs. Prior to the visit of a New Zealand team to Australia in 1971–72 it was reported that the NSWWCA were attempting to raise money for the tour: their efforts included a jumble sale at Campsie and washing cars at Liverpool. The proceeds from a social match against the men of the Dubbo Rugby Union Club also went

---

RAELEE THOMPSON (b 1945) was active in netball in primary school but discovered cricket when she attended Shepparton High School. She left school at an early age and began working in the pathology unit of a local hospital.

Thompson began playing A grade softball in Melbourne and finally moved there when she was twenty. At the instigation of Dawn Rae she joined the Collingwood Cricket Club and took 6-8 in her third game for the club against YWCA. Thompson was selected for the Victorian 2nds in 1969 and made the state team in 1970.

She played her first Test against New Zealand in 1972 — securing her opportunity when Anne Gordon broke her arm — and was a member of the 1973 World Cup side.

Thompson, along with Sharon Tredrea, spearheaded the Australian attack by the time of the 1975 tour to New Zealand and was the chief wicket-taker on the 1976 tour to the West Indies and England. She was appointed Vice Captain of the Australian side for the 1982 World Cup.

The Jubilee Test series of 1984–85 represented the pinnacle of Thompson's career. She began the series as Vice Captain but took over the captaincy for the Second Test after Captain Sharon Tredrea tore her Achilles tendon. Thompson had an outstanding series taking 18 wickets at an average of 15.72 and taking 5-33 in the final and deciding Test of the series at Bendigo.

She retired from international cricket at 39 but continued to serve as an Australian and Victorian selector. After almost twenty years of service, she resigned from the police force, partly out of disappointment with the lack of recognition provided for her status as an international cricketer. Working in the fingerprint bureau at Melbourne's Russell Street Police headquarters, she had played a role in solving a number of crimes.

Raelee Thompson was a dedicated cricketer who always worked hard at her game. 'I used to practise, practise, and then practise some more.'

towards the tour. In order not to overextend the budget the interstate tournament was not held in this season. There was, however, the beginning of some encouraging signs from sponsors with Rothman's National Sports Foundation paying for a fourteen week coaching course for the leading twelve NSW women cricketers at Barry Knight's cricket centre.

The one Test of the series was played at the St Kilda ground, Melbourne, and began on 5 February 1972. Given the succession of Test draws — Australia had not won a Test since 1957 — it was decided to extend the Test match to four days. The match was also the first women's Test to include Sunday play.

The additional day proved to be of benefit to New Zealand who achieved a first ever Test victory against Australia in an exciting match. The first day was dominated by Australia who dismissed New Zealand for only 89 and were 2–109 at stumps. Left-arm spinner, 34-year-old Lesley Johnston, who was not afraid to give the ball plenty of air, had a dream debut taking 7–24 off 13.2 overs. Johnston, who was the mother of three, stated that she had not represented her country earlier because 'every other time I had a chance of being selected I was having a baby'. She had a supportive husband, who was also a club cricketer, and her children also went to watch her play each Saturday.

Brilliant catching brought the visitors back into the game as Australia lost its last 8 wickets for just 20 runs and were all out for 129. A fine opening stand by New Zealanders Janice Stead (95) and Judi Doull (56) enabled New Zealand to accumulate what proved to be a winning total of 335. Set 296 to score on the final day Australia could only manage 152.

After the Australian tour New Zealand continued on to South Africa where they won a three-Test series by 1–0. It was the second tour of South Africa as England had won a four Test series there in 1960–61 also by 1–0. Plans were well advanced for a South African tour of Australia, beginning in December 1966, but it was cancelled by the South Africans. There were to be no further tours of South Africa in the next two decades. The IWCC cancelled a proposed English tour of South Africa in 1972 on the grounds that it would jeopardise tours of the West Indies.

Perhaps buoyed up by the the success of the World Cup in 1973 two Australian teams travelled overseas in 1974–75. The senior side travelled to New Zealand and the one Test of the series was drawn after both sides scored large totals in the first innings. New Zealand scored 359 and 6–276 decl. and Australia replied with 362 and 1–47. The Australian team were undefeated with four wins and six draws, with rain interfering in many matches.

Meanwhile an under-25 side embarked on a five week tour of India and the program included three three-day 'Tests' in

Betty Butcher and daughter, Susanne, prior to leaving for India in 1975. Susanne, who was already playing cricket, subsequently represented Victoria in Under 21s.

Calcutta, New Delhi and Poona. The tour to India was a bold initiative to build up youth cricket in Australia and was an attempt to promote women's cricket in India which, in the opinion of Ann Mitchell, had a 'bright future'. A makeshift and inexperienced side, captained by Cecilia Wilson, gave a very good account of itself and became a formidable combination. Although women's cricket was still in its infancy in India, it was reported that the sport was played by 600 players in ten provinces.

Government assistance for women's sport was more forthcoming in the 1970s. The Australian women's softball team received a

> **BETTY BUTCHER**
> (b 1925) developed an interest in cricket from her father, who was an RSL cricketer and a member of the Melbourne Cricket Club. He taught her to score even before she went to school.
>
> She attended Williamstown High School where she was a fine athlete and became the state 50 and 75 yard champion. Her mother was not keen on her participation in athletics because she regarded the costume (shorts) as unladylike; however, her parents had no objection to Betty playing cricket and she joined her first club, Blue Socials, at the age of ten. Before that she had played cricket with the boys of her street.
>
> World War II prevented Betty playing cricket while a student at Melbourne University but she later joined the Richmond Club and remained there for five years. She then joined the Olympic Club as a player and coach and during a twenty year association the Club won its first premiership followed by six more. At age twenty she was a member of the state squad but was told that she was too old for the national championships.
>
> Betty Butcher has contributed much to women's cricket as an administrator, coach and historian. She was Treasurer of the AWCC from 1970–76, Acting Secretary in 1977 and 1988, and Secretary in 1975 and has been made a life member. She was Secretary of the IWCC from 1982 to 1988 and has held various posts with the VWCA. She managed the Under 25 team which toured India in 1975. Her research on the beginnings of women's cricket in Victoria, *The Sport of Grace*, was published in 1984.

grant of $11,000 — which paid half the air fares for the team — for a tour of North America which began in July 1974. Women's cricket did rather less well receiving a paltry grant of $880 towards the New Zealand tour and nothing towards the Indian tour, on the grounds that support would only be given for one tour. Ann Mitchell, President of the NSWWCA at that time, spoke out forcefully on the question:

> But this is an unusual year for the AWCC; they have never been faced with two tours before — and are never likely to again.
>
> Indian officials wanted us to come last October when, it seems, we could have been helped. But we were not ready for the tour then.
>
> So the 'kids' have to pay themselves.
>
> The captain, Cecilia Wilson, who is a 20-year-old Sydney University student, has had to pay out $800 for fares, uniform and equipment.
>
> Our association helped its three representatives by raising $100 for each.
>
> The trouble is our sport is so strictly amateur that we are continually bleeding our players for trips within Australia, never mind tours overseas.[14]

Even if the young Australians had to dig deep in their pockets the rewards of playing on the subcontinent outweighed the initial hardships. They played a one-day game at Bangalore in front of a reported crowd of 25 000 and the 'Test' at Poona attracted 'more than 40 000'.[15] Prime Minister Indira Gandhi was openly supportive of the tour.

The Australian women in India must have wondered why there was so much public interest in a junior national side when any equivalent match in Australia would be lucky to attract a handful of spectators — essentially their friends and relatives. They must have been puzzled why Indian women's cricket, still very much in its infancy, seemed to generate such instant support. Perhaps they sensed that women's cricket in India benefited from the novelty factor as had women's cricket in Australia in the 1880s and 1930s. They must have recognised that the love of cricket in urban India was similar to Australia's love affair with the game in the 1930s when crowds flocked to all forms of cricket. However, none of these explanations fully account for the apparent great public acceptance of women's cricket in India and the yawning indifference in Australia for the majority of its history. It is hard to resist the conclusion that the prejudices against women playing certain team sports have been far deeper in supposedly enlightened Australia than the more openly-patriarchal society of India.

An added attraction of the next tour of England in May 1976 was a three-week tour of the West Indies in April with two Tests

Chapter Six

in the West Indies and another three in England. By the mid-1970s the cost of representing one's country had become very high indeed. Each woman was asked to raise $1 875. Patsy May, Convenor of the NSWWCA fund-raising committee, was irate at the lack of government support for the tour:

> These girls also have to give up their jobs or go on leave without pay during the three months tour.
>
> What a strange society ours is in which national sportsmen and women win so much honour for their country and yet receive no help from their Government.
>
> It's just as important to help these unemployed ambassadors overseas as it is to help the unemployed at home.[16]

Many of the women would not have toured at all but for the generous fund-raising activities of local clubs, male and female. The cause of nineteen-year-old Marie Lutschini, the first woman from the NSW country town of Wellington to gain an Australian blazer, was taken up by the men's Wellington District Cricket Association because there wasn't even a women's team there. The local association expressed pride in her selection and set up a fund-raising campaign to support her.

Women's cricket tours, like men's, had their share of controversies. Before the tour even got underway opening bat, Bev Wilson, felt so strongly about selection that she withdrew from the tour. Wilson wrote to the AWCC that she 'did not consider the selected team to be truly representative of the standard of women's cricket in Australia'. The young and relatively inexperienced side did not let the selectors down and melded into an effective and successful unit.

Australia played its first ever Tests against the West Indies at Montego Bay and Sabina Park, both of which were drawn. Spinner Marie Lutschini starred with the ball taking 4–48 in the First Test and 5–51 in the Second Test. A number of her wickets were snared behind the stumps by Margaret Jennings, who created a record for the number of stumpings in an innings — four — in the First Test.

It seems that by 1975 the MCC was having second thoughts about women playing a Test at Lord's in 1976. It was reported in the *Sun-Herald* of 21 December 1975 that Rachael Heyhoe Flint would report the Club to the Equal Opportunities Commission for refusing permission for the coming series to celebrate the golden jubilee of women's international cricket.

Symptomatic of the changing character of women's cricket the Test series was assisted 'by the generous sponsorship from the St Ivel department of the Unigate group'.[17] The first Test of the tour was held in Manchester. Sent in to bat on a cloudy and chilly day

Facing page:
Raelee Thompson.
(Courtesy Menna Davies)

Australia soon established that it had a strong batting side and was able to declare at 6–273 with Janette Tredrea (67) and Jan Lumsden (65) the top scorers. England's strong reply of 6–254 declared included Rachael Heyhoe Flint's first century (110) against Australia. With the large scores and the loss of play due to weather there was no possibility of a result. Australia were 6–128 at close of play. The Test was the first in England to include Sunday play but it was still played over only three days.

The second Test at Edgbaston followed the pattern of the first with both sides scoring well in the first innings. After England declared at 9–242, Australia declared at 7–236 with Margaret Jennings (104) scoring her maiden Test century. After England hit up quick runs to declare at 2–228 Australia were set 235 to win in three hours. They made a brave effort but the task was too much and the match finished in another draw with Australia 6–169.

In the interests of securing a result the final Test at The Oval was extended to four days. England had long opposed a four-day Test arguing that results could be achieved through initative. When England was bundled out for just 134 at 5.15 p.m. on the first day it seemed that a result was more than likely. Australia confirmed its advantage by scoring 379 — the largest Test total in Anglo-Australian Tests — with Scottish-born Jan Lumsden (123) scoring the first century at this venue in women's Tests. To save this Test England had to bat out the best part of two days. They found a rescuer in captain Heyhoe Flint who batted for eight hours and forty-one minutes for her 179. Australia's attack had been restricted when its champion fast bowler Raelee Thompson had broken her finger fielding a ball in slips. Although the final Test was drawn, as were the previous two, the balance of international cricket was now tilting towards the young Australians who were undefeated on tour: they won seven games, drew thirteen and one was abandoned.

Although the young Australian side could not defeat England when it 'wavered on the brink of defeat' as Ann Mitchell later put it, they did have the satisfaction of performing well even though they were defeated in the one-day series by two matches to one.[18] They lost the first ever women's cricket match played at Lord's on 4 August. Women did not get on to the Lord's turf easily as the second one-day international was originally scheduled for Sunbury. It was only after the failure of the men's Middlesex team — whose home ground was Lord's — to make the Gillette Cup quarter-finals, that the August 4 slot became available for the women. In front of a crowd of 1 000, and 'amidst a considerable flurry from the Press', Australia were all out for 161 — with Sharon Tredrea scoring 54 and having the distinction

---

ANNE GORDON
(b 1941) of Victoria is one of only three Australian women (the other being Betty Wilson and Karen Price) to have taken ten wickets in a Test. A left-arm pace bowler (but right-hand bat) she achieved this in her Test debut against England in 1969 when she took 5–61 and 5–57.

Anne Gordon attended Moe High School and later became a credit officer by profession. She played first for the YWCA Club in Melbourne and later joined the South Hawthorn Club and was also a gifted athlete who excelled at the 100 metre sprint. When she made her debut for Australia she was Secretary of the VWCA and held that position for many years.

During a men's match in 1972 held to raise money for an overseas tour Anne Gordon broke her arm and was never able subsequently to straighten it fully. She was often no-balled because of her unusual action as a result of this accident. Despite the handicap, she made a good comeback and captained Australia on the 1976 tour to the West Indies and England. She was the first woman to lead Australia in a Test against the West Indies and the first to captain the side in a four-day Test against England.

Gordon later moved to England and was a selector for England in 1991.

> **MARGARET JENNINGS**
> (b 1949) of Victoria was a good opening bat and an outstanding wicketkeeper who achieved twenty-four dismissals — fourteen catches and ten stumpings — in eight Tests and scored, in addition, a century and two half centuries.
>
> She played first for the Essendon Club but later formed, and was first President of, the Brunswick Park Club in the 1970s.
>
> Jennings made her debut against New Zealand in 1972 and took three catches and one stumping and repeated the feat in her next Test against New Zealand in 1975. By the time she toured the West Indies and England in 1976 she was an accomplished bat and when she scored 104 in the Second Test at Edgbaston she was the first Australian keeper to score a Test century. In her final Test against India in 1977 Jennings captained Australia and contributed to the victory with 57 runs and two catches. She also captained the successful 1978 World Cup side.
>
> A physical education teacher by profession, Jennings was coach of the Victorian team which won the Open National Championship in 1990/91.

of making the first female half century at Lord's. England passed the Australian score for the loss of just two wickets with Enid Bakewell 50 and Chris Watmough 50 not out.

Australia eventually broke its Test drought a year later winning its first test for some two decades when an Indian side, returning from a tour of New Zealand, played a Test at the WACA in January 1977. Australia, under new Captain Margaret Jennings, scored 266 and 1–152 declared and comfortably beat India 122 and 149. Elaine Bray scored 86 in the first innings and Lorraine Hill (74 not out) and Margaret Jennings (57) put on a century partnership in the second innings.

The Australian side at this time did not include 'five of our best young cricketers' who had toured England in 1976 because they had not been able to afford to travel to Perth for the interstate tournament and had not been considered for selection. The five were: Janette and Sharon Tredrea (Victoria), Karen Price and Julie Robinson (NSW) and Kerry Mortimer (SA). Having just come back from an international tour, the players in question were unable to raise an additional $500 to travel to Perth let alone deal with the problems of obtaining leave from their employers. Ann Mitchell reflected on the emerging finance problem in *Australian Cricket Yearbook* of 1977:

> With so much international competition occurring nowadays, the problem of finance has come right to the fore.
>
> Our strictly amateur players are finding it hard to keep up.
>
> Jobs are not secure for young people today and they can't afford to be trotting around the globe or even just Australia, every six or 12 months.

On the field, however, it was the beginning of a golden decade for the Australian women cricketers. They won the second World Cup in India in 1978 and then defeated New Zealand by 1–0 in Australia in 1978–79 in the the first three-Test series between the two countries.

The second World Cup was a much smaller, less well organised and less successful event than the 1973 triumph. Netta Rheinberg, in her account of the event in *Wisden 1979*, outlined the wide range of problems:

> In the months before the World Cup, information from that country was scarce, so that progress with preparations became difficult. Six teams had indicated their willingness to take part, but owing to political and financial difficulties, both Holland and West Indies withdrew, leaving only Australia, New Zealand, England, and India. By the time these teams arrived, there had been a change of management in India and political innuendos had crept into the organisation, which unfortunately left much to be desired. Furthermore, too little cricket had been arranged for the visitors.

LORD'S GROUND

England won by 8 wickets

(5p) — (5p)

ENGLAND v. AUSTRALIA
LADIES' INTERNATIONAL MATCH
60 overs each side (No bowler may bowl more than 12 overs)

Wednesday, 4th August, 1976

AUSTRALIA — Innings

#	Name	State	Dismissal	Runs
1	L. Hill	Victoria	c Hodges b Stephenson	0
*2	M. J. Jennings	Victoria	l b w b Bakewell	18
3	J. Tredrea	Victoria	b Hullah	9
4	J. K. Lumsden	N.S.W.	run out	8
†5	D. A. Gordon	Victoria	c Hodges b Bakewell	3
6	S. A. Tredrea	Victoria	c Flint b Allen	54
7	W. J. Hills	W. Australia	run out	27
8	K. Price	N.S.W.	c Hullah b Allen	4
9	P. May	N.S.W.	l b w b Thomas	1
10	M. A. Lutschini	N.S.W.	run out	27
11	W. A. Blunsden	S. Australia	not out	7
			B , l-b 3, w , n-b ,	3
			Total	**161**

FALL OF THE WICKETS
1—0 2—15 3—34 4—38 5—41 6—112 7—118 8—127 9—127 10—

ANALYSIS OF BOWLING

Name	O.	M.	R.	W.	Wd.	N.b.
Stephenson	10.4	3	27	1	...	...
Hullah	11	0	23	1	...	...
Bakewell	12	3	30	2	...	...
Court	12	3	34	0	...	...
Allen	9	2	28	2	...	...
Thomas	5	1	16	1	...	...

WOMEN'S CRICKET ASSOCIATION — ST. IVEL INTERNATIONAL CRICKET

ENGLAND — Innings

#	Name	Region	Dismissal	Runs
1	L. Thomas	West	c Price b May	30
2	E. Bakewell	East Midlands	run out	50
3	C. Watmough	Kent	not out	50
†4	R. Flint	West Midlands	not out	17
5	M. Lear	Kent		
6	J. Court	Middlesex		
7	J. Allen	Sussex		
8	J. Cruwys	West Midlands		
9	J. Stephenson	Yorkshire		
10	G. Hullah	Middlesex		
*11	S. Hodges	Sussex		
			B 1, l-b 13, w , n-b 1,	15
			Total	**162**

FALL OF THE WICKETS
1—85 2—93 3— 4— 5— 6— 7— 8— 9— 10—

ANALYSIS OF BOWLING

Name	O.	M.	R.	W.	Wd.	N.b.
S. Tredrea	12	4	23	0	...	1
Price	10	2	26	0	...	...
Gordon	12	3	37	0	...	...
May	12	1	24	1	...	...
Blunsden	10.2	1	37	0	...	...

Umpires—M. Bragger & I. Nowell-Smith
Scorers—K. Mortimer, E. Solomon & E. Stuart-Smith
† Captain   * Wicket-keeper
Play begins at 11.00   Stumps drawn at 7.00
Luncheon Interval 1.15—2.00
Tea Interval 4.30—5.00 (may be varied according to state of game)

Australia won the toss

SHARON TREDREA (b 1954) was brought up in Summer Hill Road, Reservoir, Victoria where she was the only girl among a tribe of boys and had no choice but to play cricket. From an early age this Victorian speedster claimed that she could hold her own and there were 'a few of them sporting my bruises'.

Her career almost did not get off the ground because of a back problem developed at the age of sixteen. However, under the coaching of former Australian player, Nell McLarty, she was good enough for selection in the 1973 World Cup. During this tour she began a very successful opening combination with Raelee Thompson: Tredrea confounding batters with her pace and Thompson with her variety. She also toured England in 1976 and became the first woman to hit up a half century at Lord's. By that tour she was regarded as the fastest bowler in women's cricket.

A bank manager, Tredrea was a member of the Australian team in all four World Cups. The back problem returned and she gave up bowling in the 1979–80 season but appeared in the Australian championships, captaining her home state Victoria. With rest and a lengthy preparation she was opening the bowling again in the third World Cup in 1982 and also represented Australia in the 1988 World Cup. She was selected Australian captain in the 1984–85 series but had to withdraw after the First Test through injury. She was a Victorian selector for many years.

Courtesy AWCC

The Australian team holding the St Ivel Trophy, Edgbaston, 1976. Back row L to R: Jan Lumsden, Julie Stockton (neé Robinson), Margaret Jennings, Sharon Tredrea, Mrs Lorna Thomas (manager), Janette Tredrea, Anne Gordon (captain), Wendy Hills, Lorraine Hill, Patsy May. Front row L to R: Betty McDonald, Marie Cornish (neé Lutschini), Karen Price, Wendy Blunsden, Kerry Mortimer.

Tour Manager, Ann Mitchell, in her report to the AWCC after the tour, confirmed the extent of the World Cup problems:

The tour will go down in history as one of the most incredible that any Australian team has ever undertaken. In the final stages of preparation there were doubts about whether the tour would proceed owing to the withdrawal of the West Indies and the lack of communication with the Indian Association ... Continual changes to the 'itinerary' while we moved around India served to frustrate the players further.

Whereas the first World Cup included many matches played over five weeks the Indian World Cup amounted to just six matches played at four venues. Each of the contestants played each other just once.

While it was a very much scaled-down tournament, Australia had still to beat the two world cricket powers, England and New Zealand. Australia and England again proved the dominant nations and both had wins against India and New Zealand setting up the last match at Hyderabad on 14 January as the final. England batting first could only manage 8–96 in its 50 overs with Sharon Tredrea taking 4–25. Australia easily passed that total in

Sharon Tredrea is well balanced in her final leap before delivering the ball. (Courtesy Menna Davies)

> LORNA THOMAS MBE
> (b 1917) began her cricket career with a piece of wood and a tennis ball when she was an eleven-year-old schoolgirl living in the Rocks area. Although she attended school at St Patrick's Church Hill, she played cricket at nearby Fort Street Girls' School. She later played district cricket for fifteen years with Annandale.
>
> A medium-paced bowler and a hard-hitting opening bat, she made the NSW side in 1937. After retiring as a player in the 1950s Mrs Thomas, affectionately known as Auntie Lorna, managed many Australian teams overseas including the 1961 tour to New Zealand, the 1963 tour to England, the 1973 and 1976 tours to England and the West Indies and the Australian team which met New Zealand in Melbourne in 1972. She also managed the NSW side, off and on, from 1959 to 1976.
>
> Lorna Thomas could not have toured without working and contributing a considerable amount of her own funds. She gained great support from her husband, Robert, who was 'more excited than me when I was chosen for a tour'. He was a 'most unselfish man' and 'we haven't had a holiday together for years' she noted in 1976.[19]
>
> Thomas was Vice-President of the NSWWCA for twenty years from 1960, was a NSW delegate to the AWCC for a number of years and was President of the AWCC from 1967–69.
>
> Journalist Jim McAuley noted that it was unlikely that the 'mild-mannered' Mrs Thomas would be ruffled by any tour problems as each day 'she handles some of the toughest ladies in town'. She was, until 1973, matron in the police department caring for women prisoners. 'We get them all through here' she noted, 'prostitutes, murderers, thieves ... you meet all types.'
>
> A major force in women's cricket for more than fifty years, she always paid her own way when managing teams and had a reputation as a tireless worker for the game — including the catering department. She became a Life Member of both the NSWWCA and the AWCC.

31.3 overs for the loss of only two wickets with Margaret Jennings scoring 57 not out and Janette Tredrea 37 not out. Sharon Tredrea was the star of the tournament scoring 56 against India and 31 against New Zealand.

Domestic, club, interstate

An annual feature on women's cricket, which appeared in *Australian Cricket Yearbook*, was proclaiming the good news by 1973: 'REVITALISATION! Greater interest! Boom times ahead!' Year by year there were reports of both new clubs and associations springing up in all states. Women's cricket began to stir again in two states which had long been dormant: Queensland organised its association again in the mid 1970s and Tasmania in 1982.

The 1973 report analysed the many factors responsible for revival. They included:

the conscious efforts of the State administrators to attract girls to the game and more coaching and publicity; the playing of more one-day, or modified cricket matches; and the impact of the World Cup Series being played in England through June and July.

But, most of all, and the girls have to admit this, the revival of women's cricket is due to the efforts of Ian Chappell and his boys. There has been a general revival of interest in cricket and young girls, just like their brothers, have been spellbound by the feats of Lillee, Massie, Marsh, Walters and the Chappell brothers.

In the next four years the number of women's cricket teams appears to have almost doubled. In the 1972–73 season Victoria reported twenty-eight teams in three grades in the Melbourne district competition and South Australia and Western Australia both had six each in their respective metropolitan competitions. By 1976–77 the Victorian figure had jumped to fifty-three teams while the other two states now had eleven metropolitan teams each.

Growth occurred at all levels of competition. In NSW the number of schoolgirls' teams involved in cricket jumped from fourteen to thirty from 1972–73 to 1974–75. There were also reports of the establishment of many new country associations in this state during this decade at Armidale, Nowra, Orange and Tamworth. With the upsurge of cricket in country areas, the NSWWCA established a country tournament over the October long weekend of 1975. Tamworth emerged the winner from the eight teams which competed.

A promotional game at Oxenham Park, Brisbane, in 1976 which featured Thommo against Thommo, marked the revival of women's cricket in Queensland. The match, which was the first organised by a reconstituted Queensland Women's Cricket Association for a decade and a half, pitted two of Australia's opening bowlers, Raelee Thompson, and Jeff Thomson, against each other. After Jeff Thomson had hit Raelee Thompson for six, she had the last laugh by scattering his stumps in her second over. As Thommo departed he quipped 'I might ask her to partner me in the next Shield match'. Four teams were established when the QWCA reformed in 1976 and Queensland returned officially to the interstate tournament in the 1978–79 season.

Another Test player, Karen Price, actually joined a men's association in 1976, playing two seasons with a B-grade side before playing another three seasons with the Normanhurst A-grade team. While it was not unusual for women to play in men's teams in the country — either because the men were short of quality players or because there was no women's team — it was far less usual for this to occur in the city.

The costumes were varied and brief in the Sun City Association (WA) in 1974. Joan Swadling is batting for Cygnets and the fielders for Postals (from left) are Janice Moy — a cricket author — Patricia Jones, Carol Cunningham (wicket keeper) and Heather Shaw. (Courtesy Betty Butcher)

Conclusion

The 1970s represented a decade of revitalisation for women's cricket. The sport made great gains in terms of publicity and public acceptance. *Wisden* published its first feature on a woman cricketer in 1970, honouring Enid Bakewell. Rachael Heyhoe

Flint was awarded an MBE in recognition of her work for the game in 1973.

There were a greater number of countries involved in women's cricket and an expanded program of tours and exchanges. The success of the World Cup in 1973 placed it firmly on the future calendar as a valuable means of promoting women's cricket.

Although there was a surge of interest in the women's game from 1970, administrators had to start all over again building up the game from a narrow base. The numbers of women playing cricket in Australia were probably not much more than those reported for England. At the time of the World Cup there were a reported 100 women's teams and about 2 000 players in England. This represented only about 0.5 per cent of the estimated number of players in men's teams, some 21 000.

While there was some prospect of a 'boom' ahead for women's cricket, there was the very real problem of who would pay for expansion. The increasing amount of international cricket and tours — which were essential for the promotion and future of the game — was beginning to place an unreasonable burden on everyone involved. At the end of the 1970s it became imperative that the trickle of government and private sponsorship in the 1970s had to be converted into something far more substantial.

The 1970s had been the best decade for women's cricket since the 1930s; there was more club and junior cricket than there had been in any intervening decade. The challenge for administrators at the end of the decade was to capitalise on this interest and to establish the game once and for all on a firm and lasting footing.

CHAPTER SEVEN

EXPANSION IN THE 1980s

The new context of women's sport

By the 1980s there was a substantial shift in social attitudes to the various issues of women's rights raised in the 1970s. Some of the ideas, which were dismissed by many as the eccentric demands of a middle-class minority in the 1970s, gradually percolated into the mainstream by the 1980s. Although many men only grudgingly changed their views on women's rights, governments and influential opinion makers began to take more notice of many feminist issues and incorporated some of them into their political agendas.

Federal and state governments recognised by the 1980s a need for more positive discrimination and greater funding of women's sport and a removal of obstacles which denied women equal opportunities for and access to sport. The issue was aired in 1975 in a Canberra Schools Commission paper on 'Girls, School and Society' in which it was demonstrated that girls suffered in many areas because they were directed towards different roles and were given different expectations. The publication of this study encouraged the various state governments to reduce sexist practices and discrimination in schools.

The NSW Government, for instance, set up the Social Development Unit within the Ministry of Education in 1977 to assist in the elimination of discrimination on the basis of sex and ethnic origin. After sport and physical education were identified as areas of 'disadvantage', the NSW Government took steps to encourage female sport. It sponsored for instance a national conference on women in sport — entitled 'Fit for Play' — which was held at the University of New South Wales from 20–23 January 1980 to address many of these problems. The Government also commissioned a discussion paper on 'Sport in Schools: The Participation of Girls' by Ms Elizabeth Coles. She concluded that girls suffered in many ways in comparison with boys:

Despite the formal aims of the education system, generally girls have access to fewer sports than boys; girls' sport is not as highly valued by the school as boys' sport, and as a consequence receives less support from teachers; girls do not have equal access to facilities; and the resources available to them, particularly financial support, are less than those available to boys. In all these areas, there is a need for change at this level of educational policy if girls' sport is to reflect the basic principles of the education system.[1]

Partly as a result of such initiatives the NSW Department of Education decided to introduce and encourage girls' cricket along with girls' soccer in the state high schools in the 1980s. Official encouragement of these two sports yielded remarkable growth by the end of the decade when it was reported that there were as many girls' cricket teams as boys' in the Combined High School knockout competition and a similar growth in girls' teams occurred in soccer.[2]

Positive discrimination in favour of women's sports also occurred in other states and at the Commonwealth level. The Australian Sports Commission established a Task Force for Women in Sport by the mid-1980s which published a report, *Women Sport and the Media* in 1985.[3] The Women's Sport Promotion Unit — now Women's Sport Unit (WSU)[4]— emerged from the recommendations of this study and this Unit started a 'Women in Sport Newsletter', *Active*, in Autumn 1988. A national conference on 'Equity in Sport' — an initiative of the House of Representatives Standing Committee — enquiring into the Status of Women — was organised in Canberra in February 1991.

It was during the 1980s that women's cricket was placed on a more secure financial footing than previously. Government now began to support women's cricket in many direct and indirect ways: there were specific grants from the Australian Sports Commission for the administration of the sport and sums of money were also given for development projects, particularly programs and camps to promote youth sport. Money was also made available for individual tours from a variety of sources. The Australian Bicentennial Authority and Film Australia produced an impressive forty-seven minute film, 'Fair Play: The Golden Eras of Women's Test Cricket'.

The changed climate of the 1980s and the government backing of women's sport encouraged a greater private sector sponsorship. Shell Australia became the AWCC's leading corporate ally and by 1990–91 had backed women's cricket for some seven seasons. The money from Shell had benefited all facets of women's cricket — at the grass roots level through the Shell Super Clinics conducted state by state for schoolgirls, in AWCC administration, coaching camps, Australian Championships and in supporting tours and international competitions in Australia. Shell also met printing costs for letterhead, business cards, promotional literature and the publication of the AWCC journal, *Between Overs*, from 1984.

By the mid-1980s Shell was the most prominent of the fourteen corporate sponsors backing women's cricket. *Between Overs*, listed some other sponsors in 1985: including the Australian Cricket Board, Ansett Airlines, TNT, A G Thompson, Budget Rent-a-Car, Phillips Industries, Gray Nicolls and Telecom. Contributions ranged from discount airfares, car, bus and truck rentals to cricket equipment, posters and cash grants.

When the Australian women went on their ten-week tour of England in 1987 they could count on a substantial amount of money from a variety of sources. Ray Sneddon, National Executive Director of AWCC, outlined the nature of tour sponsorship:

The [male] Australian Cricket Board had given $500 a player and the Sports Commission $15,000 towards the cost of the tour. Qantas helped with the airfares and $5 000, the Wool Corporation had given $1 000 towards uniforms, Gray Nicolls put $5 000 towards clothing and Puma had helped with training gear and shoes worth $5 000.[5]

Even though the days were clearly gone when women cricketers had to raise virtually all the money to tour, the 1987 team each had to pay the smaller sum of $1 500, which was part payment of fares and other costs.[6]

Ray Sneddon has elaborated on the reasons why there was such increased corporate support for women's cricket. In the changed political climate of the 1980s there was a positive incentive for a company like Shell to be associated with a women's sport — such support could only enhance the status of Shell with the Minister for Sport, who also happened to be the Minister for

'Lefty' Lyn Fullston says no to a run (vs England, 1st Test, 1987, Worcester) and she and the umpire enjoy the situation. (Courtesy Ann Mitchell)

the Environment. Greater support from the government and the private sector meant that women's cricket was placed on a sounder financial and administrative structure with the potential for future growth.

The AWCC also benefited by the support of the male cricket establishment, which came to the sensible conclusion that the growth of women's cricket could only benefit cricket as a whole. The Australian Cricket Board (ACB) assisted women's cricket in many direct and indirect ways: there were some direct grants such as $10,000 given by the Board at the beginning of the 1984–85 series and there was more sharing of coaching and administrative facilities in many states. The support of the ACB was also an important reason why women were admitted to the MCG in 1988 when the World Cup Final was played there. The new spirit of cooperation was reflected in the close liaison between men's and women's cricket in NSW: the administration of women's cricket was housed in the men's NSWCA and a representative of NSW women's cricket was given a vote on the NSW Cricket Association.

There were some limits to the acceptance of women by the men's cricket authorities. When the Australian Institute of Sport established a Cricket Academy at Adelaide in 1987, it was announced that all twenty live-in scholarships were reserved for men. The decision led to a heated public debate. Despite the protests and the opinion of Equal Opportunities Commissioner Josephine Tiddy that this represented a contravention of the Commonwealth Sex Discrimination Act, the ACB remained unmoved. ACB General Manager Graham Halbish argued that the Board was entitled to its stance as it had already been very generous to women's cricket: 'We have made available Test match grounds, financial grants and Kanga cricket involvement to the women ... Kanga cricket is egalitarian and the academy is unashamedly elitist.'

Behind the scenes there have been some more encouraging developments. The Victorian Institute of Sport announced in 1990 that three women had been included in its cricket squad to be coached by Keith Stackpole and Dav Whatmore. The three selected — Natalie Challis, Sue Karasz and Melissa Papworth — joined a squad of twelve male cricketers receiving assistance from the Institute. The program included individual and fitness testing and advice on personal and career development.

Funded salaries enabled women's cricket to establish more permanent posts for professional administrators, such as the National Executive Director and the National Development Officer. Ray Sneddon became the first National Executive Director in the 1982–83 season. Sneddon, who had played district cricket in Melbourne and for the Victorian Colts, had had an extensive career in advertising and marketing. Although his post was only a part-time position, it was an advance on what was before

A thrill for Kanga kids.

It's always been a buzz for Kanga kids to play on a Test ground but this summer the thrill will be bigger than ever. They'll be there with their schoolmates and teachers as just one school will be chosen to represent the entire state.

KANGA CRICKET

achieved by voluntary effort — a recognition that the demands of organising sponsorship required a more ongoing and professional approach. Sponsorship also enabled the establishment of greater administrative support and more coaching, the holding of seminars and workshops at state level, more international meetings and competitions, greater youth development, including camps, and better preparation of the national team.

During the 1985–86 season the AWCC created the new position of National Development Officer. Test all-rounder Karen Price, who had a sound background in management and finance, became the first officer.

The development of modified cricket games is also likely to have added to the number of female cricket players. The modified game of Kanga cricket, which involved both boys and girls, was aimed at the two million pupils in primary schools and was launched in the 1984–85 season. The principle aim of Kanga cricket was 'to provide the means and incentive to schools, so that girls and boys may play a game of cricket, with a minimum amount of organisation and material, and a maximum amount of fun' in a more non-competitive environment.[7] The broader aim was to encourage junior development at the grass roots level so as to maintain cricket's national popularity in the more competitive

Captain Lyn Larsen leads a jubilant Australian team from the field during the First Test against England in 1987 at Worcester. (Courtesy Ann Mitchell)

LYN FULLSTON (b 1956), who developed an orthodox left-hand slow bowling action which accounted for 41 wickets in twelve Tests, acquired the nickname 'Lefty' at primary school. Originally a member of the Adelaide CAE College team she became captain-coach of Flinders University in 1982 and then joined the Eencee Club as captain/coach in 1988. She is a physical education teacher by profession.

Fullston, who represented South Australia from 1978 and captained the side for several years, became a member of the Australian World Cup team in 1982 when she topped the Australian bowling and batting averages — taking 23 wickets at a cost of 12 and with a batting average of 41. An unorthodox batter, she performed well in this tournament. She made her Test debut in India in 1984 and took 20 wickets in the series. In the final Test of the series she took 7 wickets in a marathon spell of 112.5 overs with 57 maidens. Fullston played an important role in the 1984–85 series against England taking 19 wickets including 4–53 off 25 overs at Gosford. She also scored some useful runs and was a fine close to the wicket fielder. Fullston bowled well on the 1987 English tour and was the star bowler in the one day international at Lord's when she took 4–12.

Fullston was a dual Australian representative playing netball for her country in 1978 and representing South Australia in this sport from 1977–84.

Former South Australian team member, Jen Jacobs, stated that 'beneath the exterior of extreme competitiveness' Lyn Fullston 'is an astute, sensitive and very amusing human being'.

sporting climate of the 1980s. The concept of Kanga cricket was developed by the ACB and endorsed by the AWCC. Bronwyn Jones, the Junior Development Officer of the AWCC, liaised closely with the ACB Development Manager, Peter Spence and was well supported by the state associations.

Bats and stumps, used in Kanga cricket, were moulded from durable plastic which made them light and safe, while the bat was closely modelled on a real cricket bat. The ball was made from plastic and was soft enough to require no protective equipment but simulated the bounce of a cricket ball. The Kanga cricket program aimed to develop specific cricket skills and more general motor skills. A feature of the three forms of the game— Kanga Couples, Kanga Co-op and Kanga cricket[8]— was that every participant had equal opportunity to bat, bowl, field and to keep wickets.

The program was initiated after ACB-commissioned market research on 203 Victorian schools indicated a high level of interest. The cost of Kanga cricket over its first three years was $1.1 million which was raised by the Federal Government, the ACB and the major sponsor, the Australian Dairy Corporation — a role subsequently assumed by Western Star Butter. After the program was launched with a flourish by Prime Minister Bob Hawke each school was sent a newsletter, a pamphlet, a hand-

JILL KENNARE
(b 1956) had no idea that women played cricket until she was nineteen when she was studying to become a physical education teacher and was introduced to the game by a fellow student. She then joined the Adelaide CAE Women's Cricket Club. Kennare came from a large family of five but was the only one to take an active interest in sport.

A right-hand top order bat, she was selected for the South Australian Juniors in 1975 and made the Open side by 1978 and was captain at one stage. Her Test debut was against New Zealand in 1979.

Kennare played in the 1982 World Cup scoring 98 in the first game. She was Australian captain — the first South Australian to do so — on the 1984 tour of India. It was on this tour that she began to realise her batting potential, scoring 131 in the Third Test of the series including a huge 6.

She had an outstanding series in the 1984–85 season scoring two Test centuries and another two in the one day internationals. Kennare was one of the most accomplished and attacking batters to represent Australia and was also one of the most consistent. Her 1976 Junior (Under 21) record score of 153 still stood in 1990.

Jill Kennare played lacrosse from 1976 and represented Australia from 1981–87.

---

book and equipment to play the game. A promotional film, featuring well-known television identity Peter Russell-Clarke, was also produced.

From its inception the response to Kanga cricket was 'tremendous' with teachers and students responding enthusiastically to the game.[9] By April 1986 it was reported by Ray Sneddon that 60 per cent of of the 5 200 primary schools had Kanga cricket equipment and the figure had increased to 65 per cent by the next season. It is not known precisely how many of possibly one million children playing Kanga were girls but the equal encouragement of boys and girls would suggest that there must be more girls playing a modified form of cricket than ever in the history of the game. It is also not clear how many girls will make the transition from Kanga cricket to junior and then senior cricket but it would be surprising if there was not considerable carryover. Sneddon believed that the game had the potential to give an increase of 'more than 65,000 more women players' in the 1990s.[10]

Indoor cricket also became immensely popular in this decade. It was one of the fastest growing sports with an estimated 200,000 men and women playing the sport in the early 1980s and an estimated 500,000 by 1991.[11] Although the majority of players were men and boys, this simpler and quicker form of cricket also led to more women becoming involved in a modified form of cricket. Since indoor cricket was a commercial operation, women were encouraged to both form their own teams and also to take part in mixed teams. Undoubtedly some women, as did men, gravitated from indoor to outdoor cricket. Sally Howard reported in *Cricketer* in December 1984 that the boom in indoor cricket was responsible for an increase in the number of outdoor teams organised by the QWCA which had increased that season from eleven to thirteen. Karen Price has captained Australia in indoor cricket while Belinda Clark and Sally Moffat have also represented their country in this sport.

A decade of Australian dominance

Australia entered the 1980s on a high note. The team was number one in the world in limited overs competition and was also challenging for the top place in Tests. The first major event in international women's cricket was the Third World Cup, held in New Zealand in 1982. This tournament was far better organised than the second World Cup: five teams — Australia, England, India, New Zealand and an International XI — played twelve games each over a period of five weeks at various venues over the North and South Island.

Prior to the final, Australia had been undefeated — with eleven wins and one tie — and were firm favourites to beat England, which had a record of seven wins, two ties and three losses. In the games leading up to the final Australia achieved its highest World Cup score (and the second highest on record) of 5–266 against the International XI. Lyn 'Lefty' Fullston, a left-arm orthodox spinner, created another record when she took 5–27 against New Zealand and Jill Kennare was unlucky to miss a century in scoring 98 against India, who 'showed remarkable progress and enthusiasm' even though they won but four of their twelve matches.

Although the home side was not represented in the final, there was a very good crowd of 3 000 in brilliant weather at Lancaster Park, Christchurch, on 7 February, and there was a live telecast of the match. The final proved a tight match which Australia won by three wickets in the second last over. After England scored 5–151 in their allotted 60 overs Australia slumped to 3–28 before the middle order in the persons of Karen Read (32), Sharon Tredrea (25), Jen Jacobs (37) and Marie Cornish (24 not out) steadied the innings to see Australia home.

In 1984 Australia had travelled to India for the first full-scale tour which included four Tests played at major centres in Delhi, Lucknow, Ahmedabad and Bombay. Unfortunately each Test was limited to three days and all four were drawn. The Indian players, while exhibiting fine skills in the spin bowling department, contributed to the draws by their defensive batting which was not surprising given that they were the minnows of Test cricket. There were, however, some good performances by the home bats. Sandhya Aggarwal scored 71, 134 and 83 in consecutive innings at Ahmedabad and Bombay. India also had a good all rounder in medium-paced bowler, Shanta Rangaswamy, who was the first Indian woman to make a Test century. Left-arm spinner, Diane Edulji, was the pick of the bowlers with 6–64 at Delhi, 5–152 (for the match) at Bombay and 3–35 and 1–52 at Lucknow.

The Australian bats scored plenty of runs. Captain Jill Kennare scored 131 at Ahmedabad and centuries were also scored by Peta Verco (105) and Karen Price (104 not out) in the same match, as Australia accumulated a record score of 525 — the highest ever in any women's Test. Verco ended up with a series aggregate of 367 runs. Verco, opening with Lindsay Reeler, was also responsible for establishing a new first wicket partnership of 105. Lyn Fullston and Christina Matthews also set a 9th wicket partnership record of 67.

Karen Price took ten wickets at Lucknow — 6–72 and 4–35 — and finished with a series total of sixteen wickets. Talented spinner Lyn Fullston had the largest Australian aggregate of 20 wickets.

While all the Tests were drawn, Australia won all four of the one-day internationals. Some of these matches were played in front of big crowds, reportedly as large as 20,000. All the games

---

PETA VERCO (b 1956), nee Cook, was a dependable right-hand opening bat and off-spin bowler who first represented Western Australia in 1974. After moving to Perth from the country town of Kulin — where she played cricket with the local boys — she helped form and played with the WA Secondary Teachers' College women's cricket team and then joined the University of Western Australia women's cricket club and then played with the Midland-Guildford Club and is still prominent both as a player and administrator.

Verco made her Test debut at Perth in 1977 but it was not until the 1984 tour of India, and in the 1984–85 series against England that her batting blossomed. She was the batting star of the 1984 Indian tour — scoring 105, 81, 78 and 67 — and batted well in the following series featuring in a century and half-century opening stands with Denise Emerson. She also became a useful bowler taking 9 wickets in the series. Initially a medium paced bowler, a shoulder injury caused her to revert to spin bowling.

DENISE EMERSON
(b 1960), who was motivated by the success of her elder brothers, Test bowler Terry and Perth club cricketer John, joined the Subiaco Club at the age of sixteen, there being no girls' cricket at her school, Newman High School. She represented WA Juniors in 1977 and made the senior side in 1978. A right-hand opening bat, with a sound technique and all the shots in the book she was particularly fond of driving. She first represented Australia in the 1982 World Cup.

After Emerson moved to NSW in 1984 — when she married cricket umpire Ross Emerson — she was the batting star of the 1984-85 series against England, scoring a century (121) in the Second Test and an additional three half centuries. She and Peta Verco set a new first wicket partnership of 114 in the Fourth Test. Emerson toured England in 1987 but did not have as much success on the slower English wickets.

---

were closely contested: the Australians won the first game with ten balls to spare and the third with just four balls remaining. Trish Dawson (77 not out, 58 not out and 46) and Lindsay Reeler (60 and 47) batted consistently.

England toured Australia in 1984-85 for the Jubilee series to mark fifty years of Tests. It was a very long time since the last tour — 1968-69 — and even longer since Australia had held the Ashes (1963) and yet longer still since Australia had won a Test against England (in 1951).

The ambitious character of the tour program reflected the improving status of women's cricket in Australia. For the first time the tour included five Tests. Each Test was of four-days' duration and three of the five were returned to major cricket venues — Adelaide Oval, the Gabba and the WACA. There were in addition three one-day internationals and a gruelling schedule of ten interstate matches included.

The First Test was played at the WACA from 13-16 December. To mark this historic occasion the coin was tossed by England's first captain, Betty Archdale. Jan Southgate, the 1984 English captain, called correctly and England elected to bat. English openers Megan Lear and Carole Hodges had to face some of the quickest women's fast bowlers in world cricket. They opened against the lethal pace bowling of Debbie Wilson, reputed to bowl at 120 kmh. She was backed up by Sharon Tredrea (who captained the home side), Raelee Thompson and Denise Martin.

After England achieved a total of 290, Peta Verco and Denise Emerson established a new first wicket record of 97 before Verco was run out for 36. Jill Kennare (56) and Emerson (84) then took the score to 157. Australia batted on till the third day reaching a total of 251 fifteen minutes before lunch. After England declared at 9-242, with Jan Brittin scoring an impressive 112, Australia were set a target of 282 in 270 minutes. Hopes of an English victory were foiled by a Jill Kennare century, 103 in 167 minutes, and the match ended in a draw with Australia 8-209 at stumps. Raelee Thompson was the pick of the bowlers with match figures of 6-97 off 47 overs.

Australia had a new captain, Raelee Thompson, for the Second Test at Adelaide Oval from 21-24 December — the first women's Test played there since 1958 — because Sharon Tredrea withdrew through injury. All-rounder Karen Price and Annette Fellows were added to the Australian side. After England won the toss they were bundled out for just 91 runs with Karen Price bowling a fiery spell: she took 4-22 off 17 overs. Australia were well on the way to passing the English total before they lost Verco at 80 and then proceeded to build up a commanding lead, totalling 262 almost half of which (121) was scored by opener Denise Emerson.

Although England were 171 runs behind they batted determinedly to reach the highest total of the match, 296, with Chris Watmough (70) and June Edney (50) the leading scorers. Set only 126 in 330 minutes to win, Australia collapsed spectacularly against the English bowlers, McConway and Starling, and subsided to 5–6. Karen Price (51) and Lyn Fullston (28) provided some spirited resistance for a time but England eventually won a very close finish by just five runs. Considering that they had been behind for the majority of the match it was a courageous last day revival. Cricket again proved a great leveller for the Australian batting star at Perth, Jill Kennare, suffered the indignity of a 'pair' at Adelaide.

After the disappointment of Adelaide the Australian selectors opted for fresh blood in the persons of three promising young players for the Third Test at the Gabba on 1–4 January — the first ever Test played on the Gabba. They were right-handed bats, Lindsay Reeler and Wendy Napier, and all-rounder Lyn Larsen. The English side remained unchanged.

England won the toss for the third time in a row and again batted first. Batting was not easy as a torrential downpour had occurred 24 hours before the Test and England took four sessions to score 275. Captain Jan Southgate top scored with 74. Larsen (4–33) and Reeler (2–27) were the pick of the bowlers.

Australia batted with much more conviction in this Test totalling 9–326 declared with Denise Emerson (84) again leading the way and Reeler (59) and Larsen (52) impressing. Although Raelee Thompson took some early wickets — when she clean bowled Lear with the first ball of her second over she had taken her fiftieth Test wicket — there was never really sufficient time for a result and with three injured Australian bowlers England batted out the day to end at 7–204.

The Australian women may well have been disappointed with the result of the series up to this point. But for one bad session they would have been leading England 1–0 (rather than the reverse) with two Tests to go. Regaining the Ashes was now a difficult assignment for Australia, requiring victories in the last two Tests to achieve their task.

However, at the same time they must have been heartened by a growing public recognition of their efforts as women's cricket started to receive greater and more serious attention than it had for decades. Matches were reported at length in the sports pages, there were longer features in some prominent weeklies, such as the *National Times*, and there were more (though brief) reports of the games on radio and television.

Women's cricket, in addition, actually started to attract back spectators, though admittedly on a far smaller scale than the 1930s. Greg Growden noted in the *Sydney Morning Herald* on

---

LINDSAY REELER
(b 1960) scored 510 runs in just ten Tests before a knee injury threatened to impair her promising international career.

Coming from a sporting family — her father was an Oxford Blue in rugby — Reeler was keen on many sports from an early age. She attended Ravenswood School, Sydney, and played in the same team as Belinda Haggett and Sally Moffat. She often practised cricket with boys from nearby Barker College and later, when playing with the women's West Pymble club, practised with male cricketers. She later returned to Ravenswood as a physical education teacher and coached the school cricket team.

A right-hand opening bat and medium-paced bowler, she made the NSW team in 1980, the Australian Under 23 team in 1983 and the national side, when she was selected to tour India, in 1984. She had a very successful 1987 tour of England making three centuries, six half centuries and taking thirteen catches. She shared a record third wicket partnership of 309 with Denise Annetts, who reflected on her partner in the *Sun-Herald* of 8 January 1989:

'She is cool looking. She has that kind of look the West Indian players have. It's a sort of arrogance. It's more than an appearance of control. She knows what she thinks'.

Renowned for her vagueness off the cricket field she has the ability to focus her mind effectively at the crease.

Reeler has kept some of her best performances for one-day internationals. She has been by far and away Australia's most prolific run scorer with 1 034 runs in twenty-three innings. During the 1988 World Cup she scored 448 runs in eight innings at an average of 149.3.

She represented NSW in hockey in 1983, 1985, 1986 and 1988.

> DEBBIE WILSON
> (b 1961), a right-arm fast bowler but left-hand bat, found inspiration (and a practice partner) in her sister, Bev, who had played for Australia in the 1970s. Debbie Wilson made the NSW Juniors in 1975 and the Open side in 1978. At Teachers' College she wrote her final thesis by comparing the bowling action of a woman (her own) with that of men.
>
> Wilson was a member of the 1983 Under 25 team which toured New Zealand but teaching commitments prevented her from undertaking the 1984 tour of India. She had a fine series against England in 1984–85 securing 19 wickets with her best figures in the Second Test: 3–25 off 20 overs. She figured, with Sally Griffiths, in a world record 8th wicket partnership of 181 against New Zealand in 1990, achieving her highest Test score of 92 not out.
>
> She was one of the fastest women bowlers in the world in the 1980s and also batted well at times. Retiring from international cricket at the end of the 1990–91 season, she continued to play for the Melville Club in Western Australia.

8 January 1985 that a crowd of about 350 turned up to watch the first day of the game between NSW and England at Pratten Park. Growden commented further on the spectators:

Sure, the attendance was not quite a world record, but it was certainly much more healthy than those at many recent Sheffield Shield matches and better than at any Sydney grade game . . . .

Surprisingly, men were in majority, with many admitting to watching their first women's cricket match. All seemed surprised by the high standard of play.

England won the toss for the fourth time in a row in the Fourth Test which was played at Graham Park, Gosford, from 12–15 January. Perhaps hoping that the ball would move around early, England sent Australia in but the move backfired when Emerson (58) and Verco (48) put on an opening stand of 114 and Australia were able to declare at 8–232. Recalled left-arm seamer Denise Martin took three wickets in four balls and spearheaded the Australian attack which dismissed England for just 140 after an opening partnership of 66.

In the interests of a result Raelee Thompson declared the Australian second innings closed at 9–153 leaving England plenty of time — seven hours — to score 246 runs to win. Despite an innings of 65 by opener Jan Brittin, England totalled only 128 with Lyn Fullston securing 4–53.

There was great interest in the final Test, with both the series and the Ashes at stake, which was played at Queen Elizabeth Oval, Bendigo, from 25–28 January — the town which was the site of the first fully recorded game in Australia. There was also considerable public support with daily crowds as large as 1 500 — the largest Test crowds since the 1950s — recorded during the Test.

England, which won the toss for the fifth straight time, elected to bat this time. They made a good start but declined from 4–139 to be all out for 196 with Raelee Thompson having the excellent return of 5–33 off 28 overs. Australia celebrated its national day, 26 January, by scoring 4–228 thanks to another Jill Kennare century (104) and yet another valuable opening stand of 90 between the reliable Emerson (43) and Verco (40). After Australia declared at 8–285 England had reached 5–131 at the end of the third day.

With five wickets in hand and an overall lead of 51 runs England might well have hoped for a draw but the Australian bowlers, with Verco (3–30) and Wilson (3–40) to the fore, disposed of the visitors for 204. There was no sensational collapse this time when the Australians were set 116 to win in an ample 59 overs. The reliable top order Verco (40), Emerson (23) and Kennare (42) set up a comfortable win by seven wickets. Adding to the drama of the last day was a 'gastro epidemic' — christened 'Bendigo Belly' — which afflicted three Australians, two English

Debbie Wilson — one of the quickest bowlers around in the 1980s — at the 1990 Commonwealth Bank Open Championship. (Courtesy AWCC)

players and an umpire. The Australian side fielded with three substitutes and there was also a substitute umpire.

Denise Emerson had an outstanding series with the bat with one century and another three half centuries, an aggregate of 453 runs and an average of 50.33. Jill Kennare, 347 runs at an average of 38.55 and two centuries, was also prominent. Raelee Thompson, Captain (in four Tests), topped the Australian bowling with 18 wickets at an average of 15.72.

Australia finished on a high note winning all three of the one-day internationals played at Melbourne. The first, played at South Melbourne on 31 January, proved the closest with Australia winning by just 6 runs. After Australia reached 6–169 in 60 overs with Denise Emerson (70) again prominent, England were in contention until the last over when they were dismissed for 163 with four balls remaining.

The second and third matches became the Jill Kennare and

Lyn 'Whisper' Larsen

(b 1963) was Australia's youngest ever captain when she led the national side in 1986 at the age of twenty-two. Raised at Tuntable Creek, Lismore, she came from a cricketing family in which her grandfather, father and brother were all keen on the game. She graduated with a Bachelor of Education from the Northern Rivers College of Education and began work for the Department of Sport, Recreation and Racing in Lismore as a recreation officer.

A middle order right-hand bat and leg spin bowler, she began playing cricket at thirteen and won selection for the NSW Country Firsts a year later. In 1978–79 she was selected for the NSW Under 21s and took her place in the Open side in the following year. She represented Australia in the Under 23 side against New Zealand at the WACA in 1981 and the Under 25s in 1983 before touring India with the national side in 1984 where she took 8–58 in one match.

She captained Australia on a victorious tour of New Zealand in 1986 and has been a successful captain ever since, leading her country to series wins over England, New Zealand, India and Ireland and to victory in the 1988 World Cup. Australia has not lost a Test under her leadership, securing four wins and five draws.

Larsen acquired her nickname because she is quietly spoken and even shy but she has proven herself as a dedicated captain, a sound tactician — who is a perfectionist when it comes to setting the right field — and a respected leader of women. She has the ability to rise to the occasion whether with both bat and ball.

Larsen is a natural competitor who enjoys many other sports including tennis, soccer, table tennis, hockey and touch football. Also an accomplished musician, she plays the piano, guitar, clarinet, mouth organ, piano and button accordion.

Denise Emerson show with Kennare scoring 122 and 100 not out — her fourth century for Australia that season — and Emerson not far behind reaching 84 and 56 not out. Australia had very big wins by 138 runs and by nine wickets.

The ABC telecast of the first one-day international was the first occasion on which a women's match has been televised in Australia. Although the amount telecast was less than what was originally hoped — the entire day's play — it was a promising development. Women's cricket authorities were well aware of the vital importance of gaining television coverage. Since 1970 television had totally altered the character of sport by creating the possibility of huge national audiences. Attracting live spectators to an event, while still of some importance, became secondary to tapping into the enormous audience available through television. Making it in this medium became of crucial importance to any sport attempting to make the transition from minor to major status and was vital in generating public interest in the sport which would in turn add to the pool of players. Success in television coverage was also essential for maximising sponsorship, as sponsors gravitated towards sports which generated television exposure.

Australia played another three one-day internationals after the series against England against the New Zealand side — on their way to a full tour of India — at Aberfeldie Park, Melbourne. With the retirement of several key players Denise Emerson was the new captain and Lyn Fullston her deputy. Although Australia easily won the first match when New Zealand were caught on a damp wicket and only made 58, the Kiwi women, like the Kiwi men, were always tough opponents. In the second match the New Zealanders won by 5 wickets to level the series. Australia suffered a catastrophic five run outs and were dismissed for 155 with Emerson scoring 54; it was their first limited overs defeat since 1976. Australia regrouped for the final match and were easy victors: Australia scored 7–214 (Denise Emerson 75 and Karen Read 56) and bowled New Zealand out for only 106.

When Australia went on a short tour of New Zealand in early 1986 the side had a new captain, Lyn Larsen, who at twenty-two was the youngest Australian women's captain ever appointed. Larsen was very much a product of the now well-established junior program: she had first represented Australia in the Under 23s (1980–81), had graduated to the Under 25 side in 1983 and had toured India with the senior side in 1984 and made a Test debut during that tour.

Probably because of the keen trans-Tasman rivalry New Zealand was the one side in the 1980s which could occasionally dent Australian pride and remind them that winning, for a champion team, did not occur as a matter of course. Australia in fact suffered a rare one-day series defeat when New Zealand won the Shell Rose Bowl series at Willeton Oval, Perth, early in 1987 by two matches to one. The Australians were slow to 'mesh together as a team' and lost the first two games due to tenacious and inspired play and the form of the Kiwi openers Debbie Hockley and Jackie Clark. Australia regrouped for the final match and had an easy win against their opposition: New Zealand managed only 9–117 and Australia replied with 2–118. It proved but a temporary setback for the Australian team as they won back the Shell Rose Bowl in the following year in New Zealand by the convincing margin of three matches to nil.

Australia travelled to England to defend the Ashes in 1987 playing three four-day Tests and another three one-day internationals to celebrate the jubilee of women's Test cricket in England. For the ten-week tour the Australian team travelled with a support staff of four: Manager, Ann Mitchell; Coach, Peter Bakker; physiotherapist, Annette Tonkin and scorer and statistician, Erica Sainsbury — who paid her own expenses.

Peter Bakker had taken over from the earlier national coach, Peter Carlstein, the former South African Test player who had toured Australia in 1964. Based in Perth in the mid-1980s, Carlstein became coach of the Western Australian women's team.[12] During the Jubilee Test series of 1984–85 he became unofficial coach of the national side, a position which was both part-time and honorary. Carlstein took his responsibilities seriously: he was 'instrumental in bringing the Australian team together, and preparing them physically and mentally for the exhausting Jubilee Test series against England'.[13] He attended the open national championships at Adelaide in 1986 as WA coach and then coached Australia in the 1987 Rose Bowl Series against New Zealand. The AWCC was sufficiently impressed by the benefits of a national coach to advertise the position prior to the 1987 English tour.

The successful applicant was level three coach and former club cricketer, Peter Bakker, who had built up a fine reputation as coach of the Victorian women's team from 1983. Under his tutelage the state secured success, including wins in all three national championships in one year. Bakker was able to assist the national team at many points. By organising practice and many behind-the-scenes activities, he was able to lighten the burden on the captain in the same way that Bob Simpson had been of great assistance to Allan Border. Bakker also had the time to enhance the tactics employed by the Australians. Like any good football coach he spent hours studying the videos of the opposition to locate their strengths and weaknesses in order to define clearly the best on-field strategies.

All four Tests on the 1984 Indian tour were drawn but there were some outstanding Australian performances. Australia had the satisfaction of winning all four one day internationals. Back Row L to R: Ann Mitchell (manager), Trish Dawson, Jen Jacobs, Denise Martin, Wendy Piltz, Glenda Hall, Lyn Fullston, Lyn Larsen, Anne Clutterbuck (physiotherapist) Front row L to R: Lindsay Reeler, Peta Verco, Karen Price, Jill Kennare (captain), Christina Matthews, Karen Read, Annette Fellows.

This was another first for Australian women's cricket: they adopted a national coach before Bob Simpson was appointed to the men's team and played an important part in the revival of Australian cricket. The English women were sufficiently impressed by this innovation to introduce a coach during the 1987 series.

For reasons which are not entirely clear, women's cricket in England was not making nearly as much progress as Australia in terms of gaining public and private sector support. Netta Rheinberg, who wrote an annual report on women's cricket for the 1988 *Wisden*, was clearly disappointed that 'despite energetic efforts, the necessary major sponsorship failed to materialise' in 1987 though 'many free services and minor sponsorships were forthcoming'. It was an ongoing problem, it seems, as she had reported in the 1985 *Wisden* that the long-overdue New Zealand visit became a reality only because of the determination and enterprise of the members of the WCA who 'refused to succumb to dire warnings of financial disaster and lack of administration to cope with a home tour'. There was in 1987 no longer a Test at The Oval: two Tests were played on county grounds at Hove and Worcester and the other at the Collingham and Linton Cricket Club. The good news for the tourists was that they were allocated a game at Lord's — the first one-day international — well in advance of the tour and Channel 4 committed itself to a ball-by-ball television coverage of the entire day's play.

It was 'very depressing', as Christina Matthews put it, that after a fine fortnight the morning of the appointed day of the Lord's match was damp and dismal. With a wet outfield and a dull sky the groundsman was not very hopeful of any play taking place at all. But the weather did improve and the game commenced at 2 p.m. with each side batting for 31 overs. Australia, led by Lindsay Reeler (69), hit up an impressive 3–174 which was too much for the English side which scored 5–104 in their allocated overs with Lyn Fullston taking 4–12.

Weather intervened in the second one-day international at Guildford which was abandoned because of rain. England won the final match — played on an artificial wicket because heavy rain had drenched the ground on the previous evening — but Australia won the series (tied at one all) on a superior run rate.

Australia had the distinction of winning the Test series by one

The Australian team, depressed at the bleak prospect of play, amuse themselves in various ways on the balcony at Lord's. The weather later brightened, spirits improved and Australia won. (Courtesy Ann Mitchell)

Lindsay Reeler has just taken a vital catch in the First Test against England (Worcester 1987) and keeper Chris Matthews and the slips cordon, Lyn Larsen and Denise Annetts, celebrate. (Courtesy Ann Mitchell)

to nil, with two Tests drawn, which was their first series win on English soil. Australia had a very commanding win in the first Test at Worcester winning by an innings and 21 runs and with a day to spare. England were dismissed for only 134 in their first innings with seamer Karen Brown (3–17) backed up well by the other quick bowlers Sally Griffiths (2–42), Zoe Goss (2–18) and spinner Jenny Owens (2–29). Australia replied with a big total of 293 with Belinda Haggett making a fine 126 — a world record score on debut. England fared little better in the second innings totalling 138 with Owens (4–18) the pick of the bowlers.

The Australians must have been thankful that the groundsman at the Collingham and Linton ground was keen to make play possible in the Second Test because overnight rain left the ground soaked each morning. England began better in this Test and at 5–160 at tea looked comfortably placed but collapsed to be all out for 201 with Owens securing 5–55. Australia lost two valuable early wickets (Emerson and Haggett) for 37 but did not lose another wicket until six-and-a-half hours later by which time 309 runs — a world record — had been scored. The star was diminutive Denise Annetts who was run out at 193. *Wisden* described her world record innings: 'She batted beautifully, her innings full of memorable cuts, leg glides and pulls through mid-wicket on a pitch that was soft, very slow and turned appreciably throughout.' Her partner, Lindsay Reeler, played an invaluable support role scoring a marathon 110 not out in 454 minutes including the slowest century on record in 440 minutes. Play on the final day did not begin until 2 p.m. which made England's task of drawing the match easier. England were 4–116 when stumps were drawn.

Australia were in command from the time they were put into bat in the Third Test at Hove beginning on 29 August. Ruth Buckstein (83) and Lyn Larsen (70 not out) were the top scorers when Australia declared at 7–366. Karen Brown (5–32) took three quick wickets and England were in trouble at 4–41. However, a determined middle order resistance, including a record stand of 110 for the 7th wicket, saw England reach the good total of 8–265 declared. Australia batted out the final day reaching 8–262 and a draw resulted.

The tour began with three one-day internationals against Ireland — the first occasion on which the two countries met. Australia won all three matches.

> **DENISE ANNETTS**
> (b 1964), known as 'Little One', she stands five ft 3/4 ins (154 cm), took up cricket when attending Abbotsleigh. After studying pharmacy at the University of Sydney she started work in her father's chemist shop at Gladesville. She played first grade at the age of fourteen and was selected for NSW Juniors in 1978 and the Open side in 1983. She has captained both the NSW Junior and Open sides.
>
> A prolific top order bat, leg spin bowler and a useful slips and short leg fielder, she first represented Australia in the 1985 Shell Cup one-day series against New Zealand. She toured with the 1987 team to England and made a record-breaking aggregate of 352 runs including her world record score of 193 in the Second Test. She scored 892 runs on this tour (av. 63.71) — including a century before lunch against Surrey — and took fifteen catches. In 1987 she was awarded NSW Sportswoman of the Year.
>
> Annetts has also represented NSW in hockey in 1982–84 and 1986 and is an enthusiastic sailor and skier. She married Ross Anderson in June 1991.

Zoe Goss — a combative and talented star — in her first Test in 1987, at Worcester. (Courtesy Pippa Levett)

The improved domestic structure

Australia dominated women's cricket — both Test and limited overs — throughout the 1980s and in fact from 1978 to 1991. They have now been world champions for almost as long as the West Indian men. While success is ultimately determined by which country has the best players — and a tradition of success generates more success — in the case of the Australian women it is also a product of better administration, greater sponsorship, superior training and preparation, a wider network of competition and a growing and larger pool of players than most of the other women's cricketing nations.

The greatest success of Australian administrators has been to organise and consolidate public and private sponsorship and to assure its future continuity. Largely due to the continuing efforts of Ray Sneddon, whose experience in marketing has proved both invaluable and essential, Australian women's cricket continued to maintain its links with corporate sponsors in 1990 and could count on much direct and indirect support from the Australian Sports Commission and other government agencies. Commonwealth funding of women's cricket for instance tripled from 1980–83 from $6 000 to $18,000.[14]

Money and indirect support enabled administrators to set up a more professional organisation, to initiate essential training and

BETWEEN OVERS

Australian Sports Commission — Shell Australia

OFFICIAL MAGAZINE OF THE AUSTRALIAN WOMEN'S CRICKET COUNCIL

The Kiwis are coming... The Indians are coming

By Ray Sneddon, Executive Director (part time), AWCC

Ray Sneddon

This coming summer is another big season for Australian Women's cricket.

With only a seasons break from the very successful 1988 Shell Bicentennial World Cup, Australia is playing host to New Zealand for the annual Shell Rose Bowl Series (three One Day Internationals) and then India for a full 3 Test Match Series and a One Day International.

At a recent Confederation of Australian Sport luncheon, Kevan Gosper, Shell Australia's Chairman and Chief Executive Officer, announced that Shell would become the major sponsor of the forthcoming India and New Zealand tour of Australia.

"Shell was delighted with the success of the 1988 Bicentennial World Cup in Australia and we are pleased to continue our major sponsorship role with this very important International Tour."

"This sponsorship is additional to our contribution to AWCC which we have supported now for over seven years" commented Mr Gosper (refer p.3 for Shell's AWCC sponsorship announcement - Editor).

The Australian Sports Commission is also a Tour sponsor.

Shell's Chairman, Kevan Gosper accepts the Award of Distinction from the Confederation of Australian Sport President, Greg Hartung

President's Message	2
International Program	**2**
Victorian Institute of Sport Accepts Women into Cricket Squad	3
1990 Australian Development Squad	4
Players of the Future	5
Commonwealth Bank Australian Championships	6
News from the States	7
Stretching	14
Practice with Peter Bakker	17
Australia v India - A History	17

development programs, to underwrite tournaments and tours and to help publicise the sport. Shell Australia helped in many areas: it underwrote international tours, it provided sponsorship for one-day competitions in Australia such as the Shell Rose Bowl annual one-day series. Shell underwrote Super Clinics which were held in all the major cities in 1985–86 and were taken to regional areas in the following seasons. Super Clinics provided coaching free of charge to participants.

Many other imaginative development programs were introduced during the 1980s. To further increase the development of the state junior (Under 21) players, the AWCC announced in 1987 the formation of a development squad to receive intensive top-level coaching for two days after the National Under 21 Championship. An elite squad of twenty was chosen on the last day of the championship.[15]

Sponsorship enabled the AWCC to extend the national junior competitions — Under 18 and Under 21 — by the mid-1980s in addition to the already-established Open competition. There had been a Junior interstate competition from 1959–60 which began as an Under 18 competition but was changed to Under 21 in the 1964–65 season. An Under 18 National Championship was held in Canberra in December 1985 and was contested by Victoria (the winner), ACT, NSW and South Australia. This had followed an experiment with an Under 19 tournament which had been held in Sydney in December 1984 and involved ACT, NSW, Queensland and Victoria. Several seasons earlier, in 1982–83, the AWCC sent another Under 25 team of thirteen overseas, this time to New Zealand, to play a series of matches including two three-day unofficial Tests. New Zealand had earlier sent an Under 23 team to the WACA to play the Australian Under 23 side in 1981.

There was also an expansion of schoolgirl competitions in the 1980s. The NSWWCA, responding to the growing number of school teams, formed a NSW Schoolgirls' Association during the 1985–86 season. Matches in this competition were played on Saturday mornings and the teams were divided into three zones.

Grants have also been of critical importance in establishing a permanent infrastructure of coaching, training camps, and general development which are all important for the maintenance and improvement of standards and for the expansion of the game. Some exciting developments in this area include increased awards and scholarships for juniors, many being provided by the private sector. For example, the ANZ Youth Sport Scholarship program which was begun in 1986, comprised a cricket camp for young cricketers and a chance to win a $10,000 scholarship. It was open to all young cricketers between the ages of 12 and 18. In its first year, twelve girls were selected from Australia-wide nomina-

Facing page: With the support of the Australian Sports Commission and Shell Australia the AWCC has produced an attractive magazine since 1984.

tions to attend a weekend live-in camp at Melbourne Grammar where they were coached by Peter Carlstein.[16] A special award designed to promote cricket in the ACT — the Chief Minister's City of Canberra Trophy — and an associated award of a return trip to England, was awarded to the best Under 21 male and female cricketers in the ACT in 1989–90.

To respond more effectively to the new climate and opportunities for women's cricket in the 1980s, there was a major restructuring of the AWCC in 1986. In the interests of streamlining decision-making and to respond more quickly and efficiently to the demands of players, government, sponsors and the media, the previous Council of seventeen was reduced to a less cumbersome total of nine: a President, a Vice President and a delegate from each affiliated body which replaced the previous practice of two delegates per state. At the same time an Executive of seven was established: a President and Vice President and five section managers in charge of administration, competition, development, finance, and marketing respectively. The restructuring had become essential, as Ray Sneddon put it, 'as the workload has greatly increased over recent years'.[17]

Australia set the lead in women's cricket in terms of establishing a professional and efficient administration to deal with the changing context in which the sport now operated. In addition to creating the post of National Executive Director, that of National Development Officer was also established. This post, first occupied by Karen Price, was subsequently filled by Helen Armitage and Christina Matthews. Price's immediate priorities were to coordinate and assist the states with their Shell Super Clinics and Kanga cricket programs. Most affiliate associations have followed suit by appointing their own development officers. Recent funding from the Australian Sports Commission will make it possible for these officers to gather for workshops each year.[18]

With the re-formation of the Tasmanian Women's Cricket Association in 1982 and with a new association emerging in the ACT in the 1977–78 season, Australian women's cricket was organised on a more national basis. The ACTWCA played in the national championships by invitation in 1978–79 and competed for points in the championships in the following season. Although NSW and Victoria remain the dominant cricket powers — Victoria won the annual Open tournament four times, and NSW three times, in the 1980s — other states are starting to threaten their hegemony. South Australia won the annual Open tournament in 1979–80 and the Under 18 tournament in 1986–87. Western Australia, captained by Karen Read, won its first ever open national championship in 1986–87 and the ACT was runner up in the first ever Under 18 tournament in 1985–86.

During the 1980s there was a continuing growth in the numbers of players and teams involved in women's cricket in all states and territories. By the mid-1980s Ray Sneddon was able to argue that 'women's cricket was entering a most exciting era both at the grass-roots and international level':

Participant level has increased in every State. Registrations, which were just 3 000 five years ago, now are more than 5 000 and increasing at a steady rate. Victoria, for example, this summer experienced an increase in players of just over 30 per cent from the previous year.[19]

The number of registered players continued to grow throughout the decade reaching 8 992 in 1990 and 12,281 in 1991. This figure did not include a large number of primary school girls involved in Kanga cricket.

The Australian World Cup, 1988

The fourth World Cup was held in 1988 in Australia over three weeks from late November to the final at the MCG on 18 December and cost $400,000 to stage — fortunately adequate sponsorship was forthcoming. The 1988 tournament was known as the Shell Bicentennial World Cup in honour of the two major sponsors, Shell and the Australian Bicentennial Authority — the latter designating the Cup a 'major event' and contributing $75,000. It was the hope of the AWCC to take the World Cup to every state but, even with support from the public and private sector, they had to settle for matches in Perth, Sydney, Canberra and Melbourne.

The Cup was contested by five nations: the three long-standing rivals — Australia, England and New Zealand — and two countries playing in their first World Cup: Ireland and the Netherlands. Women's cricket had been played for fifty years in Ireland but it was not until 1982 that the Irish Women's Cricket Union was formed and Ireland began to take part in international competition. The Netherlands was one of the newer cricket nations: while there were about 4 500 men playing cricket there, there were only about forty women's teams with not many more than 500 players.

Australia stamped its dominance on the Cup during the preliminary rounds. Ruth Buckstein (100) and Lindsay Reeler (143 not out) created a record opening partnership of 220 in the opening match against the Netherlands at Perth. It was a very lopsided match: while Australia scored 1–284, their opponents could manage only 29. Their form was equally good against more fancied opposition. England could only manage 8–84 in their allotted overs against Australia in a match at North Sydney Oval and Australia won easily scoring 210 with the evergreen Sharon Tredrea top scoring with 69.

The classical and balanced style of Lindsay Reeler. (Courtesy Chris Matthews)

Australia, with seven wins, and England with six headed the competition yet again at the end of the preliminary rounds. One week before the final the home side had received a timely warning not to underestimate their opposition when they were beaten by England by fifteen runs at the Richmond Cricket Ground with Carole Hodges top scoring with 62.

When the Australian women took to the field at the MCG on 18 December it was the first time that women had played there for almost forty years, since the Test match of January 1949. Unfortunately the match, watched by some 4 000, and a live television audience, was not a great spectacle. England found it difficult to score runs against a tight attack and on a slow outfield drenched by overnight storms. England took 6 overs to score a run off the bat and after a middle order collapse could only total 7–127 in their 60 overs. Although Australia lost two early wickets a record undefeated stand between Lindsay Reeler (59 not out) and Denise Annetts (48 not out) assured Australia its third successive World Cup victory, this time by the margin of 8 wickets.

Three Australians were among the stars of the tournament. Lindsay Reeler scored 448 runs at an average of 149.3. Lyn

Fullston was the leading bowler with sixteen wickets at an average of 11.9. Karen Brown (Australia) and Carole Hodges (England) both took twelve wickets. New Zealand's Debbie Hockley accumulated 446 runs at an average of 63.7.

Conclusion

By 1990 women's cricket, in terms of the numbers of women playing in senior competition, had surpassed the heady days of the 1930s and the game had more than made up the ground which had been lost in the late 1950s and 1960s. It was not an easy task for administrators for there was no public memory of the achievements of women's cricket in the 1930s — the public had to be re-educated about this sport.

In the area of media publicity it is quite clear that women's cricket today is not receiving the 'heaps of publicity' showered on the game in the 1930s. The competition for media attention in the 1990s is far greater due to the wide range of both men's and women's sports and it is unlikely that women's cricket can expect that degree of publicity, at least in the foreseeable future.

However, the foundations for the future survival and growth of the sport now appear sounder than they were in the 1930s. No sport can hope to survive in the long term without public acceptance, a sound financial and administrative basis, and, above all, a well-distributed network of teams, clubs and players from the junior and school level to senior competition. Women's cricket now has a sounder foundation than it has ever had before. The novelty, or fad factor, is less of a reason for people to watch and participate in the game. Also, nowadays women playing cricket, or running marathons, participating in triathalons, or even lifting weights and boxing raises fewer eyebrows than it did in previous decades.

Although many of the old prejudices still remain — particularly amongst some males — there is a slow but continuing change in the public perception of women playing all manner of sport. During the 1970s and 1980s some of the long-established gender boundaries underwent redefinition. A large number of Australians have dispensed with the gender blinkers and now view sports participants — whether men or women — simply as individuals or teams, playing sport.

KAREN PRICE (now Hill) (b 1955), an all-rounder, began playing cricket in the backyard with her brothers. Her father, Colin, who coached her brother Lawrence's cricket team, encouraged Karen to train and play with the side. There was no girls' cricket played at Asquith Girls' High School so she joined the Mirrabooka Club instead. For one season she was Secretary of the Men's Normanhurst Club before she joined the Gordon Club, which was formed in the mid-1980s when Mirrabooka amalgamated with the Pymble Club.

Karen Price was selected in the NSW Under 21s in 1970–71 and made the Open side in 1972–73. She made her international debut against New Zealand in 1975 and toured the West Indies and England in 1976 taking 5 wickets in the final Test.

Since she could not afford to participate in the National Championships, Price did not qualify for the 1977 Test match against India and she disappeared from women's cricket until 1984. During this period she developed her game by playing in men's competitions.

Selected again for the 1984 Indian tour, Price starred with the ball in the Second Test (6–72 and 4–35) and the bat (104) in the Third Test. Injury restricted her availability in the 1984–85 series when she played in only two Tests.

Price was the first part-time National Development Officer for the AWCC and has since worked as an accountant in industry. She has been a state selector since 1988. She has also been involved in managing and coaching many teams since 1985 including the NSW Under 18 and 21 teams and the Australian Under 21 Development Squad.

Price has represented her state both in hockey and indoor cricket. She was selected in the NSW Indoor Cricket side in 1984 and was captain from 1986–88.

CHAPTER EIGHT
THE MEDIA

An improving media?
Ray Sneddon, forthright publicist for women's cricket in the 1980s, was extremely pleased with the extent of publicity generated by the Jubilee Test series in 1984–85. He reflected on the media response in *Cricketer* of October 1985:

Last summer, the coverage of women's cricket was at an all-time 'high' and we look forward to further acceptability and credibility through these columns in *Cricketer*, which are being backed by one of our most important sponsors, Shell Australia.

The coverage of season 1984–85 was fantastic, both in newspapers, magazines and radio, as well as on television where we enjoyed an hour and a half of national exposure through the ABC.

Sneddon's comments underlined the relative improvement in media attention to women's cricket compared with the lack of notice in the 1960s. However, he would have been the first to acknowledge that women's cricket had a long way to go before it reached the pinnacle of publicity of the 1930s.

> RAY 'TWOPENCE' SNEDDON (b 1940) has had a long involvement with cricket; he played for the Melbourne, Toombul and Richmond clubs from 1957–75 and then was Captain/coach of the Camberwell side in 1976–77. Selected for the Victorian Colts in the early 1960s, Sneddon is a member of the Richmond Cricket Club Board and coaches the Camberwell Women's Cricket team.
>
> Sneddon's marketing career began in the 1960s and he spent ten years with an international agency. After a brief stint with a sports marketing company he formed his own company, The Sports Connection, in 1981. Since then his company has played an important role in promoting women's cricket tours in Australia. The Sports Connection has also marketed many other sporting events including Funs Runs, the 1986 New Zealand America's Cup Challenge and the NSW Men's Tennis Open Championship.
>
> Ray Sneddon has been National Executive Director of the AWCC since 1986 and its marketing manager. He has been very successful in attracting a wider range of sponsors and in creating a higher profile for women's cricket. He has also assisted women's cricket in many other ways, writing numerous articles for newspapers and cricket magazines. He has also been a committee member and marketing consultant for the Women's Sport Unit at the Australian Sports Commission.

Yet Sneddon was right to suggest that there was a welcome increase in media attention to women's cricket. During the early 1980s reports on women's cricket in magazines such as *Cricketer* were confined to a column or half a column at the end of the club and other sections. The sponsorship of Shell altered this from the 1985–86 season when women's cricket achieved more substantial coverage and a prominent two to three page spread in this magazine.

A larger number of male cricketers and journalists were writing about women's cricket with greater sympathy and insight in this time. Former Test player Peter Philpott compared women's cricket favourably with the men's game in the *Sydney Morning Herald* of 7 February 1985, noting that while the men had 'jazzed' up cricket 'in many ways the girls still play it as a symphony'. He added that while women's cricket 'lacks two things — strength and experience' — there was 'nothing lacking as far as their technique goes'.

Prominent Sydney journalist Philip Derriman, who attended the Commonwealth Bank Open Age state championships in Canberra, wrote a sympathetic and reflective piece in the *Sydney Morning Herald* on 12 January 1988:

The cricket has been good. To watch women play cricket today is to be reminded of the cricket men played 20 or 30 years ago. There is plenty of wristy stroke play, and you frequently see batters skipping down the pitch to drive. All very attractive . . . .

It is not easy to explain why men have been so unwilling to accept women's cricket. They take women's tennis and women's athletics seriously, so why not women's cricket? It is as if cricket were a peculiarly male ritual. As many men see it, the idea of women playing cricket is contrary to nature — rather like women becoming priests.

Sneddon would have noted some other encouraging signs in that influential journals, such as the now-defunct *National Times* and later the *Bulletin*, were beginning to give voice to some of the inequalities in cricket and more generally in sport. The *Bulletin* of 5 June 1990 published a more general feature entitled 'Why We Are Bad Sports':

Traditional male sports such as these (Cricket, Rugby League, Rugby Union, Australian Rules) portray their participants as warriors and gladiators. It fits the macho image, says sociologist Elizabeth Darlison. 'Sport and war are the two last bastions of old-style masculinity. If you look at some sports, they are symbolic war, really. The rituals and ceremonies are very much the same; even the language is the same' . . . The sporting field, says Darlison, is where men learn to be men. 'The notion of manliness, masculinity, courage, strength — all the things that are literally present on the playing field and are symbolic of what it means to be a man — can be found in sport.'

A further encouraging development has been the gradual and tentative beginning of women — who were likely to be more comfortable, more sympathetic and better briefed on the matter — reporting on women's sport. During the 1980s Tracey Holmes and Tracey Watts on radio and Karen Tighe on television became a regular part of ABC sports service and the ABC set aside its custom of four decades in 1991 when Tighe hosted the ABC Sports Awards for 1990. Women featured prominently on this program: Holmes was a guest presenter and the coveted individual award went to champion swimmer Hayley Lewis. Other notable female sports reporters include Kerryn Pratt, Tracey Parrish and Debbie Spillane on television and radio as well as journalists Mary Boson, Helen Eva, Louise Evans, Amanda Lullham, Elaine Canty, Heather Smith and Kathryn Wicks. Boson has been a regular commentator on women's cricket in *Cricketer* and the *Sydney Morning Herald*, while Lullham has written on a wide variety of sports and in particular sailing in the *Telegraph Mirror*.

Launch of the video 'Fair Play'—Australian stars promoting their own game. Back: Zoe Goss, Lyn Larsen, Ann Mitchell, Belinda Haggett, Denise Annetts. Front: Chris Matthews, Lindsay Reeler. (Courtesy Ann Mitchell).

Government also began to play a more important role in the 1980s in creating a better context for women's sport. A report entitled *Women, Sport and the Media*, which was published by a Working Group on Women in Sport, was presented to the Federal Government in 1985. The Group had been charged to investigate and make recommendations on the following issues: the adequacy of current media coverage of women's and girls' sporting activities; the methods by which women's sporting groups liaise with the media; the problems of running women's sports such as sponsorship, administration, government funding, promotion and training; and ways in which the media coverage of women's sport could be increased and enhanced.

The Women's Sport Promotion Unit, which became the Woman and Sport Unit (WSU) in 1991, was set up in 1987 as a result of this report. WSU was a committee of the Australian Sports Commission. The brief of WSU was a wide one. It was to provide advice to the Federal Government on all aspects of women's sport in Australia and to liaise with government departments and authorities; it was to facilitiate, promote, monitor and report on the coverage of women's sport in the media; and it was to report on the allocation of government funding to women's sport. Media assistance and sponsorship advice was also to be provided for women's sports associations. WSU was also to organise conferences to promote women's sport and to deal with administrative and other problems. Finally the Unit was to act as a tribunal to investigate and act upon complaints brought to its attention.

The WSU, and affiliated State units, have played an important role in increasing the status of women's sport. It has, among other things, developed a series of registers of sportswomen. Its quarterly newsletter, *Active*, which has a circulation of 25,000, highlights the achievements of women in every sporting area, provides publicity for important coming events and airs issues of national importance. The Unit also produces a wide range of promotional and educational material aimed at women of all ages, from schoolgirls to the elderly.

Conferences on women and sport have helped to both focus public attention on the issue and also assist women's sporting associations. A two day seminar entitled 'Equity for Women in Sport' was held in Canberra during the Women in Sport Week, 25 February–1 March 1991, and was organised jointly by the Australian Sports Commission and the House of Representatives Standing Committee on Legal and Constitutional Affairs. It attracted considerable media attention including an ABC 'Couchman over Australia' program which was screened on

6 March 1991. The WSU also organised an international conference in Sydney on 'Women and Coaching and Sport Management' which was held from 28–30 June 1991. The Unit also organised other conferences in conjunction with state governments such as a seminar on 'Sportswomen Speaking Out' which was held in Sydney on 23 February 1991 in conjunction with the NSW Department of Sport, Recreation and Racing.

The 1990 appointment of Ros Kelly as Federal Minister for Arts, Sports and the Environment has proved another boost for women's sport. Kelly, who was the first female attached to the sports portfolio, had pledged to place the issue of women's sport high on the political agenda. One of her first initiatives was to create a committee of Sportswomen of Excellence which included Jane Flemming, Debbie Flintoff-King, skier Kirstie Marshall, Victorian Sportsperson of the Year and basketball coach Jenny Cheeseman, gymnast Monique Allen, TV sports presenter Kerryn Pratt and former Australian netball captain Anne Sargeant. Kelly and her 'A-Team', as she refers to them, aim to enhance the profile of sportswomen in the media and attempt to attract greater corporate sponsorship.

Ros Kelly has undertaken many initiatives to improve the status of women in sport. She has called on the Australian Sports Commission to accelerate their plans for women and, to encourage greater corporate sponsorship, has presented a video of the achievements of outstanding sportswomen to major companies throughout the country and encouraged them to consider the benefits of greater sponsorship of women's sport. At a meeting of State Sport and Recreation Ministers in August 1990, Kelly called on them to endorse the principle of equity in sport and to establish a working group to develop and implement equity policies in a nationally co-ordinated way.

Women and sport was one of the topics taken up by the House

WOMEN'S SPORT PROMOTION UNIT

active

SUMMER 1990/91
WOMEN IN SPORT NEWSLETTER
THE AUSTRALIAN SPORTS COMMISSION VOL 3 No 4
ISSN No. 1031–282X
1990 WORLD ROWING CHAMPIONSHIPS
by Kate Dearden

of Representatives Standing Committee on Legal and Constitutional Affairs which conducted an enquiry into Equal Opportunity and Equal Status of Australian Women. Equity in sport was a topic targeted by the Committee and many sportswomen testified about inequities such as prize money. During the enquiry Federal Sex Discrimination Commissioner Quentin Bryce was moved to comment that 'sport, the great Australian obsession, is riddled with sexism' in that 'it is an area where women continue to suffer blatant discrimination in opportunity and status'.

Some of the media welcomed this enquiry. The *Daily Telegraph Mirror* of 23 November 1990, for example, ran an editorial entitled 'Why Women Athletes Deserve Better'. It argued that 'any reasonable appraisal of Australian sport would show our women athletes have to battle harder and longer for the money and recognition they deserve'. There is a case, it continued, for 'a better deal in prize money for our women sporting stars' as the federal parliamentary committee had found. 'It is strange,' the article concluded, 'how sportswomen are popular enough to sell anything from chewing gum to government services, but aren't good enough to get top money on the field.'

The changed context of women's sport seems to be slowly bringing about some changes in male perceptions of women participants. Prominent cricket commentator Bill Lawry more than once chided a Victorian (or some other) player in the early 1980s as batting 'like a girl/woman/old woman'. It was an expression which easily rolled off the tongue of this commentator because — as Bill O'Reilly had noted in 1948 — the comparison had a long history, as old in fact as the deep-seated prejudices against women. Whatever Lawry's attitude to women playing cricket a decade ago he was certainly making an effort by 1991 when he attended the women's Test at Richmond, Victoria, commenting sympathetically on their play on ABC radio and even attempting to use non-sexist language by using the rather awkward term 'batsperson'.

Some other male Test cricketers have made supportive remarks about women's cricket, with Allan Border expressing sympathy for the problems faced by women cricketers:

I have never had the time to go to a ladies' game but obviously the team is very good, and I keep track of its scores. I don't know much about Lyn [Larsen] except that she is very good ... I have seen her on television and she is obviously very good.

The poor old girls don't get much publicity ... the publicity's so low you don't hear anything about them. It would be good to organise a match against the team as a promotional thing but given our schedule it would be hard to get a chance.[1]

Former Test player, Rod Marsh, who was one of the commentators at the 1987 one-day international at Lord's, praised the standard of play.

The persistence of prejudice

Despite the greater airing of more progressive and enlightened views concerning women playing sport, some leading male cricketers and prominent media personalities don't seem to have altered their views one iota. In fact many of them would agree wholeheartedly with the comment made by Len Hutton many decades ago that women playing cricket was almost as absurd as men knitting.

There was a sizeable backlash in Adelaide after it was suggested in some quarters that some women, in addition to the twenty men, should be given scholarships at the newly-established Cricket Academy of the Australian Institute of Sport. The Adelaide *Sunday Mail* of 13 September 1987 made no attempt to hide its bias suggesting that women 'should be back in the pavilion buttering scones and making tea'. The newspaper then chided what it clearly saw as 'uppity' women for the temerity of their claims:

That men's cricket has finally received Federal and State Government funding for the (Australian Institute of Sport) academy is most welcome. It is, after all, our one true national sport. But that shouldn't automatically mean a handful of ladies can hitch their skirts (or culottes) on to the same organisation. The cost to the taxpayer would be enormous ... next this feminist lobby will be demanding equal space to men's and women's cricket.

The then State captain David Hookes attempted to deliver a few home truths in an article in the *Advertiser* headed 'women's cricket a bit of a yawn' in which he stated that 'women's recent attempted inroads into male bastions have raised a few eyebrows' and presumably hackles. Hookes was critical of the slow scoring in women's cricket and, to underline his contempt for the quality of women's sport, challenged the top female tennis player to meet him (at tennis, not cricket) on the surface of her choice 'if she is game'. Hookes also took a swipe at Olympian Glynnis Nunn by questioning her ability to withstand a physical clash with an Australian Rules footballer, conveniently ignoring the fact that she was an athlete — body contact is not any part of the heptathalon — and not a footballer.

Hookes is not the only Shield cricketer who is critical of women's cricket. Test wicket-keeper Christina Matthews was shocked to discover the views of one of the more prominent Western Australian male cricketers during the 1990–91 season. With scant respect for her achievements — she became a world

The heated newspaper debate about women and the AIS Cricket Academy at Adelaide. (Courtesy Christine Garwood)

record-holder during the Tests against India — and that of her team he informed her point blank that he did not think women should play cricket.

Some prominent media personalities were not reticent in criticising the Federal Government for attempting to encourage greater equity (and more prize money in particular) for women in sport. Don Lane, who achieved great popularity for his incisive presentation of American football, defended the existing inequalities and claimed that female sport could never expect to generate the same interest as men's sport. He commented on 2KY radio on 23 November 1990 that:

People are intrinsically more interested in men's sport than they are in women's — what's the big deal? . . . I mean, if you really want to talk about it, this money that women are getting today is far more than what they would have gotten ten years ago or fifteen years ago, so it's not like there hasn't been a price hike, it's not like they've stood still and the men's prize money has gone ahead. It hasn't happened that way. I think the ratio is even and I think it's a very good ratio.

I don't say that it [basketball] isn't exciting to watch them [women], it just doesn't have the same magnetism that men's sports do, especially marathons. I mean, they always say this is the first woman to cross the finish line — I mean, nobody really cares.

Talk-back identities John Laws and Alan Jones joined in the chorus of criticism of the Federal Parliamentary Committee. Laws informed his audience on Radio 2UE on 23 November 1990:

But I certainly ask the question about just why a Federal Parliamentary Committee is going to be set up to investigate why male sporting people get paid more than female? Why? Why do we need to waste time and money on such matters? . . . I mean it's a lot of rubbish . . . We really have got screwed up priorities here haven't we!

Alan Jones weighed in on the same day and on the same station:

Everyday you read or hear of some other piece of bureaucratic nonsense. Well try this for the piece that takes the cake today. We're strapped for cash, but there's a Federal Parliamentary Committee going to investigate why male sporting competitors often get more prize money than their female counterparts . . . Is Liza Minelli paid less than Tom Jones? I don't think she is. Why? They perform the same act . . . If Boris Becker is superior to Steffi Graf, should he be paid more than Steffi Graf? I would have thought simply, yes. It's got nothing to do with sex.

The willingness of popular and high-rating broadcasters to speak so openly and so scathingly about women's sport attests to the continuance of deep-seated prejudices against women's sport as a whole and explains why women's sport still gets limited air space and is for the most part ignored. A 1989 survey by Sandy Gordon of the University of Western Australia[2] found that only about 2.5

per cent of total sports reporting space in newspapers was devoted to women's sport. The study, which was based on fifteen major daily newspapers across the country, also indicated that photographs of men's sports outnumbered those of women's by roughly twelve to one. While it may be true that some of the 97.5 per cent of sports coverage is of sports which are not solely male — horseracing for instance has many female followers and even a few female participants — there is an obvious media discrepancy between many much-publicised male sports and largely-hidden female ones. Gordon found a similar result when he examined the average amount of women's sport on six major television channels, which he found was 1.3 per cent of the total sport time. A disturbing feature of Gordon's research is that there had not been any real improvement in media attention to women's sport over the previous eight years.

The disparity is all the more glaring because women, according to the 1990 *Australian Sports Directory*, now constitute about 23 per cent of sports participants. Australian women, in addition, have a better record than men both at the Olympic and Commonwealth Games. From 1948 to 1988 women have constituted only 390 of the 2 030 Australians at the Olympics, 19 per cent, and have participated in only 22 per cent of the events but they have won 42 per cent of the fifty-seven gold medals won by Australians. Women were also the first to win a gold medal in a team sport (other than a relay event) when they won the hockey gold medal in 1988. There has been a similar pattern at Commonwealth Games. During the 1990 Auckland Commonwealth Games Australian women, representing 38 per cent of the national squad, won sixty-eight of the 162 medals won by Australians — 42 per cent. Swimmer Hayley Lewis, with an unprecedented five gold medals, was the star of the Australian team.

Negative images

Various theories have been floated as to why women's sport continues to gain miniscule media attention when compared with men's sport. Ron Casey, 2KY sports director, believes that there is a tendency for women's authorities to blame the media. He argued on the 'Couchman over Australia' program in March 1991 that the public was largely indifferent to women's sport and that administrators could not expect the commercial media to broadcast sport unless there was a demand for it and an audience.

Casey stated that the blame should be placed rather more on women's administrators who had failed to market their sports attractively. He added that once there was a public demand for a sport and it was clear that a women's sport rated, there would be

Courtesy Phil Schofield

no trouble gaining air time. Peter Couchman himself raised the question as to whether women's sports stars might well be promoted in more glamorous, and even sexy terms — in the tradition of Warwick Capper of the Sydney Swans — in the interests of greater public attention.

Casey's criticism of the administrators of women's cricket, and for that matter of netball and other sports, is both unfair and uninformed. Administrators have worked long and persistently — and mostly on shoestring budgets — to market their respective sports. They have in fact a very keen awareness of what is required to gain broader media acceptance and are confronted with a classic chicken-and-egg situation faced by all minor sports. Getting on television on a regular basis is a vital ingredient for greater public interest but the media for the most part is reluctant to take risks with unproven sports and to educate the public to a new sport. Minor sports are caught in a classic vicious circle: they do not get major coverage because they are defined as minor sports, and because there is limited media exposure they do not have the opportunity to improve their status. A few minor sports which have succeeded in gaining television exposure, such as basketball and snooker, have subsequently boomed in popularity.

The growth in women's cricket by the 1990s occurred because some women's cricket authorities bombarded the media, targeting the radio stations first. Christina Matthews elaborated on the tactics in the *Sydney Morning Herald* of 25 March 1991:

Our policy was to hound the media and keep on hounding it ... The reality is that the media won't chase women's sport. Women's sport has got to chase the media and that's what we did. It worked.

Media exposure is also vital for all women's sports in order to overcome the deep-seated prejudices held against it. This is the major reason why the demand for more women's sport has been relatively sluggish even in the 1980s. Ron Casey has underestimated the problems faced by women's authorities in changing public perceptions of women playing sport.

Three negative images concerning women playing sport can be identified and have been a staple part of the media coverage of women's sport for almost as long as it has existed in Australia. They have persisted, to some extent, into the 1990s partly because a significant part of the sports audience — both male and female — believe in them to some degree.

The dolly-bird image

Jim McKay, a sociologist at the University of Queensland, made reference to this image at a 1991 conference on 'Equity in Sport' when he noted that the media frequently suggest that women's athletic achievements were frivolous. A 'dolly bird' style of sporting journalism concentrated on the appearances of female athletes rather than their actual achievements.

This image has a long history. The first newspaper account of an Australian women's cricket match, at Bendigo in 1874, concentrated rather more on their costume and their appearance than their play. Even when the media started to report some details of female sporting achievements in the 20th century — when Australian women such as Fanny Durack became world champions — there was still a preoccupation with costume, body shape, marital status and whether a competitive athlete could retain her femininity. One journalist, who commented on Fanny Durack's body shape, was pleased to note that she had no unsightly muscles.

While most male sports have gained a ready audience and media attention, only the more 'feminine' women's sports have been encouraged by the media. Helen King has noted that sports such as diving, figure skating, tennis and gymnastics, which emphasise grace, rhythm and balance, have achieved acceptance and some coverage. Individual sports, such as swimming and athletics, have long been defined as suitably feminine. Other sports which require strength, endurance and body contact, with more obvious competition and aggression and which infringe on male territory, have received far less media coverage.[3]

Until recently women's sport has also been trivialised by sexist

186 CHAPTER EIGHT

GN500 Pro-balanced and GN100 5 Star Scoops can be bought for as low as $79; Batting Helmet with Visor for $63; Special prices on balls. A free fully illustrated catalogue and mail order form available on application — a must for every club secretary and cricket connoisseur.

Send for your free catalogue now to Australia's mail order cricket specialists since 1973

THE CRICKET CENTRE P /L 15 Dover Street, P.O. Box 234, Albion, Brisbane, QLD. 4010 Ph (07) 262-3166

A dolly bird 'at bat'
Australian Cricket
December 1979.

comments — particularly by headings which have obviously been dreamed up with some relish by male sub-editors. An English cricket magazine headed its feature on women's cricket 'Crumpet Cricket'. One Australian heading of the 1980s treated women's cricket as a bit of a joke and denigrated the sport at the same time by sexual innuendo: the heading stated, 'A princess who dreams of Lord's and the ultimate Test'. The player was defined in 'dolly bird' terms as a princess and the heading implied that she was interested in finding a man. Sexual innuendo was part of another heading: 'Petticoat cricketers are hoisting their skirts'.

During the 1980s the American custom of cheer leaders was introduced by many Rugby League and Australian Rules teams to add to the 'entertainment'. While the male heroes strutted on the real sporting stage, the 'dolly birds', such as the Swanettes, had the privilege of dancing and gyrating to encourage the footballers to greater effort and to celebrate success on the field.

The media has perpetuated the 'dolly bird' image in many subtle ways. Roy Masters of the *Sydney Morning Herald* noted in 1991 that up till a decade ago newspapers had published photographs of women athletes which emphasised their grace and rhythm, whereas illustrations of men frequently stressed aggression and competition.

Fortunately, Masters noted, this stereotyped presentation had been breaking down in more recent times — possibly because of changing gender definitions due to a greater awareness of gender stereotyping. Editors had also realised the media mileage to be gained by publishing pictures which reversed the popular public image: publishing photographs of aggressive and competitive women athletes and the graceful and lithe male participants.

Ultimately the 'dolly bird' image will not be properly dismantled until the public becomes more familiar with women's team sports and its stars. This negative image is based mostly on ignorance of the nature of women's sport. Greater familiarity with the athletes involved in cricket and netball, along with gymnastics and tennis, will enable the public to view the participants as individuals and athletes and thereby realising that many sports, both male and female, can combine both grace and strength, rhythm and body contact.

The butch image
By far the greatest handicap for women playing team sports such as cricket, which have been dominated by men and regarded as central to male culture, is that any female attempting to enter the inner sanctum of 'male' sport is regarded as a closet male, or butch. Although this is a view which is not stated openly and

Women's role in the development of cricket has been badly underrated.

With today's emphasis on the more macho variety, the impact that women have had on this genteel game has been frequently overlooked.

It is generally agreed that over-arm bowling began in the early 19th century when John Willes, a Kentish sportsman, adopted the style after watching his sister, Christina, bowling round arm so that she would not be hampered by her long dress.

A Mrs Martha Grace is understood to have taught her son, the renowned W G Grace, the game and was his most severe critic.

The great West Indian batsman Sir Learie Constantine paid tribute to his sister who coached him.

In the 18th cent...

'Petticoat cricketers' are hoisting their skirts

...BY GREG GROW...

What a frill, England win the Cup

EE-AYE-HEY-HOE, we won the Cup.

...nd's male cricke struggling at t things couldn or our women

Heyhoe-Flint 92-run victory Edgbaston t 'orld Cup t men's cricke chael recei 'rincess An

...that rs of th ful set they ly har the shire win sec me

cored at will

Scoring almost at will for a ll she failed by only two runs obtain her century before h when England had am...

Bakewell cooks up a mum's special

By BRIAN MARSHALL in Birmingham

INSPIRED by an exciting century by their opener Enid Bakewell, a mother of three, England inflicted Australia's first defeat of the series to win the women's World Cup cricket competition in this deciding match by 92 runs.

Watched by Princess Anne, who presented the trophy to England's captain, Rachael Flint—she has done more to enhance women's cricket than any other individual at the present time—the game was a fitting climax to the sponsored series.

England were given an excellent start by their openers, Bakewell and Lynn Thomas. They put on 101 for the first wicket and from this solid foundation England progressed to 279.3—a record for the series. In reply Australia scored 187.9 off their alloted 60 overs.

Bakewell who completed the double of 1,000 runs and 100 wickets on the tour of Australia in 1968, certainly enjoyed herself in this match and following the dismissal of Thomas for 40, she found an admirable partner in her captain, Flint.

CRUMPET CRICKET

No longer on cricket's outskirts

FRANK KEATING on the women's World Cup which starts today

While the blokes in the Long Room are still debating which sponsors to chat up for their World Cup, the women cricketers have knuckled down and organised their own competition, the first of its type the game has known. The tournament starts today on Kew Green, London, when Jamaica play New Zealand, and continues around the country until July 28.

The other sides in the competition, which consists of twenty-one 60-over matches, are Australia, Trinidad and Tobago, England, Young England, and an International XI.

Predictably, the tournament has met with a patronising greeting from Fleet Street and television (at net practice last week the photographers were traipsing away, moaning that the players' skirts were such that they didn't allow so much as a glimpse of knicker as they bowled) as well as from the Lord's hierarchy who, in their mind-boggling male chauvinism, say they have no changing facilities for women's teams. What a national quacking there would be if Wembley or Wimbledon, let alone the council tennis club down the road, came out with that one!

Though she World Cup organisers are far too nice to say so, they were hugely disappointed at getting no invitation to play their final match at Lord's. Edgbaston, of course, said "with pleasure". Since then the president of MCC, Aidan Crawley, has patronisingly gone on record as telling them that if women's cricket proves itself this "------mer to be as graceful as -----------" ard's sport, then...

(ch) MAYOR of Bath, Coun Tom Cornish greeted the Australian women's cricket team (pictured above) at the Guildhall before their civic tour of the city today.

The 15-strong party — which arrived in Bath last night for Wednesday's game with West of England women, at North Parade Batts and Bump Room as before lunching with the Monarchy 1000 committee at...

batting: necessary dimensions that, alas, the stronger men's game now so often ignores. There will certainly be many a surprised cricket lover watching the World Cup during the next five weeks.

Although the Women's Cricket Association is now 47 years old the game was intriguing the ladies long before that. "eleven maids in "eleven maids of notches to 119" mon, near Guildf Arlott of the day they bowled, batt caught as well as in that game." And Mrs Grace, the Down wife, herself a right a had first introduced and toddling son to the they watched Clarke's A XI play a local Twenty-her pony carriage, Mrs Stevens was screaming advice (not, as it w unminged with abuse) famous husband, the gr Hambledon CC.

Bradman's suppor

Into this century, and that l vellously diverting player writer, R. C. Robertson-Glasg (Oxford and Somerset) was ac ally coached by a woman, a Swiss governess with more zeal than precision "Ron, Ron or you will nevair egg-sell at the athletics"—and he also had an Aunt Emily who would never walk when given out lbw. Much later, Sir Neville Cardus was reportedly quite beside himself at watching the talents of the tiny Australian tweaker, Antonio, in the pre-war women's team that toured England; and in the late fifties Sir Donald Bradman voiced huge delight at watching Kdna Barker of England...

lacrosse players met at the still gracious Edwardian village of Colwall, near Malvern, in Worcestershire, to amuse themselves by playing cricket together. They formed the Women's Cr- ciation and to plea- year to .

A LONG LEG AND A SLIP OR TWO AT LORDS

19-6-73

G. probably turned in his grave but Lib and all it was no real -dies Day on the hal- -mbers

A side full of fine legs

There they were to receive the Edgar medals presented to all sportsmen taking part in Monarchy celebrations.

"It's been a grand party so far," said party manager Lorna Thomas. "especially as we've reached the final of the World Cup. We are playing England on Saturday."

The team, aged between 19 and 35, is looking forward to Wednesday's tussle. "We need a game before Saturday, as we were washed out at Swansea over the weekend," said captain Miriam Knee, from Melbourne.

The girls were planning to build up to Wednesday's game with a visit to Longleat Park tomorrow.

The party leaves Bath on Thursday for Edgbaston and Saturday's final.

for a tough 60-over encounter with a West of England side that includes four of Bath-based Somerset Wanderers Jane Gough, Christine Bradley, Judy Goodwin and Nicola Tran...

You just can't keep a good bra down

Some of these newspaper headlines of the 1970s while clever were decidedly sexist.

directly in public, it is frequently hinted at or even voiced directly in private, in dressing rooms and pubs around the country.

A public hint has always been sufficient to activate male prejudice in that many men have always been keen to sniff out 'butch' cricketers. The seemingly innocuous comment in one newspaper of the 1930s that Betty Archdale's hair was cropped close in the style of a boy must have been sufficient to set some male tongues wagging. The issue was also a concern to an elderly spectator who attended the January 1985 Test at Gosford and who confided to a male journalist that he had never seen so many 'manly'-looking women watching the game.

On the eve of the 1951 Australian tour to England the Melbourne *Sporting Globe* of 5 April 1951 published the following banner headlines: 'Women Cricketers for England', 'Average 26 Years' 'Only One Married'. The one married player, it informed its readers, was 'Dot Laughton, of South Australia, whose husband is a Government servant'. By contrast the marital status of male cricketers, and the occupation of their wives, has rarely been commented upon.

Such is the strength of this perception that the onus has always been on women, according to Ann Mitchell, to disprove the 'butch' image of women's cricket. Mitchell noted that one of the reasons why Australian women opted for culottes rather than trousers, was to counter the 'butch' stereotype, presenting a more acceptable feminine image.

Gender stereotyping has long played an important role in both men's and women's sports. Boys who have been unwilling to play 'manly' team sports — cricket and football — have been defined as 'wimps' and dismissed as effeminate. It is ironic that the reverse is true for women — any female who is keen to play cricket or football is immediately under suspicion of being a terminal spinster or, in more recent times, of being butch.

Once men have made the national cricket or football team there has been little public interest or discussion of their sexual orientation off the field — whether they are straight or gay, married or single. They are treated as athletes whose essential manliness is asserted by their deeds on the field. It is only in recent times that there has been largely private discussion amongst male cricket followers as to whether some male Test players might be gay. The on-field antics of Merv Hughes and his much-discussed kissing of fellow players has generated considerable pub speculation as to whether he, or any other players, might be gay. The issue has not in any way reduced Merv's popularity as it seems that his essential manliness has not been questioned — whatever his sexual orientation — in that he is a whole-hearted cricketer who has the ability to bowl his heart out

MEET THE BRADMAN OF WOMEN'S CRICKET

SPARKLING FINALE TO SEASON

BRADMANESQUE BATTING

Women's Sport Feature By Heather McCulloch

With a Bradmanesque off-drive to the fence, Miss Florrie McLintock reached her thousand runs for the season at the Premiers versus The Rest cricket match at University Square yesterday.—A grand finale to the season.

She stole all the limelight in a match in which the "creme de la creme" of women's cricket were competing.

Florrie moved out to every ball, hit two sixes and three fours in one over, and then was caught brilliantly by Miss Pat Nye, for 53.

It was a grand innings, made up of the sort of cricket that's good to watch.

She didn't take long in moving spectators from the possible danger zone, and I began to get a bit anxious about my own safety away in the pavilion.

It's a long time since Miss M. Flaherty the fast bowler has been treated so disrespectfully.

The ball was bouncing high, and Miss McLintock merely hit them a little higher. Everyone was hoping she'd try for the tennis courts—but nothing happened that way.

Miss Dive's Crash

Miss Dive surprised, too. She made only five—and her parents were there to see it, too!

It was a lovely five—a single, a four that should have been caught on the way and then a similar hit with not such a lucky result.

Premiers had little difficulty in winning, for The Rest didn't field as well as they might have done, and opportunities were not appreciated. Only one mishap marred the match.

Miss J. Shaw, who made her debut from Goulburn not so very long ago, was hit on the head by a rising ball from Miss...

"Bradman" of the women

By VIC SIMONS

Joyce Dalton, a 24-year-old schoolteacher from Uki, near Murwillumbah, is the "Don Bradman" of the N.S.W. women cricketers this season.

It is her best season in five years of cricket.

She has been dismissed three times and has scored over 500 runs for a batting average of 160.

Her highest score was 125 in a club match.

Joyce is a prolific batswoman, but, unlike men cricketers, the women do not keep averages.

"Although we have a competition in Sydney, the emphasis is more on the game than the result," said Miss Mollie Dive, manageress of the present Australian team.

"We play hard, but the principle of women's cricket, in general, is to play the game to enjoy it.

"They have no competition in England, but play friendly matches between various clubs," she added.

Other games, too

Miss Dalton was a member of the Australian team to meet England in the first Test which was to have commenced at North Sydney Oval last Friday, but rain washed out play in the three days' match.

All of Miss Dalton's family are keen cricket supporters.

Her father, who runs a general store at Uki, played first grade in Brisbane, and her brother Jack has represented the Tweed district.

Joyce, a right-handed batswoman, who usually goes in first wicket down, played for N.S.W. in her first year of cricket.

That was during the 1952-3 season when she...

...been making the cricket her mammoth double-Nothing unusual? Except a woman — and one of ing women cricketers. ounced her retirement, SMITH talks to her...

LASHED OUT
Bradmans In Skirts

Top scorers for their respective teams in yesterday's women's cricket matches, Misses Bloomfield and Milham, each hit 11 fours.

Miss Bloomfield, batting for Cypress, made 55 and Miss Milham (Annandale Waratahs), 57.

Miss Medcalf (Vice Regal), however, took the honors of the day. She rattled up a sparkling 90 not out, the highest score made in grade matches this season.

She played interhouse cricket with Vice Regal last season. This is her first year in N.S.W.W.C.A. competitions.

Annandale Girls' Brisk Exhibition of Hitting

The Annandale Waratahs, comprising a first and second eleven of women cricketers, did not take long to absorb the finer points of the game. Last season the first eleven, with only five playing months behind them, captured the B grade premiership for 1931, and were elevated to A grade. This season, in four matches played, the first team has won three matches.

On Saturday, in a game against Cypress, Annandale lost six wickets for 233 (E. Jenkins 83, D. Milham 57, T. Ryan 11, A. Hudson 15, N. and E. Milham 12½). Cypress, first innings 126; second innings 4–118 (E. Bloomfield 55, A. Wigemund 52 not out).

E. Jenkins 13 and D. Milham 12 fours for the victors, and E. Bloomfield 11 fours for the losers. Between them the two teams, in three hours' play, knocked up 264, which is not so bad for every one of our grade teams, let alone girls.

CRICKET IN HER BLOOD

Annandale v. Newcastle

The Annandale Waratahs met the Newcastle girls in a second match at the Sports Grounds, No. 2 today. Annandale won the toss and sent Newcastle in to bat, losing first Miss E. Crossley quickly and then dismissed her account before she had opened.

Scores:—
NEWCASTLE—First Innings
...

Women cricketers are not viewed in their own right as are tennis players. Women players have long been compared with men — particularly Sir Donald Bradman.

for his country. Merv's antics have also been treated by the media as just an amusing byplay of an exuberant individual.

It is to be hoped that a greater familiarity with the stars of women's cricket in the future will also help focus attention on their achievements on the field as athletes. In these days, when the ideal of equal opportunity has been accepted, it should not be relevant as to whether one player is 'straight' and another 'gay'. The private lives of many male stars have frequently been a disaster — there have been criminals, sex offenders, alcoholics and others who have later become derelicts or taken their life — but this should not diminish their one area of success in life: that of genuine sporting achievement.

Women playing inferior sport

Comparison with men's sport, invariably unfavourable, has been the bane of many women's sports. Women participants are reminded time and time again that they are less strong, can bowl the ball at a lesser pace and hit the ball with less ferocity than men. Women's sport is slower and less interesting in the opinion of many men and lacks what Don Lane referred to as the 'magnetism' of men's sport.

Part of the so-called magnetism of men's sport has, in the opinion of many, been the greater display of aggression, within and often on the fringe or even outside the rules. The physical clash of forwards in football, the intimidation of the bumper in cricket, bouts of fisticuffs and all-in player brawls, certainly draw a louder response from spectators than more regular play.

Comparisons between men's and women's cricket are both odious and unfair. Men's cricket is played by almost fifty times as many participants as women's — therefore the standards cannot be fairly compared. Women, until recently, have often played far less cricket than men at an early age.

Women's cricket, as Zoe Goss pointed out, should be judged on its own terms, as she states in the *Sydney Morning Herald* of 26 January 1991:

> You have to appreciate it's a different game. It's like tennis where women do not play such a powerhouse game as the men.
> Strength should not be an issue. The essence of the game and technique is still there and cricket purists can appreciate that.

There should be recognition, as there was in tennis, that the women's game emphasises different facets and skills. Some more informed commentators, such as Peter Philpott, have recognised this point and have suggested that women's cricket has retained some of the traditional virtues of the game now partly lost by the men.

Some of the comparisons between men's and women's cricket

are made out of ignorance. When Denise Annetts featured on the ABC Sports Award program of 8 January 1988 — the Australian Women's team was then nominated for the Team Award — compere Tim Lane, alluding to the hours that it took Annetts to achieve her memorable 193 in 1987, commented that 'women are not as physically strong as men and take longer to make runs'. With great diplomacy Annetts replied: 'Yes, Tim, it took me just over seven hours but why don't you ask Allan [Border] — I think, if memory serves me correctly, he took over eight hours to score his 200!' This retort brought a smile to Border's face.

Due to its wider exposure there has been more recognition and appreciation of women's tennis as a different game from the men's. There have also been occasions over the past two decades when the women's game, featuring all court play and longer rallies, has been as popular with the public, and sometimes even more so, than the men's game which has become a more predictable and duller serve-volley contest.

The popularity of women's tennis suggests that the sporting public is able to view a game in its own terms once the sport has sufficient exposure in the media. Women don't hit the ball as hard as men, they play shorter matches in many tournaments and there is a dearth of McEnroe-style outbursts of unbridled aggression, yet the sport has an undoubted appeal.

The new world of televised sport

Ann Mitchell, President of the AWCC, has long been aware of the crucial importance of greater media coverage for women's cricket and particularly wider television exposure. She recognised that it was vital for the sport to secure a whole match on television to 'allow the drama to unfold' rather than edited snippets of play. Mitchell noted that:

If women received the saturation coverage of men's cricket then people could get involved in the drama of live cricket. The men's faces are on bubble-gum cards and on posters in McDonald's, so they have a high profile in marketing as well as television, but television is the secret because it plays such a dominant role in our society.

Access to television has now become an essential factor for any sport to prosper and to achieve major status and has substantially altered the world of sport. Although television was introduced to Australia in 1956 at the time of the Melbourne Olympics, it was not until the 1970s that its potential was fully realised. Before that time, cost and technical problems restricted the extent and quality of television sports coverage. The 1970–71 men's cricket series against England was the first Test series broadcast nationally and in its entirety.[4] The television audience for this series

Syd Miller Says—

WRITING ABOUT LADIES' CRICKET, PATSY HENDREN STATES — "WHATEVER GIRLS ARE DOING"—

"CRICKET!"

"THEY'RE NOT—"

"HULLO! WHERE YOU GOING?— FANCY DRESS BALL OR SOMETHING?"

AND WHAT'S MORE — "IT IS IMPOSSIBLE FOR WOMEN TO BECOME EXPERT WITH THE BAT!"

"PLAYING—"

—AND YET WE DUNNO!

was huge. While there was an average daily live attendance of 20,279 the home audience reached one million per day — fifty times the live audience — as the series progressed. With the introduction of colour television and slow motion replays in 1975, televised sport became even more popular. Since that time, satellite technology has added to the range of sport presented on television providing easier access to world sporting events which are now shown around the clock on Australian television.

Australian men's cricket enjoyed a television-related boom in the first half of the 1970s. Improvements in television coverage coincided with a resurgence in the performance of the Australian XI. The side had highly marketable stars — the charismatic Lillee–Thomson combination, an aggressive captain, Ian Chappell, and the laconic Doug Walters.

Men's cricket was ripe for the picking by commercial television in 1977. Thwarted by the Australian Cricket Board, who denied him a monopoly of cricket television coverage, Packer took the novel step of attempting to take over the sport by contracting the leading international players and organising an alternative competition. It was a bold and expensive investment which underlined what a rich plum men's cricket had become by this time.

Commercial television has transformed and revitalised a number of other men's sports, particularly Rugby League and Australian Rules football, in the last two decades, with the potential of larger and larger audiences having far reaching ramifications. In the battle to tap new audiences games have been scheduled at changed times (with more games being played on weekdays in addition to weekends) and new clubs have been formed and some old ones disbanded in the interests of creating more national audiences.

Commercial television, not surprisingly, has chased those lucrative sports with an established audience as they represent a safe investment and an assured return. The main beneficiaries of larger and larger windfall television profit since the 1970s have been the established men's team sports, cricket, and the various codes of football. Tennis, golf, and horseracing — other sports well established before the television era — also benefited from the expansion of television sports broadcasting.

Basketball appears to be the one relatively new sport (in Australia) to profit from television. Its American connection has obviously been beneficial as there has been an increase in the coverage of American sports on Australian television in the last decade. The quality of Australian basketball has also benefited by the importation of ready-made American 'stars'. Slick American marketing, including all the razzamatazz and hoop-la of the American sport, has also been a factor in its growth in Australia.

The tragedy for minor sports — including most women's sports and particularly team sports — is that television has favoured the already well-established and well-funded sports. It has in fact widened the gulf between the rich major sports and what are fast becoming the 'third world' sports — those which, if not becoming poorer and poorer, are less rich in comparison with the favoured few sports. Regrettably for minor sports there is no easy way to ease this sporting poverty trap. Effective promotion in the now highly competitive and lucrative sporting world requires a massive injection of funding, the likes of which are only available to the privileged sports.

Unlike men's cricket and basketball, women's sports such as cricket only surface occasionally on television. A tentative beginning has been made to televise the coverage of women's cricket on ABC television. A one-day match was televised during the 1984–85 season and the final of the World Cup in 1988. ABC radio Grandstand broadcast some of the final Test match live during the 1990–91 series — when women were fortunate there was no men's first class cricket on the weekend of the Test at Richmond. Results of matches were mentioned on nightly television news though usually without pictures.

Greater attention was paid to women's cricket on Channel 9 during the 1990–91 season when the scores of women's matches were reported regularly during breaks in the live coverage of the men's series against England. The Wide World of Sports Team attended the First Test against India at North Sydney and compiled a short but informative piece which was subsequently screened during one of the intervals of the men's Test.

The cause of women's sport has not been helped by the fact that most of the decision-makers at the sports desks of newspapers, radio and television stations, have been and continue to be male. While some may have a low opinion of women's sport, others are not necessarily biased against women's sport as such — they are simply more familiar and comfortable with men's sport. On the whole they are not likely to have a clear grasp of the growing appeal of women's sports, such as netball, hockey and cricket, and a sure appreciation of the potential television audience for these sports.

Some men are aware of the changing character of sport and sympathetic to the introduction of new ones. Ian Frykberg, executive producer of sport at Channel 9, was quoted in the *Sydney Morning Herald* on 31 January 1991:

We ought to give it [women's sport] more exposure. It is one of our roles to lead public interest. There is a clear case for increased coverage of women's sport; not only the male-dominated sports like soccer and cricket, but netball — the Australian team is very successful. But you must remember it isn't only women's sport that needs coverage; a lot of minority sports demand it.

Former Olympian, academic and sports administrator Shirley de la Hunty was pessimistic about whether women's sport would gain greater media exposure in the immediate future. She noted that despite the efforts of the WSU, the efforts of women administrators to promote their sports, and the increasing numbers of female sports participants, there had been no real increase in the coverage of women's sport in the 1980s. De la Hunty hinted that more drastic action in the form of affirmative action legislation, may well be required to redress the balance. This suggestion was supported by politicians such as Senator Rosemary Crowley.[5]

Josephine Tiddy, the South Australian Commissioner for Equal Opportunity, was coming to a similar conclusion when she floated three proposals to reduce discrimination against women in sport at the seminar on 'Equity for Women in Sport' in 1991. Tiddy argued that a national sports policy, based on the South Australian junior sports policy, should be implemented. The introduction of sanctions against sporting organisations which did not encourage women to participate in sport and to share administrative roles was a central element of this policy. She also contended that the Sexual Discrimination Act should be amended to end comparisons between men's and women's sport as a measure of its worthiness. Finally, she suggested that this Act should be amended to allow complaints of victimisation to be pursued through a confidential complaint process rather than through the more public (and embarrassing) court of law.

Lack of positive media exposure has been detrimental to all women's sports. Various reports have indicated that girls tend to drop out of sport earlier than boys. There are of course a variety of reasons for this which were cited in a 1988 report: lack of opportunity (30 per cent), skill (49 per cent) and time (59 per cent) were some of the main reasons. Interest in other activities (88 per cent) and boys in particular (39 per cent) also distract girls from sport.

Other reasons for lesser female participation in sport relate more directly to a continuing limited public acceptance of women in sport which is all too faithfully reflected in media coverage. Girls are variously discouraged from participation by peer group pressure, disinterested or discouraging parents, embarrassment about physical maturity, ridicule from boys and a lack of female role models. Adult women have also not received a great deal of encouragement to continue playing sport and to return to it after motherhood.

Conclusions

Women's sport has made some progress towards greater media acceptance during the 1980s, as Ray Sneddon has noted, but the pace of change has been ever so slow. Long-held prejudices against women in sport will not be erased overnight. Greater television coverage is the solution to the problems of women's sport — the public will then be more inclined to view the game in its own right and the participants more as athletes — but there is no prospect that this will be realised in the immediate future.

The most promising line of action to redress the media balance is through education. The growth and cultivation of girls' cricket in schools is an encouraging development. With the backing of Departments of Education and teachers, cricket and football for girls now has more social legitimacy than previously. The promotional work of the WSU has also helped raise the profile of women's sport: regular newsletters and seminars are providing greater encouragement for sports administrators and are helping to place the political issues relating to women's sport on the public agenda. Education, supplemented by government support through direct assistance and through legislation, represents the main hope of women's cricket for greater media attention in the future.

The long term goal is that the faces of women cricketers will become sufficiently familiar to the public — through television exposure — that people will recognise them. The stars of the game will then be acknowledged as heroines and role models for women, young and old.

CHAPTER NINE

THE FUTURE OF WOMEN'S CRICKET

During the 1980s what Ray Sneddon referred to as *that* question — the future of women's cricket — was frequently asked as it had been in previous decades. Sneddon's column in *Cricketer* of April 1986 was headed 'Has Women's Cricket a Future?'

Many people have asked *that* question of me as I have moved from State to State as the part-time national executive director.

People involved in sport, male and female members of the media, corporation executives and interested parents have, from time to time, asked me *that* question.

Unlike one commentator, who was unsure of the future of the game in 1970, Sneddon was able to answer the question confidently by listing all the positive developments in the 1980s. Participant levels had increased; more girls were now playing Kanga cricket from an early age; media acceptability of women's cricket had also expanded as had sponsorship and Federal and State government support while the ACB had also been a 'tremendous help'. The AWCC was functioning in a more effective way and the women's international game was becoming increasingly attractive and more visible to the public than it had been for a long time. Long-held prejudices about women playing team sports were diminishing and sexual discrimination was being reduced.

Sneddon could have added that there were a growing number of women and girls playing organised sport on a regular basis. While the number of women playing sport was still well below the men, it was increasing. Tables of the numbers involved in the top ten male and female sports, derived from the *Australian Sports Directory* of 1991, indicated that many women's sports had developed a substantial following. For every seven males involved in these popular sports, there were approximately three females involved in equivalent sports.

Leading Men's Sports (1991 registrations)

	Senior	Junior	Total
Cricket			550 000
Aust. Football	139 680	335 310	474 990
Soccer	42 179	305 371	347 550
Golf			346 324
Tennis	130 000	150 000	280 000
Bowls			274 943
Fishing	122 300	24 300	146 600
Rugby League	32 300	96 600	128 900
Baseball			106 000
Rugby Union	43 570	59 610	103 180
Total			2 758 487

Leading Women's Sports (1991 registrations)

	Senior	Junior	Total
Netball	196 381	177 027	373 408
Tennis	130 000	150 000	280 000
Bowls	148 547		148 547
Fishing	61 200	12 200	73 400
Basketball	40 448	27 628	68 076
Touch Football	47 000	9 000	56 000
Softball	22 684	14 535	37 219
Volleyball	20 000	12 500	32 500
Hockey	20 767	10 836	31 603
Squash	24 430	4 340	28 770
Total			1 129 523

Mixed Sports (1991 registrations)[1]

Cricket (Indoor)	500 000
Soccer (Indoor)	347 550

WOMEN'S CRICKET IS CATCHING ON

Australian Sports Commission — Shell Australia

A further encouraging sign was that some women were beginning to take up a few of the traditional male sports such as power lifting, soccer, rowing and surfriding. Although the figures were small, they indicated that some long-established sporting gender boundaries were crumbling.

Female participation in some minor sports (1991 registrations)

	Senior	Junior	Total
Surfriders	2 287	3 766	6 053
Rowing	3 000	1 450	4 450
Soccer			4 387
Power lifting	122	305	427

Despite the grounds for optimism, women's cricket still is very much a minor sport in 1991 — after more than a century of organisation. Even with 12,281 registered players in 1991, the sport has a long way to go to make the top ten women's sports. A central question about the future of women's cricket is whether it will make the transition from a minor to a major sport. Ann Mitchell acknowledged the importance of this issue:

Women's cricket has got to become more than a minority sport ... we may never have the numbers like netball because it can be difficult to find women to give up a whole afternoon every weekend but there can be a lot more growth.

We should look to a time where we are more structured like the men who even have national championships for primary level boys.[2]

Mitchell recognised that women's cricket had to experience growth and development in order to survive in the highly competitive and diverse sports world of the 1990s. To make the transition from a peripheral minor sport to a well recognised major one was essential for the future viability of the sport. Minor sports in Australia have never had an assured future; there have been many instances of sports which have flourished for a decade or two but which have slipped from public notice subsequently. Professional sculling was a popular sport in the late 19th century, when Australia produced a succession of world champions, but it faded from public notice in the 20th century. Cycling boomed in the 1890s but suffered a decline in the first decades of the 20th century. Boxing has had a very chequered history in Australia, experiencing periods of expansion (such as immediately before World War I) but declining dramatically at other periods.

The problem for these sports in particular, and minor sports in general, was that they failed to lay a solid foundation for the sport — in terms of school and junior programs, club organisation, and a sound administrative and financial structure — in their years of prosperity. This has occurred because public and media acceptance has been conditional and at times even superficial and lacking this support, they have been unable to survive. Minor sports have often been taken up as a fad and then discarded once the novelty has worn off. They lack the legitimacy of more established sports which can count on continuing support and promotion by government and educational authorities and business leaders.

Until recent decades women's cricket has suffered from this classic minor sport syndrome. The boom of the 1930s was not soundly based — media and public acceptance was conditional — to carry it through the leaner years of the late 1950s and 1960s. Some of the gains of the 1930s were diminished in the 1960s and women's cricket authorities had to start from scratch in the 1970s.

There is considerable evidence in the 1980s and 1990s that women's cricket is in the process of overcoming the handicap of

A star of the future. Olivia Magno (NSW) had a batting average of 80 at the 1990 Under 18 Australian Championships (Courtesy Chris Matthews)

minor sport status, really for the first time, and the related negative cycle of growth and decline. Women's cricket may never acquire the popular following of netball but its future growth now seems assured. Ray Sneddon's hope that there may be a five-fold increase to a playing strength of 65,000 may not be too far distant. The future of the sport seems far more certain than it was in the 1930s because of changes in four areas: the support of government and business for women's sport in general and women's cricket in particular; a greater amount of promotion of, and public education about, women's sport; the establishment of a strong network of school and junior programs and more support for women's cricket from men's cricket authorities.

Government support has played and will continue to play a vital role in the future expansion of women's cricket. It has occurred in many ways and at many levels: assistance in publicity, promotion, and in direct financial grants. However, the most important contribution has been to provide women's sports with greater legitimacy by introducing positive discrimination in favour of women's and girls' sports. The decision of the NSW Department of Education to actively promote girls' cricket and soccer in high schools in the early 1980s was an extremely important one in that it enhanced the status of women's cricket and has added and will continue to add to its future player strength.

Greater government support for women's sport is occurring in many other societies as well. The fares of the Indian women cricketers, who toured Australia in January and February 1991, were paid by the Government of India. Women's cricket in India is now subsidised to a considerable extent by the government. The majority of the players are employed by the Railways and receive generous leave entitlements, including touring Australia on full pay. Kersi Meher-Homji believed that the cautious play of the Indians — who have been renowned for the number of drawn Tests — is partly a result of a fear that losing Tests might mean a loss of more than face. Meher-Homji stated that if India loses a Test 'the [Indian] Ministry of Sports is reluctant to release foreign exchange for an overseas trip'.[3]

Government policy has been one reason why business has taken women's sport more seriously. Business, of course, is equally sensitive to shifts in public opinion as well and the advantages of being associated with women's sport. Greater sponsorship has played a vital role in the revival of women's cricket given the spiralling costs of conducting international competition and the need to promote sport in a highly competitive market place.

Government initiatives, the promotional efforts of sports

CHRISTINE BRIERLEY
(b 1949) became Manager of the Australian Cricket Team in 1989 after the retirement of Ann Mitchell. She played club cricket for Kuringgai from 1965–71 and then after a break of eleven years due to ill health, played for Gordon from 1982–86. She then returned to Kuring-gai, playing with the club until 1990. During her professional career she has been involved in photography, public relations and communications.

Brierley managed the NSW team from 1984–88 and held many administrative positions in the Sydney WCA and NSWWCA before she became President of the NSWWCA in 1988. She was NSW delegate to the AWCC from 1987 and became Chairperson of the NSWWCA Board from 1988.

Christine Brierley believes that one of the strengths of women's cricket administrators in Australia has been that 'they have all been players', at one level or another, and 'are professional in their approach'.

Sponsors find women's cricket a safer wicket

By JUDITH FRIEDLANDER

IT'S the cricket season and this month mad dogs and Englishmen and 5000 Australian women will venture out under the noonday sun to compete in this established sport.

Cricket is attracting more and more women and all State cricketing organisations report increases over last year's figures.

Tasmania and the ACT, for example, which a few seasons ago had only a small number of female cricketers, this year boast a 145 per cent increase in playing numbers.

Women's cricket is also starting to attract sponsors with companies such as Ama and Shell backing last season's locally-played Test series between England and Ausalia. This was supplemented by funding from the Government, the Australian Women's Cricket Council (AWCC) and the Australian Cricket Board.

A major sponsor for women's cricket over the next three years is expected to be announced in about two weeks.

Sponsors are possibly feeling that women's cricket is a safer bet than the men's game: while Australia's male crickers were being convincingly beaten by the West Indies last season, their female counterparts were riding high against England, winning the Test series 2-1 and the one-day internationals 3-0. In fact, Australia has been the world champion in women's cricket since 1979.

The indications are that there is an even bigger boom ahead for the women's game. Organisations such as the Australian Women's Cricket Council have been busy for some years laying the groundwork with schools and cricket clubs and are now starting to reap the rewards.

The first national Australian championships for under 18-year-old female players will be held this year and Kanga cricket — modified cricket for boys and girls aged from six to 12 — has just been introduced to about two million children in Australian primary schools.

Many would assume that women's cricket is only a recent development — judging by the new attention from sponsors and women themselves.

But it's a heightened awareness, rather than an interest in the sport, that is propelling it to greater popularity.

Women's cricket was first played in England in the mid-1700s and it was some years after colonisation that the game was played here. The first Australian match is reputed to have been held on the outskirts of Sydney in 1815.

History has credited a woman with inventing the over-arm bowling action. Christina Willes, sister of Kent cricketer John Willes, tried the round-arm action in order to avoid her voluminous skirts.

Her brother was so impressed that he tried the new method at Lords in 1822 but was "no balled" by the umpire. It took another six years for the technique to be accepted.

Just as the sponsors have started to regard women's cricket a little more seriously, the media is also learning that the game has credibility and is worth watching.

Today's reporting of women's cricket is a far cry from the tone used 50 years ago. "A women's cricket match at the MCG — can such a thing be possible? Even in the memory of the oldest member there has never been a similar occurrence and the shock may be nearly too much for those who consider that women should keep to the gentle sports," commented *The Star* in 1934.

So why has cricket in the past few years ceased to be considered a purely male preserve and started to attract more players and fans?

Anne Mitchell, president of the International Women's Cricket Council, believes that the general public is noting the success of Australia's female cricketers. "Australians like to hear of winners," she said. "And the interest in the women's team was heightened last season when the men weren't playing too well."

The appointment of Ray Sneddon as national executive director of the AWCC in 1983 made him the first paid administrator — albeit a part-time one — that the council has taken on.

Anne Mitchell said his appointment has led to a positive follow-on in promotional and marketing circles. "You can't have a national or international cricketing organisation run by amateurs for the simple reason that amateurs have other jobs and can't afford to devote a lot of time to other concerns," she said.

"One of the most important functions of a cricketing organisation is to ensure that journalists know about you."

Ray Sneddon commented that women's cricket was "looking better" than it did three years ago. "Then, we didn't have anything in the way of sponsors and media attention," he said. "Now, I strongly believe government and business are taking a stronger interest in the sport."

He said he expected the companies that had supported the 1984-85 Tests between England and Australia to continue their sponsorship of the AWCC. "We're still negotiating but most companies have indicated they'll continue supporting us. The Government has also agreed to fund the council $34,000 which will cover aspects such as coaching projects and international competitions. And there'll soon be a big announcement of a major women's cricket sponsor for the next three years."

Mr Sneddon said he had to "drag" male cricket reporters to watch the last Test series. "But once they saw the game they were impressed. Our role is to get them to the game — once they're there the cricketers will do the rest."

Denise Emerson, regarded as one of the best batswomen in the world and vice-captain of Australia last season, said women's cricket was receiving greater recognition but she would "still like to see the day when women get paid for playing the game".

Ms Emerson works as a secretary at Norglass Laboratories, a Sydney paint manufacturing firm, and during the cricket season trains at nights and weekends. She said last season's sponsorship helped the sport considerably but all players had had to contribute about $1000 of their own money.

"Any sporting team representing the country should not have to be out of pocket — especially the best team in the world," she said.

Denise Emerson . . . one of the world's top bats

administrators and shifting gender ideologies have all had some impact on media and the public which is beginning to become better informed and educated about women's sport. Prejudices still abound but the public is starting to become more familiar with women as jockeys, bodybuilders, marathon runners and power lifters.

The growth of public interest in health has also led to more involvement of women and girls in sport. Various studies have suggested that it is beneficial for females to exercise more than they do and other research has focused on why females have higher 'drop out' ratios from sport than males. Ken Dyer, for instance, from the University of Adelaide, conducted one such study in November 1986 on 'Girls' Physical Education and Self-Esteem — a Review of Research Resources and Strategies' which was published as a report to the Commonwealth Schools Commission. He argued that female sport and physical education should be encouraged and extended because sporting participants had better self-concepts, self-esteem and body images than non-participants.[4]

The future of women's cricket, however, rests even more on the development of school and junior cricket. Without channels of recruitment from the earliest age women's cricket can never hope to expand and even consolidate its present position. It is quite surprising to discover how many former Test stars did not discover cricket, or begin to play it seriously, until post-school years. For every player recruited to cricket at the age of seventeen or eighteen — at university, as was the case of Mollie Dive — there must have been dozens of others forever lost to the game because they had no access to the sport at school in these years. Or, because cricket was not accessible to girls in the majority of Australian primary and secondary schools, most girls must have opted for other sporting alternatives such as hockey, netball and tennis.

The growth of school sport, then, is vital to the future health of women's cricket. The backing of educational authorities and its promotion by teachers provided the sport with greater legitimacy both in the eyes of students and parents. Playing the sport from an early age will help develop the skills of the game and improve the standards of women's cricket.

The most encouraging sign for women's cricket in fact has been the expansion of school and junior cricket in the 1980s and 1990s. NSW led the way in terms of an impressive expansion of school cricket at both the primary and secondary level. By 1990–91 some of the benefits of Kanga cricket were beginning to flow through and resulted in an increased demand for a girls' cricket competition. Neil Sherring, a Senior Education Officer

Kanga cricket, with Dean Jones and Simon O'Donnell, encouraging girls to bat. (Courtesy ACB)

involved in primary schools sport,[5] reported that there was a perceived need, a few years ago, to start a separate cricket competition for girls. It began with twenty-five teams but by 1990–91 there were seventy teams organised in a knockout competition. There were also, he added, a number of girls playing cricket in 'boys' competitions'.

The rapid expansion of girls' cricket in secondary schools was even more impressive. There were 173 separate girls' teams in the Combined High Schools (CHS) competition in 1989–90, who competed in the Marie Cornish Knockout competition, and the figure had increased to 191 in 1990–91. The schools came from ten different regions in the city and country. A healthy sign for girls' cricket was that school cricket was stronger in the country areas — where women's cricket organisation was traditionally less strong — than the city. Wellington High School won the tournament in 1990–91 and all four semi-finalists came from the country. Graeme Errington, Convenor of CHS cricket in 1990–91, noted that schoolgirls' cricket was in fact much stronger and taken more seriously in the country than the city, whereas for schoolboys' cricket the reverse was true. Country schoolgirl teams benefited from coaching by men who were sympathetic to the game. In just a decade the number of girls' teams had increased to such an extent that Grant Parker, a Senior Education Officer, reported that there were about the same number of girls' teams as boys' in the CHS competition.[6] There were, in addition to CHS teams, some thirty-two schoolgirl teams competing in the state's Catholic colleges. The annual census of the AWCC for the 1989–90 season reported a total of 392 schoolgirl teams in the metropolitan area and another 153 teams in country NSW.[7]

The same census conveyed the dramatic increase in numbers of schoolgirls playing cricket particularly in NSW and the ACT. In just one season the numbers of players in NSW more than doubled.

The growth of competitions has led to the need for new institutions. A NSW Schoolgirls' Sub-Committee dealing with schoolgirls' cricket was formed in 1989 of representatives from the CHS, the Independent Girls' Schools Sports Association (IGSSA) and the Catholic Girls' Secondary Schools Sports Association (CGSSSA). A NSW Schoolgirls' Championship was initiated in 1989 and hosted by the CHS. The 1990 championship, this time sponsored by IGSSA, was held at Macquarie University between two representative CHS teams, and one each from Independent Girls' Schools and Combined Catholic Colleges. The CHS First XI was successful in 1990–91.

With such a strong network of schoolgirl and junior competition NSW has been dominant in recent years in the Australian Under 18 and Under 21 Championships. During the 1989–90 and 1990–91 tournament the NSW Under 18s did not lose a game and the Under 21 side was also successful. The NSW Under 18 side was drawn directly from the NSW Schoolgirls' Championships of the previous year.

There were promising developments in junior and school cricket elsewhere. School cricket in Victoria was sponsored by the Health Promotion Foundation. Finalists in the 1990–91 Food and Nutrition Schoolgirls' Championships were Carey Grammar, Greenwood Secondary College, Loreto and Penleigh & Essendon

> ZOE 'ZED' GOSS
> (b 1968) was born in Australia but lived in Germany until the age of ten. After returning to Australia, she discovered cricket and was an instant success. She joined the Subiaco Club in 1979, then made the WA Juniors in 1980 and the Open side in 1983. Standing at 5 ft 11 in (181 cm) she was a natural sports player and enjoyed hockey, squash and basketball.
>
> Goss was the youngest member of the 1987 Australian side to tour England and is a player of great future potential both with the bat and ball. She is currently a Bachelor of Science student at the University of Western Australia.
>
> She captained the WA side in the 1991 Open Championship.

Schoolgirls' Cricket: Numbers of players 1988–89 Season

	Metro-politan Nos	Country Nos	Non-affiliated Nos	Total
NSW	1 560	888		2 448
VIC	409	20	1 500	1 929
ACT	86		200	286
SA	110		140	250
WA	165		80	245
QLD	90		50	140
TAS	50		60	110
Total	2 470	908	2 030	5 408

Schoolgirls' Cricket: Numbers of players 1989–90 Season

	Metro-politan Nos	Country Nos	Non-affiliated Nos	Total
NSW	4 000	2 000	—	6 000
VIC	397	20	1 500	1 917
ACT	81		352	433
WA	176			176
QLD	110			110
SA	84	–		84
TAS	20			20
Total	4 868	2 020	1 852	8 740

Grammar with Greenwood winning the championship. Victoria was the second strongest state in schoolgirl cricket with a total of ninety teams and 1 917 players by 1990–91. The Victorian Junior state squad was sponsored by the Lord's Taverners. Victoria's Junior Development Officer for 1991, Sue Crow, was active in promoting Kanga cricket and organising clinics in primary and secondary schools.

A State Schoolgirls' team was selected in Western Australia in 1972 and half the side went on to represent the state in the Under 21s and in the Open side. A Primary Schools' competition was formed in 1974 and contained ten teams by 1978 but it did not continue in the 1980s. Officials in the state realised that a more integrated competition structure was needed to encourage girls to progress through the ranks to senior cricket. To cater to this need in the 1980s they introduced Under 15 and Under 18 competitions, making use of modified rules. Former Test player Peta Verco was chosen to become coaching/development co-ordinator working specifically with sub-junior and junior players. She later became state Development Officer, concentrating particularly on schools.

More young girls are playing cricket than ever before. The NSW team at the inaugural Under 18 Championships at Canberra in the 1985–86 season. Back L to R: *Karen Price (Manager), Sally Hughson, Elizabeth Keen, Karen Haybittle, Alison Pool, Denise Toohey, Linda Ward, Rebecca Dam.* Front: *Karen Daws (captain), Kate Lunney, Leisl Stimpson, Gabbie Skinner.* Absent: *Belinda Clark.*

A schoolgirl competition, involving seven private schools, was begun in Queensland in 1986. This initiative was the result of cooperation between a number of teachers[8] and the Secretary of the QWCA, Ailsa Rowell. Since this time the QWCA has targeted the state schools, organising coaching clinics along with umpiring seminars for upper primary and secondary schools. A senior development camp was held at the Gabba in August 1990. The QWCA reported in *Between Overs* of March 1991 that it was making great progress towards realising its aim of introducing girls' cricket to the state primary and secondary schools. The progress in junior cricket in this state enabled Queensland to enter a side in the Under 18s Australian Championship for the first time in 1986.

There have been some recent initiatives to promote schoolgirl cricket in Tasmania. By 1988–89 the TWCA had four affiliated clubs which fielded five senior and four junior teams. Two Shell Clinics were held in 1989 for girls from nine to sixteen and attracted sixty girls who were keen to join the juniors or B Grade competition. Although the scale of operations in Tasmania was far more modest than NSW and Victoria, Jacqui Triffit, publicity

CHRISTINA MATTHEWS
(b 1959) is the most successful Australian wicketkeeper — she broke the world record for Test dismissals (36) achieving 47 by the end of the 1990–91 season — and also has had the most appearances (18) in Tests of any Australian player. As a girl she wanted to play football but chose cricket instead.

Matthews made the Victorian Junior side in 1977 and the Open side in 1983. She first played for Australia in 1984. When she moved to NSW in 1988 she was the incumbent Australian wicketkeeper but was unable to displace the state keeper, Cathy Smith. Although she lived in Sydney and represented the United Club, she was also eligible to play for ACT — as she played for the Ginninderra Club (ACT) — which enabled her to continue to play for Australia. She was Vice Captain of ACT in 1990 and 1991.

Matthews toured with the Australian team to India in 1984 and has been virtually a permanent fixture behind the stumps in the Test side ever since. Her chirpy good humour and ready quips have played an important role in maintaining team morale.

She also plays indoor cricket (representing NSW in 1989), golf, and at one stage was Secretary-Administrator of the Australian Women's Hockey Association. She subsequently became National Development Officer for the AWCC.

1990

Pioneer Victorian Ladies' Cricket Association

(Past and Present Players Association)

Organised 1905   Disbanded 1916
Re-organised Socially 1930

OFFICE-BEARERS

President: Mrs. E. Stephens
Secretary: Miss L. Taylor
Vice-Presidents: Misses G. Wilson, H. Thompson, D. Purchase
Committee: Mesdames P. Graf, D. Padley, M. Reid
Misses J. Bath, V. Beasley, I. Beasley, M. Goring, N. Murray
Treasurer: Mrs. I. Grant

LIFE MEMBERS

Miss Hilda Striezel, Mrs. Mather, Mrs. Henderson, Miss Ann Latham, Mrs. Edna Stephens, Mrs. Mary Armstrong, Miss Gwen Wilson, Mrs. Marie Reid, Miss Hilda Thompson, Miss Dot Purchase, Mrs. Phyllis Graf, Mrs. Irene Grant, Miss Joyce Bath, Miss Dorothy Padley, Miss Marian Goring.

60th REUNION DINNER

will be held on
Friday, 9th November, 1990
at
TOWNHOUSE HOTEL — (Lincoln Room)
701 Swanston Street, Carlton
Start 7.00 p.m.
— all tickets to be paid for by 31st October, 1990 —
— Distribution of tickets on receipt of order —

$27.00   **LADIES ONLY PLEASE**

---

officer for TWCA, reported in *Between Overs* in March 1991 that the future of junior cricket in the state was hopeful:

At present the local competition is undergoing a period of transition... The growing number of girls involved in primary school competition should provide a solid foundation for the development of Tasmanian women's cricket and ensure that our younger girls have the best opportunity to develop their skills and so aspire to state and national selection.

Schoolgirl competition is also on the increase elsewhere, particularly in the ACT. With the encouragement of both the Federal and ACT Government and business, the number of schoolgirl teams increased from nine to fifteen and the players from 200 to 352 from seasons 1988–89 to 1989–90. An ACT Schoolgirls' team is

WOMEN PUT GRACE INTO CRICKET

sufficiently strong to take on a NSW CHS team in annual competition.

Another hopeful sign for women's cricket is that more and more men's officials, from the ACB and state associations, are forging closer and stronger links with women's cricket authorities. There are many benefits from this development including sharing of facilities, cash grants to women's cricket and easier access to major cricket grounds. A less tangible but more important benefit has been the greater legitimacy for women's cricket.

Ray Sneddon, who had helped to bring about a closer working relationship between the ACB and the AWCC, advocated more future amalgamation between men's and women's cricket. He referred in the Melbourne *Herald* of 14 April 1987 to the example of the Camberwell Cricket Club (Victoria) which fielded both a men's and women's first XI. The 'social events', he added, 'have never been so well attended.' Ann Mitchell believes that in the future there will be only one game — cricket — as played by men and women.

It is only in recent decades, in the more competitive sports market place, that it has finally dawned on the majority of male cricket administrators that the growth of women's cricket will be beneficial for cricket as a whole. Greater encouragement of women to play cricket at school, junior and senior levels can only enhance female appreciation of the game, add to the number of spectators at men's games and encourage more mothers to introduce both their sons and daughters to the game. When so many sports compete for the sponsorship dollar and for adoption at the school and junior level, it would be foolhardy for men's cricket authorities not to encourage girls and women to play the game.

It is surprising that it took the best part of a century for men's cricket authorities to arrive at a more sympathetic understanding of women's cricket. The blinkers of prejudice against women playing cricket, which have been held as strongly by male cricket players and the establishment as by the general public, was the primary factor. The complacency of men's cricket officials was another reason — at least until the 1970s, when men's cricket seemed firmly established on top of the national sporting pedestal with a confirmed mass following and an assured future.

The many sponsors of cricket for women.

Men's cricket didn't need women's cricket. The rapidly changing world of sponsorship and media presentation and the rise of new sporting challengers, such as basketball, has demonstrated that no sport, however powerful, can be complacent about the future and must make the most of its resources. Given the current priorities in favour of more equal opportunities in sport, the discovery of women's cricket can only be an asset for the men's game.

Conclusion

Australia entered the 1990s on a high note by comfortably defeated the visiting Indian side by two Tests to none (with one drawn) in the 1990–91 season. India, trying desperately to stave off defeat in the Second Test at Adelaide, tried the patience of spectators when they registered some of the slowest batting ever recorded — scoring only 102 runs for 3 wickets in one entire day. The Indian bowlers were unable to make much of a dent in the powerful Australian batting side which was not dismissed once in six innings.[9] Belinda Clark scored 104 in her Test debut in the First Test at North Sydney. Wicketkeeper Christina Matthews rewrote the record book during the series achieving three world records: the number of dismissals in a match (nine, eight catches and a stumping), in a series (nineteen) and the total number of dismissals (forty-seven). Prior to the Test series Australia retained the Shell Rose Bowl in a three match encounter with New Zealand by two matches to one. Belinda Haggett was the leading bat, scoring 80 and 70, while Zoe Goss and Jo Broadbent were the pick of the bowlers.

With the continuing success of the national team, women's cricket can anticipate a more promising future in terms of expanded numbers and greater public acceptance. Women's cricket has arrived at an exciting threshold, as it did in the 1930s, but the foundations for a future 'take off' seem more secure now than in those days.

There has been a slow but remarkable change in the public and media's attitude towards team sports. Whereas women have been discouraged from playing cricket and football in many direct and indirect ways in the past, they are now receiving encouragement at least from some quarters to play any manner of sports. Far from treating women's sport as a joke many influential women and men are encouraging women to involve themselves in the gamut of sporting experience. A journalist and international rugby player, Peter Fitzsimons, expressed surprise in the *Sydney Morning Herald* of 6 April 1991 that Australian women had not organised a rugby team to participate in the inaugural Women's World Cup in Wales in 1991. There was no disparagement of women playing rugby in this article and the likely effect of this story is that some women will be encouraged to form a team some time in the future. In an increasingly health-conscious society it is likely that women will become more involved in all

---

BELINDA 'BIN' HAGGETT
(b 1962) played cricket with boys in a Saturday morning competition while she was at primary school but by age fourteen she was playing first grade cricket with North Sydney Women's Cricket Club before transferring to the Kuring-gai Club. She made the NSW Junior team in 1979 and the Open side in 1981. She became a physical education teacher and is also a Level 1 Coach.

Haggett made her international debut in the 1985 Shell Cup one day tournament against New Zealand. Touring England with the 1987 side, she had the distinction of making 126 on her Test debut and aggregated 224 runs in the three Tests. A right-hand bat she has become a permanent fixture in the Australian side.

A keen sportswoman who also plays golf and tennis, she was state softball representative for many years before she decided to concentrate on cricket.

The Australian team entered the 1990s—as they had left the 1980s—as champions. As winners of the 1991 Shell Rose Bowl they displayed their latest uniform. Back row L to R: Kerry Saunders, Karen Brown, Zoe Goss, Sally Moffat, Meg McIntyre (physiotherapist), Debbie Wilson, Bronwyn Calver, Tunde Juhasz, Joanne Broadbent, Peter Bakker (Coach, Belinda Haggett. Front row L to R: Christine Brierley (Manager), Denise Annetts, Lyn Larsen (Captain), Belinda Clark, Sharlene Heywood. (Courtesy AWCC)

manner of sports; it is also probable their efforts will achieve greater recognition in the future.

For much of the past century sport has been one of the great bastions of male culture but many of the gender walls are now crumbling. While there will be some diehards who will not welcome storming the battlements of a once comfortable male territory, the majority will soon start to recognise, if they have not yet begun to do so, that greater female involvement in sport in general, and cricket in particular, will add to the richness and diversity of the Australian sporting world and make it more accessible to all Australians.

Ann Mitchell believes that the minority sport known for a century as 'women's cricket' — a term accepted both by those within and outside the sport[10] — will cease to exist as such in the future. Women, she believes, will take part alongside men as players and administrators in the one game and cricket will be stronger as a result of the equal involvement of men and women. Mitchell believes that while women and girls will continue to play in separate teams and have their own administrative structures, there will be a greater pooling of resources in the future — particularly in terms of sharing coaching, training and administrative facilities. Women and girls who were for so long confined to the margins of cricket — whether it be making tea and scones for the male players or playing largely unnoticed beyond the boundary — are beginning to take their place at the wickets themselves.

Statistics of Australian Women's Cricket

Prepared by Erica Sainsbury

TEST CRICKET

Summary of Test Matches

VS	PLAYED	WON	LOST	DRAWN
England	32	6	6	20
New Zealand	11	4	1	6
West Indies	2	0	0	2
India	8	3	0	5
	53	13	7	33

Summary of Tests against England

YEAR	VENUE	DATES	TOSS	RESULT
1934–35	1 Brisbane	Dec. 28,29,31	Aust (Bat)	Eng by 9 wickets
	2 Sydney	Jan. 4,7,8	Aust (Bat)	Eng by 8 wickets
	3 Melbourne	Jan. 18,19,21	Eng (Bat)	Draw
1937	1 Northampton	June 12,14,15	Aust (Bat)	Aust by 31 runs
	2 Blackpool	June 26,28,29	Eng (Bat)	Eng by 25 runs
	3 The Oval	July 10,12,13	Aust (Bat)	Draw
1949	1 Adelaide	Jan. 15,17,18	Aust (Bat)	Aust by 186 runs
	2 Melbourne	Jan. 28,29,31	Aust (Bat)	Draw
	3 Sydney	Feb. 19,21,22	Eng (Bat)	Draw
1951	1 Scarborough	June 16,18,19	Eng (Bat)	Draw
	2 Worcester	Jun 30, July 2,3	Eng (Bat)	Aust by 160 runs
	3 The Oval	July 28,30,31	Eng (Bat)	Eng by 137 runs
1958	1 Sydney	Feb. 7,8,10	Match abandoned	
	2 Melbourne	Feb. 21,22,24	Eng (Bowl)	Draw
	3 Adelaide	Mar. 8,10,11	Aust (Bat)	Draw
	4 Perth	Mar. 21,22,24	Eng (Bat)	Draw
1963	1 Edgbaston	June 15,17,18	Aust (Bat)	Draw
	2 Scarborough	Jun 29, July 1,2	Eng (Bat)	Draw
	3 The Oval	July 20,22,23	Eng (Bat)	Eng by 49 runs
1968–69	1 Adelaide	Dec. 27,28,30	Eng (Bat)	Draw
	2 Melbourne	Jan. 10,11,13	Eng (Bat)	Draw
	3 Sydney	Jan. 25,27,28	Aust (Bat)	Draw
1976	1 Old Trafford	June 19,20,21	Eng (Bowl)	Draw

	2 Edgbaston	July 3,4,5	Eng (Bat)	Draw
	3 The Oval	July 24,27,28	Eng (Bat)	Draw
1984–85	1 Perth	Dec.13,14,15,16	Eng (Bat)	Draw
	2 Adelaide	Dec.21,22,23,24	Eng (Bat)	Eng by 5 runs
	3 Gabba	Jan. 1,2,3,4	Eng (Bat)	Draw
	4 Gosford	Jan.12,13,14,15	Eng (Bowl)	Aust by 117 runs
	5 Bendigo	Jan 25,26,27,28	Eng (Bat)	Aust by 7 wickets
1987	1 Worcester	Aug. 1,2,3	Eng (Bat)	Aust by inns & 21
	2 Collingham	Aug. 21,22,23,24	Eng (Bat)	Draw
	3 Hove	Aug. 29,30,31 Sept.1	Eng (Bowl)	Draw

Summary of Tests against New Zealand

YEAR	VENUE	DATES	TOSS	RESULT
1948	Wellington	Mar. 20,22,23	Aust (Bat)	Aust by inns & 102
1957	Adelaide	Jan. 18,19,20,21	Aust (Bat)	Aust by inns & 88
1961	Dunedin	Mar. 17,18,20	NZ (Bat)	Draw
1972	Melbourne	Feb. 5,6,7,8	NZ (Bat)	NZ by 143 runs
1975	Wellington	Mar. 21,22,23,24	NZ (Bat)	Draw
1979	1 Sydney	Jan. 12,13,14,15	NZ (Bat)	Draw
	2 Adelaide	Jan. 19,20,21,22	Aust (Bowl)	Aust by inns & 74
	3 Melbourne	Jan. 26,27,28,29	Aust (Bat)	Draw
1990	1 Auckland	Jan. 18,19,20,21	NZ (Bowl)	Draw
	2 Wellington	Jan. 26,27,28,29	NZ (Bowl)	Draw
	3 Christchurch	Feb. 1,2,3,4	NZ (Bat)	Aust by 8 wickets

Summary of Tests against West Indies

YEAR	VENUE	DATES	TOSS	RESULT
1976	1 Jarrett Park	May 7,8	WI (Bat)	Draw
	2 Sabina Park	May 14,15,16	WI (Bat)	Draw

Summary of Tests against India

YEAR	VENUE	DATES	TOSS	RESULT
1977	Perth	Jan. 15,16,17	Aust (Bat)	Aust by 147 runs
1984	1 Delhi	Jan. 21,22,23	Ind (Bat)	Draw
	2 Lucknow	Jan. 28,29,30	Aust (Bat)	Draw
	3 Ahmedabad	Feb. 3,4,5	Ind (Bat)	Draw
	4 Bombay	Feb. 10,11,12	Ind (Bat)	Draw
1991	1 Sydney	Jan. 26,27,28,29	Ind (Bowl)	Draw
	2 Adelaide	Feb. 2,3,4,5	Ind (Bat)	Aust by 10 wickets
	3 Melbourne	Feb. 9,10,11,12	Aust (Bowl)	Aust by 9 wickets

Scores of 300 and Over

1984	Ahmedabad	vs India	3rd Test	525
1976	The Oval	vs England	3rd Test	379
1990	Auckland	vs New Zealand	1st Test	371
1987	Hove	vs England	3rd Test	7–366
1975	Wellington	vs New Zealand		362
1984	Bombay	vs India	4th Test	8–358
1957	Adelaide	vs New Zealand		9–354
1987	Collingham	vs England	2nd Test	3–346

1968/9	Adelaide	vs England	1st Test	7–339
1948	Wellington	vs New Zealand		6–338
1984/5	Brisbane	vs England	3rd Test	9–326
1990	Wellington	vs New Zealand	2nd Test	9–325
1979	Melbourne	vs New Zealand	3rd Test	311
1991	Melbourne	vs India	3rd Test	3–307
1937	Blackpool	vs England	2nd Test	302
1991	Sydney	vs India	1st Test	4–301
1937	Northampton	vs England	1st Test	300

Test Batting Averages

NAME	STATE	TESTS	INN	NO	HS	100	50	AGG	AVER
ALLITT M	NSW	11	20	—	76	—	1	348	17.40
AMOS E	VIC	4	7	1	55	—	1	182	30.33
ANNETTS D	NSW	9	12	2	193	1	6	671	67.10
ANTONIO P	VIC	6	12	1	37	—	—	128	11.64
BANFIELD S	VIC	1	2	—	21	—	—	41	20.50
BATH J	VIC	3	3	1	8*	—	—	9	4.50
BATTY V	VIC	7	12	1	70	—	2	272	24.73
BAYLISS M (nee CRADDOCK)	VIC	6	6	3	9*	—	—	22	7.33
BLADE F	NSW	1	2	1	4	—	—	4	4.00
BLUNSDEN W	SA	7	5	1	23*	—	—	53	13.25
BRAY E	VIC	5	8	1	86	—	2	261	37.29
BREWER J	QLD	2	4	—	34	—	—	100	25.00
BROADBENT J	SA	5	4	2	36*	—	—	88	44.00
BROWN K	VIC	8	6	—	65	—	1	132	22.00
BUCK H	NSW	3	5	—	47	—	—	169	33.80
BUCKSTEIN R	VIC	1	2	—	83	—	1	85	42.50
CHRIST J	NSW	8	10	—	73	—	2	255	25.50
CLARK B	NSW	3	6	2	104	1	2	322	80.50
CORNISH M (nee LUTSCHINI)	NSW	9	8	2	46*	—	—	90	15.00
COULTHARD F	SA	1	2	1	3	—	—	3	3.00
DALTON J	NSW	3	4	1	59*	—	1	104	34.67
DAWSON P (nee KELLY)	NSW	6	10	1	72	—	1	142	15.78
DEANE E	VIC	1	2	1	1*	—	—	2	2.00
DENHOLM L	VIC	8	14	2	93	—	1	349	29.08
DIVE M	NSW	7	11	—	59	—	2	177	16.09
DOW R	SA	3	5	1	58	—	1	120	30.00
EDWARDS M	VIC	1	0	—	—	—	—	—	—
EMERSON D (nee ALDERMAN)	NSW	7	11	0	121	1	3	454	41.27
FELLOWS A	SA	3	5	0	25	—	—	53	10.60
FITZPATRICK C	VIC	2	0	—	—	—	—	—	—
FLAHERTY M	NSW	6	8	3	14*	—	—	54	10.80
FULLSTON L	SA	12	14	5	41*	—	—	285	31.67
GEORGE W	SA	3	6	2	62*	—	1	170	42.50
GOLDSMITH J	VIC	3	4	—	58	—	1	129	32.25
GORDON A	VIC	9	11	1	38*	—	—	195	19.50
GOSS Z	WA	9	13	3	48	—	—	252	25.20
GRIFFITHS S	NSW	6	6	1	133	1	—	197	39.40
HAGGETT B	NSW	9	14	2	144	2	4	730	60.83
HALL G	NSW	2	2	0	12	—	—	17	8.50

Name	State	M	I	NO	HS	100	50	Runs	Avg
HILL L	VIC	7	10	2	118*	1	2	499	62.38
HILL S (nee FITZSIMMONS)	VIC	3	4	—	38	—	—	80	20.00
HILLS H	VIC	1	1	1	2*	—	—	2	—
HILLS W	WA	9	12	1	69*	—	1	351	31.91
HOLMES P	NSW	3	6	—	70	—	1	176	29.33
HUDSON A	NSW	9	16	3	81*	—	2	451	34.69
JACOBS J	SA,VIC	7	11	1	48	—	—	136	13.60
JAMES J	WA	1	2	—	7	—	—	7	3.50
JENNINGS M	VIC	8	12	—	104	1	2	341	28.42
JOHNSTON L	VIC	1	2	—	22	—	—	28	14.00
JONES M	VIC	3	4	1	17	—	—	19	6.33
JUDE M	SA	1	2	—	5	—	—	9	4.50
JUHASZ T	SA	3	5	4	9*	—	—	17	17.00
KENNARE J	SA	12	19	0	131	3	2	702	36.94
KETTELS L	VIC	2	4	—	9	—	—	19	4.75
KNEE M	VIC	8	14	2	96	—	3	319	26.58
KUTCHER L	VIC	4	5	2	52	—	1	68	22.67
LAING J	NSW	3	4	0	84	—	1	119	29.75
LARSEN L	NSW	14	13	4	70*	—	2	324	36.00
LARTER L	VIC	7	10	2	17	—	—	72	9.00
LAUGHTON D	SA	1	1	—	47	—	—	47	47.00
LEE H	NSW	2	3	1	25*	—	—	60	30.00
LUMSDEN J	NSW	6	8	—	123	1	1	345	43.13
MACPHERSON T	NSW	1	2	—	3	—	—	3	1.50
MCCAULEY A	SA	1	1	—	8	—	—	8	8.00
MCDONALD B	SA	1	—	—	—	—	—	—	—
MCDONOUGH M	WA	1	—	—	—	—	—	—	—
MCLARTY N	VIC	5	10	—	23	—	—	68	6.80
MCCLINTOCK F	NSW	2	4	1	20	—	—	40	13.33
MARTIN DEBBIE	NSW	3	4	—	36	—	—	73	18.25
MARTIN DENISE later PLAIN	WA	7	7	4	17	—	—	41	13.67
MARVELL M	NSW	5	5	2	15	—	—	22	7.33
MASSEY E	VIC	4	6	3	32	—	—	53	17.67
MASSEY N	VIC	3	6	1	40*	—	—	98	19.60
MATTHEWS C (nee WHITE)	VIC/ACT	18	21	5	34*	—	—	177	11.06
MAY P	NSW	7	6	4	17	—	—	38	19.00
MOFFAT S	NSW	5	2	2	10*	—	—	13	—
MONAGHAN R	NSW	2	4	—	12	—	—	29	7.25
NAPIER W	VIC	2	3	—	9	—	—	21	7.00
NEED J	SA	2	2	1	4	—	—	4	4.00
NEWMAN D	WA	3	5	—	76	—	2	154	30.80
ORCHARD B	SA	2	3	1	17*	—	—	21	10.50
OWENS J	WA	3	2	1	14	—	—	26	26.00
PAISLEY U	VIC	12	17	—	108	2	—	471	27.71
PALMER A	VIC	3	6	—	39	—	—	92	15.33
PARKER J (nee WADY)	VIC	5	8	1	60	—	2	172	24.57
PEDEN B	NSW	4	8	1	33	—	—	94	13.43
PEDEN M	NSW	6	12	2	34	—	—	87	8.70
PICTON M	NSW	7	10	4	29	—	—	111	18.50
PILTZ W	SA	1	1	0	8	—	—	8	8.00
POTTER J	NSW	1	2	1	51	—	—	78	78.00
PRICE K	NSW	8	12	1	104*	1	1	278	25.27

PRITCHARD H	NSW	6	12	—	87	—	3	340	28.33
RAE D	VIC	1	2	—	38	—	—	53	26.50
RAYMOND K	NSW	2	3	—	6	—	—	11	3.67
RAYMONT K	QLD	3	5	—	47	—	—	142	28.40
READ K	WA	3	6	2	21	—	—	62	15.50
REELER L	NSW	10	15	2	110*	1	3	510	39.23
ROBERTS J (nee TREDREA)	VIC/SA	5	7	0	67	—	1	210	30.00
SCHMIDT J	VIC	7	12	—	42	—	—	206	17.17
SHEVILL E	NSW	3	6	1	63*	—	1	110	22.00
SHEVILL R	NSW	2	3	1	10	—	—	15	7.50
SLATER V	QLD	1	1	—	9	—	—	9	9.00
SMITH K	QLD	6	12	—	88	—	2	335	27.92
SMITH O	NSW	4	2	—	4	—	—	4	2.00
STOCKTON J (nee ROBINSON)	NSW	3	4	—	117	1	—	162	40.50
THOMPSON R	VIC	16	22	8	25	—	—	162	11.57
THOMSON P	NSW	4	6	2	30	—	—	107	26.75
TREDREA S	VIC	10	14	3	63	—	1	346	31.45
VERCO P (nee COOK)	WA	13	20	1	105	1	4	765	40.26
VOGT A	VIC	1	1	—	3	—	—	3	3.00
WALSH A	NSW	3	6	—	24	—	—	56	9.33
WEGEMUND A	NSW	2	4	1	5	—	—	14	4.67
WEIR W	NSW	2	1	—	25	—	—	25	25.00
WHITE C	VIC	1	1	—	1	—	—	1	1.00
WHITEMAN N	NSW	7	10	4	36*	—	—	151	25.17
WILSON Betty	VIC	11	16	1	127	3	3	862	57.47
WILSON Bev	NSW	2	4	—	51	—	1	88	22.00
WILSON D	NSW/WA	11	9	6	92*	—	1	171	57.00
WILSON M	NSW	1	1	—	0	—	—	0	0
WILSON N	VIC	3	5	—	9	—	—	19	3.80

Test Centuries

ANNETTS D	193	vs England	1987	2nd Test	Collingham
HAGGETT B	144	vs India	1991	3rd Test	Melbourne
GRIFFITHS S	133	vs NZ	1990	1st Test	Auckland
KENNARE J	131	vs India	1984	3rd Test	Ahmedabad
WILSON Betty	127	vs England	1958	3rd Test	Adelaide
HAGGETT B	126	vs England	1987	1st Test	Worcester
LUMSDEN J	123	vs England	1976	3rd Test	The Oval
EMERSON D	121	vs England	1984	2nd Test	Adelaide
HILL L	118*	vs NZ	1975		Wellington
STOCKTON J	117	vs NZ	1979	1st Test	Sydney
WILSON Betty	111	vs England	1949	1st Test	Adelaide
REELER L	110*	vs England	1987	2nd Test	Collingham
PAISLEY U	108	vs NZ	1948		Wellington
VERCO P	105	vs India	1984	3rd Test	Ahmedabad
PRICE K	104*	vs India	1984	3rd Test	Ahmedabad
JENNINGS M	104	vs England	1976	2nd Test	Edgbaston
KENNARE J	104	vs England	1985	5th Test	Bendigo
CLARK B	104	vs India	1991	1st Test	Sydney
KENNARE J	103	vs England	1984	1st Test	WACA, Perth
PAISLEY U	101	vs NZ	1957		Adelaide
WILSON Betty	100	vs England	1958	2nd Test	Melbourne

Century at First Appearance

HAGGETT B	126	vs England	1987	1st Test	Worcester
HILL L	118*	vs NZ	1975		Wellington
STOCKTON J	117	vs NZ	1979	1st Test	Sydney
PAISLEY U	108	vs NZ	1948		Wellington
CLARK B	104	vs India	1991	1st Test	Sydney

Over 400 Runs in Tests

NAME	TESTS	RUNS	AVER
WILSON Betty	11	862	57.47
VERCO P	13	765	40.26
HAGGETT B	9	730	60.83
KENNARE J	12	702	36.94
ANNETTS D	9	671	67.10
REELER L	10	510	39.23
HILL L	7	499	62.38
PAISLEY U	12	471	27.71
EMERSON D	7	454	41.27
HUDSON A	9	451	34.69

Highest Average (over 400 Runs)

NAME	TESTS	RUNS	AVER
ANNETTS D	9	671	67.10
HILL L	7	499	62.38
HAGGETT B	9	730	60.83
WILSON Betty	11	862	57.47
EMERSON D	7	454	41.27
VERCO P	13	765	40.26

Highest Series Aggregate

3 Tests	ANNETTS D	1987	vs England	352 runs
4 Tests	VERCO P	1984	vs India	367 runs
5 Tests	EMERSON D	1984/5	vs England	453 runs

Test Record Partnerships

1st*	178	HAGGETT B CLARK B	vs India	1991	1st Test Sydney
2nd	177	HAGGETT B ANNETTS D	vs India	1991	3rd Test Melbourne
3rd*	309	ANNETTS D REELER L	vs England	1987	2nd Test Collingham
4th*	163	PAISLEY U WILSON Betty	vs N Z	1948	Wellington
5th*	135	WILSON Betty BATTY V	vs England	1958	3rd Test Adelaide
6th*	125	KNEE M ALLITT M	vs England	1963	2nd Test Scarborough

7th	88	TREDREA S HILL L	vs N Z	1975	Wellington
8th*	181	GRIFFITHS S WILSON D	vs N Z	1990	1st Test Auckland
9th	67+	FULLSTON L MATTHEWS C	vs India	1984	4th Test Bombay
10th	39	WILSON Betty JONES M	vs England	1951	1st Test Scarborough

* Indicates World Record + Indicates unbroken

Test Bowling Averages

NAME	STATE	TESTS	OVERS	BALLS	MDNS	RUNS	WKTS	AVER
AMOS E	Vic	4	2	12	1	8	0	—
ANNETTS D	NSW	9	4	24	2	10	0	—
ANTONIO P	Vic	6	165	990	39	431	31	13.90
BATH J	Vic	3	55.4	334	22	80	7	11.42
BATTY V	Vic	7	3	18	3	0	0	—
BAYLISS M (nee CRADDOCK)	Vic	6	207	1242	75	314	16	19.63
BLADE F	NSW	1	10	60	2	24	0	—
BLUNSDEN W	SA	7	251.4	1526	111	377	7	53.86
BRAY E	Vic	5	4	26	2	6	0	—
BREWER J	Qld	2	2	12	0	3	0	—
BROADBENT J	SA	5	151.1	907	63	212	8	26.50
BROWN K	Vic	8	230	1380	96	297	17	17.47
BUCK H	NSW	3	13	78	9	11	2	5.50
CHRIST J	NSW	8	99	594	35	188	6	31.33
CLARK B	NSW	3	2	12	2	0	0	—
CORNISH M (nee LUTSCHINI)	NSW	9	267.6	1844	93	503	25	20.12
COULTHARD F	SA	1	6	36	1	11	0	—
DAWSON P (nee KELLY)	NSW	6	1	6	1	0	0	—
DEANE E	VIC	1	3	18	0	7	0	—
DENHOLM L	VIC	8	37.5	301	4	118	5	23.60
DIVE M	NSW	7	16	96	4	22	1	22.00
DOW R	SA	3	116	696	44	177	10	17.70
EDWARDS M	VIC	1	3.3	21	1	7	1	7.00
FELLOWS A	SA	3	8	48	1	18	0	—
FITZPATRICK C	VIC	2	93	558	36	141	3	47.00
FLAHERTY M	NSW	6	138	828	49	244	8	30.50
FULLSTON L	SA	12	601.4	3610	238	1046	41	25.51
GOLDSMITH J	VIC	3	62.3	499	13	214	3	71.33
GORDON A	VIC	9	253	1808	80	508	22	23.09
GOSS Z	WA	9	259	1554	117	379	17	22.29
GRIFFITHS S	NSW	6	96.3	579	34	192	5	38.40
HAGGETT B	NSW	9	1	6	1	0	0	—
HALL G	ACT	2	47	282	12	134	1	134.00
HILL L	VIC	7	24	144	9	59	0	—
HILL S (nee FITZSIMMONS)	VIC	3	45	360	23	54	4	13.50
HILLS W	WA	9	44	288	19	78	1	78.00
HOLMES P	NSW	3	37	222	11	85	2	42.50
HUDSON A	NSW	9	101.4	610	25	260	16	16.25
JACOBS J	SA/VIC	7	135.4	838	37	330	8	41.25

JAMES J	WA	1	24	144	8	47	3	15.67
JOHNSTON L	VIC	1	46.2	370	10	112	8	14.00
JONES M	VIC	3	75	450	25	131	1	131.00
KENNARE J	SA	12	17	102	8	23	1	23.00
KETTELS L	VIC	2	22	132	8	34	0	—
KNEE M	VIC	8	323.4	2274	116	570	35	16.29
KUTCHER L	VIC	4	137.3	881	41	298	16	18.63
LAING J	NSW	3	21	168	6	69	1	69.00
LARSEN L	NSW	14	340	2040	154	469	25	18.76
LEE H	NSW	2	48.4	292	18	70	4	17.50
LUMSDEN J	NSW	6	16	106	9	23	0	—
MACPHERSON T	NSW	1	31	248	6	88	6	14.67
MCCAULEY A	SA	1	16	96	6	22	1	22.00
MCDONALD B	SA	1	11	66	3	27	0	—
MCLARTY N	VIC	5	148	888	67	224	11	20.36
MCLINTOCK F	NSW	2	21	126	15	8	0	—
MARTIN DEBBIE	NSW	3	2	16	1	1	0	—
MARTIN DENISE later PLAIN	WA	7	223	1338	123	306	17	18.00
MARVELL M	NSW	5	205	1230	93	305	6	50.83
MASSEY E	VIC	4	84	504	29	176	3	58.67
MATTHEWS C (nee WHITE)	V/A	18	1	6	0	4	0	—
MAY P	NSW	7	154	996	52	319	6	53.17
MOFFAT S	NSW	5	170.5	1025	90	191	15	12.73
NEED J	SA	2	27	216	5	79	0	—
ORCHARD B	SA	2	17	102	4	26	1	26.00
OWENS J	WA	3	98.1	589	34	193	14	13.79
PAISLEY U	VIC	12	227.3	1365	62	436	19	22.95
PALMER A	VIC	3	46.2	278	9	120	10	12.00
PARKER J (nee WADY)	VIC	5	13	92	2	34	3	11.33
PEDEN B	NSW	4	20	120	4	50	1	50.00
PICTON M	NSW	7	128	818	33	305	8	38.13
PILTZ W	SA	1	18	108	6	43	1	43.00
PRICE K	NSW	8	288	1728	112	528	26	20.31
RAE D	VIC	1	18.1	145	6	26	1	26.00
RAYMOND K	NSW	2	1	6	0	1	0	—
REELER L	NSW	10	28	168	10	84	2	42.00
SHEVILL E	NSW	3	15	90	1	49	1	49.00
SLATER V	QLD	1	10.1	61	6	13	4	3.25
SMITH K	QLD	6	175	1050	39	410	13	31.54
STOCKTON J (nee ROBINSON)	NSW	3	3	24	0	13	0	—
THOMPSON R	VIC	16	649.3	4303	276	1040	57	18.25
THOMSON P	NSW	4	70	420	16	147	2	73.50
TREDREA S	VIC	10	373.6	2456	133	784	30	26.13
VERCO P (nee COOK)	WA	13	313.4	2058	126	492	21	23.43
VOGT A	VIC	1	15	90	8	18	0	—
WALSH A	NSW	3	55	330	9	207	5	41.40
WEIR W	NSW	2	53	376	8	178	4	44.50
WHITE C	VIC	1	5	40	1	10	0	—
WHITEMAN N	NSW	7	272.3	1635	102	452	22	20.55
WILSON BETTY	VIC	11	480.5	2885	172	803	68	11.81

WILSON D	NSW/WA	11	467.1	2803	160	881	48	18.35
WILSON M	NSW	1	5	40	0	34	0	—

20 or more Wickets in Tests

	TESTS	WKTS	AVER
WILSON Betty	11	68	11.81
THOMPSON R	16	57	18.25
WILSON D	11	48	18.35
FULLSTON L	12	41	25.51
KNEE M	8	35	16.29
ANTONIO P	6	31	13.90
TREDREA S	10	30	26.13
PRICE K	8	26	20.31
LARSEN L	14	25	18.76
CORNISH M	9	25	20.12
WHITEMAN N	7	22	20.55
GORDON A	9	22	23.09
VERCO P	13	21	23.43

Best Average

NAME	TESTS	AVER	WKTS
WILSON Betty	11	11.81	68
ANTONIO P	6	13.90	31
KNEE M	8	16.29	35
THOMPSON R	16	18.25	57
WILSON D	11	18.35	48
LARSEN L	14	18.76	25

5 Wickets or more in an Innings

WILSON Betty	1958	England	7-7*	1st Test (1st inn)
PALMER A	1934/5	England	7-18	1st Test (1st inn)
JOHNSTON L	1972	NZ	7-24	1st innings
WILSON Betty	1949	England	6-23	1st Test (1st inn)
WILSON Betty	1948	NZ	6-28	2nd innings
ANTONIO P	1934/5	England	6-49	3rd Test (1st inn)
ANTONIO P	1937	England	6-51	1st Test (1st inn)
WILSON Betty	1958	England	6-71	2nd Test (1st inn)
PRICE K	1984	India	6-72	2nd Test (1st inn)
WILSON D	1991	India	5-27	3rd Test (1st inn)
ANTONIO P	1937	England	5-31	2nd Test (2nd inn)
BROWN K	1987	England	5-32	3rd Test (1st inn)
THOMPSON R	1984/5	England	5-33	5th Test (1st inn)
KNEE M	1963	England	5-35	2nd Test (1st inn)
WILSON D	1990	NZ	5-42	3rd Test (2nd inn)
KNEE M	1968/9	England	5-49	1st Test (1st inn)
KUTCHER L	1968/9	England	5-49	3rd Test (1st inn)
CORNISH M	1976	W Indies	5-51	2nd Test (1st inn)
OWENS J	1987	England	5-55	2nd Test (1st inn)
GORDON A	1968/9	England	5-57	2nd Test (1st inn)

KUTCHER L	1963	England	5-59	3rd Test (1st inn)
GORDON A	1968/9	England	5-61	2nd Test (1st inn)

* includes hat trick

8 or more Wickets in a Test

11	WILSON Betty	1958	England	7-7* 4-9	1st Test
10	WILSON Betty	1948	NZ	4-37 6-28	
10	PRICE K	1984	India	6-72 4-35	2nd Test
10	GORDON A	1968/9	England	5-61 5-57	2nd Test
9	WILSON Betty	1949	England	6-23 3-39	1st Test
9	WILSON D	1990	NZ	4-50 5-42	3rd Test
9	ANTONIO P	1937	England	6-51 3-40	1st Test
8	THOMPSON R	1979	NZ	4-14 4-17	2nd Test
8	KNEE M	1963	England	5-35 3-22	2nd Test
8	ANTONIO P	1937	England	3-34 5-31	2nd Test
8	KNEE M	1968/9	England	5-49 3-19	1st Test
8	ANTONIO P	1934/5	England	6-49 2-55	3rd Test
8	JOHNSTON L	1972	NZ	7-24 1-88	

* includes hat trick

Best Series Aggregate

	TESTS			WKTS	AVER
WILSON Betty	3	1958	England	21	9.70
FULLSTON L	4	1984	India	20	19.70
ANTONIO P	3	1937	England	19	11.20
WILSON D	5	1984/5	England	19	22.32
FULLSTON L	5	1984/5	England	19	26.68
THOMPSON R	5	1984/5	England	18	15.72
WILSON Betty	3	1949	England	16	12.60
TREDREA S	3	1979	NZ	16	13.60
KNEE M	3	1963	England	16	14.25
WILSON Betty	3	1951	England	16	16.70
GORDON A	3	1968/9	England	16	16.75
PRICE K	4	1984	India	16	22.18
WILSON D	3	1991	India	15	17.67

Wicketkeeping Records

	TESTS	CATCHES	STUMPINGS	TOTAL
MATTHEWS C V/A	18	38	9	47
JENNINGS M Vic	8	14	10	24

LARTER L Vic	7	7	9	16
SMITH O NSW	4	6	5	11

Most Catches in an Innings
5   MATTHEWS C   1991   India   3rd Test (1st inn)

Most Catches in a Test
8   MATTHEWS C   1991   India   2nd Test

Most Stumpings in an Innings
4   JENNINGS M   1976   W Indies   1st Test (1st inn)

Most Stumpings in a Test
5   WEGEMUND A   1937   England   2nd Test

Most Dismissals in an Innings
5   MATTHEWS C   1991   India   2nd Test
     (4 c, 1 st)
5   MATTHEWS C   1991   India   3rd Test
     (5 c)

Most Dismissals in a Test
9   MATTHEWS C   1991   India   2nd Test
     (8 c, 1 st)

Most Dismissals in a Series
19   MATTHEWS C   1991   India
     17 c, 2 st

Most catches other than Wicketkeeper in an Innings
3	McLARTY N	1934–35	England	1st Test (1st inn)
	CHRIST J	1949	England	2nd Test (1st inn)
	SCHMIDT J	1949	England	3rd Test (1st inn)
	WHITEMAN N	1951	England	2nd Test (1st inn)
	FULLSTON L	1984	India	3rd Test (1st inn)
	VERCO P	1984–85	England	1st Test (1st inn)

Most Catches other than Wicketkeeper in a Test
4	CHRIST J	1949	England	2nd Test
	WHITEMAN N	1951	England	2nd Test
	VERCO P	1984–85	England	1st Test

Most Catches other than Wicketkeeper in a Series
(i)	3 TEST			
7	ANNETTS D	1987		England
(ii)	4 TEST			
9	FULLSTON L	1984		India
(iii)	5 TEST			
6	FULLSTON L	1984–85		England
	VERCO P	1984–85		England

Captains

NAME	TESTS [AS CAPTAIN]	WON	LOST	DRAWN
PEDEN M	6	1	3	2
DIVE M	7	3	1	3
PAISLEY U	4	1	0	3
PICTON M	4	0	0	4
ALLITT M	3	0	1	2
KNEE M	1	0	1	0

BLUNSDEN W	1	0	0	1
GORDON A	5	0	0	5
JENNINGS M	1	1	0	0
TREDREA S	4	1	0	3
KENNARE J	4	0	0	4
THOMPSON R	4	2	1	1
LARSEN L	9	4	0	5
	53	13	7	33

Most Appearances in Tests

NAME	APPEARANCES
MATTHEWS C	18
THOMPSON R	16
LARSEN L	14
VERCO P	13
FULLSTON L	12
KENNARE J	12
PAISLEY U	12
ALLITT M	11
WILSON Betty	11
WILSON D	11
REELER L	10
TREDREA S	10

ONE DAY INTERNATIONAL MATCHES

Averages — All One Day Matches

VS	PLAYED	WON	LOST	TIED
England	18*	11	5	1
India	9*	8	0	
NZ	25*	18	6	
International XI	4*	3	0	
Ireland	5	5	0	
Neth	2	2	0	
Young England	1	1	0	
Jamaica	1	1	0	
Trinidad-Tobago	1	1	0	
Total	66	50	11	1

* 1 game abandoned — rain

Batting

Record team totals

	HIGHEST			LOWEST LOSING	
Overall:	1–284 vs Neth	1988	60 overs	9–119 vs England	1976
vs England:	7–253	1985	60 overs	9–199	1976
vs NZ:	7–214	1985	60 overs	155	1985
vs India:	6–227	1982	55 overs		
vs Ireland:	3–208	1987	55 overs		
vs Neth:	1–284	1988	60 overs		

Records team totals against

	HIGHEST			LOWEST LOSING		
Overall:	3-279 England	1973	60 overs	29 The Neth	1988	
England:	3-279	1973	60 overs	8-84	1988	60 overs
NZ:	9-207 (losing)	1986	60 overs	58	1985	
India:	6-219 (losing)	1984	50 overs	74	1982	
Ireland:	103	1987		77	1987	
Neth:	85	1988		29	1988	

Most Runs

	RUNS	AVER	INNS
Reeler L	1034	57.4	23
Emerson D	820	41.0	21
Kennare J	789	43.8	19
Annetts D	711	37.4	26
Haggett B	556	32.7	20
Tredrea S	528	27.8	22
Buckstein R	511	42.6	14

Best Average

	AVER	RUNS
Dawson P	91.0	182
Potter J	83.5	167
Reeler L	57.4	1034
Kennare J	43.8	789
Buckstein R	42.6	511
Emerson D	41.0	820
Annetts D	37.4	711

Highest scores against each country

England	Kennare J	122	1985
India	Kennare J	98	1982
Ireland	Buckstein R	90	1987
Neth	Reeler L	143*	1988
New Zealand	Reeler L	108*	1988

Centuries

Reeler L	143*	vs Neth	1988
Kennare J	122	vs England	1985
Reeler L	108*	vs NZ	1988
Hill L	106	vs England	1976
Buckstein R	105*	vs Neth	1988
Kennare J	100*	vs England	1985
Buckstein R	100	vs Neth	1988

NAME	I	NO	HS	AGG	100	50	AVER
Albon L	4	1	17	28	—	—	9.3
Annetts D	26	7	75	711	—	6	37.4
Blunsden W	2	1	10	17	—	—	17.0
Bray E	5	0	40	89	—	—	17.8
Broadbent J	4	1	18	32	—	—	10.7
Brown K	17	4	38	199	—	—	15.3
Buckstein R	14	2	105*	511	2	1	42.6
Calver B	1	1	17*	17	—	—	—
Clark B	3	0	53	111	—	1	37.0
Cook L	1	0	0	0	—	—	0
Cornish M (nee Lutschini)	11	5	55*	147	—	1	24.5
Davis J	1	0	10	10	—	—	10.0
Dawson P (nee Kelly)	4	2	77*	182	—	2	91.0
Emerson D (nee Alderman)	21	1	84	820	—	8	41.0
Esmond J	1	1	2*	2	—	—	—
Farrell V	2	0	17	28	—	—	14.0
Fellows A	3	1	35*	48	—	—	24.0
Fullston L	19	11	27	134	—	—	16.8
Gordon A	3	1	50*	65	—	1	32.5
Goss Z	17	3	96*	348	—	2	24.9
Griffiths S	7	1	32	92	—	—	15.3
Haggett B	20	3	80	556	—	4	32.7
Hall G	2	0	0	0	—	—	0
Heywood S	11	1	76	243	—	2	24.3
Hill L	6	0	106	143	1	—	23.8
Hill S (nee Fitzsimmons)	12	3	76	184	—	1	20.4
Hills W	4	0	64	93	—	1	23.3
Hunter L	2	0	8	9	—	—	4.5
Jacobs J	13	2	43	225	—	—	20.5
Jennings M	9	2	57*	221	—	1	31.6
Juhasz T	2	0	21	24	—	—	12.0
Kendall R	3	1	40	71	—	—	35.5
Kennare J	19	1	122	789	2	3	43.8
Knee M	5	2	30*	86	—	—	28.7
Larsen L	21	6	54*	320	—	1	21.3
Leonard F	1	0	2	2	—	—	2.0
Macpherson T	1	0	14	14	—	—	14.0
Martin Denise (later Plain)	7	3	5*	17	—	—	4.3
Matthews C (nee White)	12	2	22	104	—	—	10.4
May P	2	0	3	4	—	—	2.0
McCauley A	1	0	7	7	—	—	7.0
Moffat S	6	3	7*	13	—	—	4.3
Mortimer K	1	1	4*	4	—	—	—
Napier W	2	0	9	11	—	—	5.5
Owens J	0						
Papworth M	3	0	19	39	—	—	13.0
Piltz W	2	0	0	0	—	—	0
Potter J	5	3	57	167	—	2	83.5

Price K	11	2	16	39	—	—	4.3
Rae D	4	0	10	16	—	—	4.0
Raymont K	1	0	2	2	—	—	2.0
Read K	18	2	56	336	—	1	21.0
Reeler L	23	5	143*	1034	2	8	57.4
Robinson J later Stockton	2	0	4	7	—	—	3.5
Russell T	1	0	0	0	—	—	0
Saunders K	7	3	15*	31	—	—	7.8
Smith C	1	0	9	9	—	—	9.0
Thompson R	13	5	50*	207	—	1	25.9
Tredrea J later Roberts	5	1	37*	66	—	—	16.5
Tredrea S	22	3	69	528	—	4	27.8
Verco P (nee Cook)	17	2	52	300	—	2	20.0
White C	2	1	16*	24	—	—	24.0
Wilson Bev	5	0	50	130	—	1	26.0
Wilson D	7	5	29*	35	—	—	17.5

Record Partnerships

1	220	Buckstein R / Reeler L	vs Neth	1988
2	176	Emerson D / Kennare J	vs England	1985
3	115*	Reeler L / Annetts D	vs England	1988
4	105	Read K / Hill S	vs NZ	1982
5	112	Annetts D / Larsen L	vs NZ	1990
6	100	Tredrea S / Goss Z	vs England	1988
7	65	Thompson R / Cornish M	vs NZ	1982
8	64	Thompson R / Fullston L	vs International XI	1982
9	37	Matthews C / Broadbent J	vs NZ	1990
10	34	Cornish M / Blundsen W	vs England	1976

Bowling

	OVERS	MDNS	WKTS	RUNS	BEST	5I	R/W	R/O	B/W
Blunsden W	37.2	4	1	129	1–7		129.0	3.46	224
Broadbent J	40	7	5	101	3–17		20.2	2.53	48
Brown K	295	90	40	608	4–4		15.2	2.06	44
Callaghan L	10	3	1	13	1–13		13.0	1.30	60
Calver B	10.3	1	0	40			—	3.81	—
Cook L	10	0	0	35			—	3.50	—
Cornish M (nee Lutschini)	145.2	42	16	273	3–22		17.1	1.88	55
Farrell V	4	0	0	16			—	4.00	—

Fullston L	394.2	80	73	971	5–27	2	13.3	2.46	32
Gordon A	50.4	12	7	149	3–25		21.3	2.94	43
Goss Z	244.1	62	29	593	3–30		20.4	2.43	51
Griffiths S	85.2	23	11	187	3–17		17.0	2.19	46
Haggett B	38	4	3	101	1–13		33.7	2.66	76
Hall G	6	0	0	26			—	4.33	—
Hill L	39.3	9	5	84	4–11		16.8	2.13	47
Hill S (nee Fitzsimmons)	57	11	9	109	3–16		12.1	1.91	38
Hunter L	51	29	5	49	2–7		9.8	0.96	61
Jacobs J	15	1	3	70	2–35		23.3	4.67	30
Kendall R	4	1	0	16			—	4.00	—
Knee M	47	12	9	130	4–26		14.4	2.77	31
Larsen L	218.4	44	18	501	3–19		27.8	2.29	73
Leonard F	8	1	0	22			—	2.75	—
Macpherson T	42.1	14	9	99	5–14	1	11.0	2.35	28
Martin Denise (later Plain)	181	65	27	376	3–8		13.9	2.08	40
May P	23	2	2	67	1–24		33.5	2.91	69
McCauley A	7	0	0	24			—	3.43	—
Moffat S	126	31	8	305	3–19		38.1	2.42	95
Mortimer K	3	0	0	18			—	6.00	—
Owens J	26.2	5	7	62	5–29	1	8.9	2.35	23
Piltz W	30	3	0	102			—	3.40	—
Price K	150.3	35	21	397	3–12		18.9	2.64	43
Saunders K	86	22	9	196	2–17		21.8	2.28	57
Thompson R	178	73	24	448	3–16		18.7	2.52	45
Tredrea S	280	88	32	521	4–25		16.3	1.86	53
Verco P (nee Cook)	136.1	29	9	329	3–9		36.6	2.42	91
White C	53	12	2	104			52.0	1.96	159
Wilson D	109.2	17	7	291	2–24		41.6	2.66	94

Most wickets

	WKTS	AVER
Fullston L	73	13.3
Brown K	40	15.2
Tredrea S	32	16.3
Goss Z	29	20.4
Martin D	27	13.9
Thompson R	24	18.7
Price K	21	18.9

Best Average

	AVER	WKTS
Fullston L	13.3	73
Martin D	13.9	27
Brown K	15.2	40
Tredrea S	16.3	32
Cornish M	17.1	16
Thompson R	18.7	24
Price K	18.9	21

Best performance against each country

England	Fullston L	4/12	1987
India	Cook P	3/9	1978
Ireland	Owens J	5/29	1987
Neth	Fullston L	5/28	1988
NZ	Fullston L	5/27	1982

Best performances

Macpherson T	5/14	vs Young England	1973
Fullston L	5/27	vs NZ	1982
Fullston L	5/28	vs Neth	1988
Owens J	5/29	vs Ireland	1987
Brown K	4/4	vs Neth	1988
Hill L	4/11	vs Jamaica	1973
Fullston L	4/12	vs England	1987
Fullston L	4/21	vs Ireland	1988
Brown K	4/24	vs Ireland	1987
Tredrea S	4/25	vs England	1978
Knee M	4/26	vs Trinidad/Tobago	1973
Fullston L	4/38	vs International XI	1982

Series—by series including captaincy

SERIES	CAPTAIN	GAMES	WON	LOST	TIED	ABANDONED
World Cup 1973	Knee M	6	4	1	0	1
vs England 1976	Gordon A	3	1	2	0	0
World Cup 1978	Jennings M	3	3	0	0	0
World Cup 1982	Tredrea S	13	12	0	1	0
India 1984	Kennare J	4	4	0	0	0
England 1985	Thompson R	3	3	0	0	0
NZ 1985	Emerson D	3	2	1	0	0
NZ 1986	Larsen L	3	1	1	0	1
NZ 1987	Larsen L	3	1	2	0	0
Ireland 1987	Larsen L	3	3	0	0	0
England 1987	Larsen L	3	1	1	0	1
NZ 1988	Larsen L	3	3	0	0	0
World Cup 1988	Larsen L	9	8	1	0	0
NZ 1990	Larsen L	3	2	1	0	0
NZ 1991	Larsen L	2	1	1	0	0
	Brown K	1	1	0	0	0
India 1991	Larsen L	1	0	0	0	1
Total		66	50	11	1	4

WORLD CUP RECORDS

VS	PLAYED	WON	LOST	TIED
England	9	6	2	1
NZ	7	7	0	0
India	4	4	0	0
International XI	4*	3	0	0

Jamaica	1	1	0	0
Trinidad-Tobago	1	1	0	0
Young England	1	1	0	0
Ireland	2	2	0	0
Neth	2	2	0	0
Total	31*	27	2	1

* 1 game abandoned — rain

Batting

Record team totals

VS	HIGHEST			LOWEST LOSING	
Overall	1-284 vs Neth	1988	60 overs	152 vs England	1988
England	210	1988		152	1988
NZ	3-211	1988	60 overs		
India	6-227	1982	55 overs		
Ireland	0-89	1988	21.4 ovs		
Neth	1-284	1988	60 overs		

Records team totals against

VS	HIGHEST			LOWEST LOSING	
Overall	3-279 England	1973	60 overs	29 Neth	1988
England	3-279	1973	60 overs	8-84	1988 60 overs
NZ	6-136	1988	60 overs	101	1982
India	7-154	1982	60 overs	74	1982
Ireland	88	1988		8-78	1988 60 overs
Neth	85	1988		29	1988

Most runs

	RUNS	AVER	INN
Tredrea S	460	27.1	19
Reeler L	448	149.3	8
Kennare J	351	39.0	19
Buckstein R	289	57.8	7
Alderman D	281	25.5	11
Read K	221	24.5	10
Verco P	217	19.7	12

Best Average

	AVER	RUNS
Reeler L	149.3	448
Potter J	83.5	167
Buckstein R	57.8	289
Annetts D	47.1	191
Jennings M	42.3	169
Kennare J	39.0	351
Tredrea S	27.1	460

Highest scores against each country

England	Tredrea S	69	1988
India	Kennare J	98	1982
Ireland	Reeler L	63*	1988
Neth	Reeler L	143*	1988
NZ	Reeler L	108*	1988

Centuries

Reeler L	143*	vs Neth	1988
Reeler L	108*	vs NZ	1988
Buckstein R	105*	vs Neth	1988
Buckstein R	100	vs Neth	1988

Record partnerships

1	220	Reeler L / Buckstein R	vs Neth	1988
2	167	Alderman D / Kennare J	vs India	1982
3	115*	Reeler L / Annetts D	vs England	1988
4	105	Read K / Hill S	vs NZ	1982
5	79	Tredrea S / Jacobs J	vs England	1982
6	100	Tredrea S / Goss Z	vs England	1988
7	65	Thompson R / Cornish M	vs NZ	1982
8	64	Thompson R / Fullston L	vs International XI	1982
9	17	Thompson R / Fullston L	vs England	1982
10	10	Blunsden W / May P	vs England	1973

Bowling

Most wickets

	WKTS	AVER
Fullston L	39	11.9
Tredrea S	32	14.9
Thompson R	23	17.1
Cornish M	15	15.8
Martin D	14	12.9
Brown K	12	10.8

Best average

	AVER	WKTS
Brown K	10.8	12
Fullston L	11.9	39
Martin D	12.9	14
Tredrea S	14.9	32
Cornish M	15.8	15
Thompson R	17.1	23

Best performance against each country

England	Tredrea S	4/25	1978
India	Cook P	3/9	1978
Ireland	Fullston L	4/21	1988
Neth	Fullston L	5/28	1988
NZ	Fullston L	5/27	1982

AUSTRALIAN NATIONAL CHAMPIONSHIPS

Winners

Year	Winner	Year	Winner	Year	Winner
1931	NSW	1956	Vic	1974	Vic
1932	NSW	1957	Vic	1975	NSW
1933	NSW	1958	Vic	1976	Vic
1934	Vic	1959	NSW	1977	Vic
1935	Vic	1960	Vic	1978	Vic
1936	Vic	1961	NSW	1979	Vic
1937	NSW	1962	Vic	1980	SA
1938	Vic	1963	Vic	1981	Vic
1939	Vic	1964	Vic	1982	Vic
1947	Vic	1965	Vic	1983	Vic
1948	Vic	1966	Vic	1984	NSW
1949	Vic	1967	Vic	1985	not held
1950	Vic	1968	Vic	1986	Vic
1951	NSW	1969	Vic	1987	WA
1952	SA	1970	Vic	1988	Vic
1953	Vic	1971	Vic	1989	Not held
1954	Vic	1972	Not held	1990	NSW
1955	Vic	1973	Vic	1991	Vic

Notes

Chapter One

1 *Sydney Mail* of 10 September 1887 reported a game between (a male) Sirocco club and Camperdown. Quite possibly the women's club had emerged out of and was supported by this club.
2 J H Heaton, *The Bedside Book of Colonial Doings*, Angus & Robertson, Sydney, 1984, p. 57. The book was first published in 1879 under the title *Australian Dictionary of Dates and Men of the Time*.
3 Unsourced newspaper clipping, possibly Sydney *Sun*, 13 December 1934.
4 Ibid.
5 This information has been provided by Lawrence Deane, a relation of Rosalie Deane.
6 *Town and Country Journal* 7 February and 7 March 1891.
7 Unsourced clipping, 13 December 1934.
8 Richard Holt, *Sport and the British: A Modern History*, Clarendon Press, Oxford, 1989, p. 8.
9 Kathleen E McCrone, *Playing the Game: Sport and the Physical Emancipation of English Women 1870-1914*, Uni. of Kentucky Press, 1988.
10 Rachael Heyhoe Flint and Netta Rheinberg, *Fair Play: The Story of Women's Cricket,* Angus & Robertson, London, 1976, p. 16.
11 Dennis Brailsford, *Sport and Society: Elizabeth to Anne*, Routledge & Kegan Paul, London, 1969, p. 240.
12 J B Buckley, *Fresh Light on 18th Century Cricket*, Cotterell & Co., Birmingham, 1935, p. 18.
13 Sonja Lilienthal, 'Tea, Talk and Tennis: An Early History of Women's Sport at the University of Sydney 1882-1918', B Educ. Hons thesis, University of Sydney p. 17.
14 John Lowerson, in Tony Mason (ed.), *Sport in Britain: A Social History*, Cambridge UP, 1989, p. 204.
15 Holt, *Sport and the British*, pp. 89–90.
16 J S Bratton, *The Impact of Victorian Children's Fiction*, Croom Helm, London, 1981.
17 Flint and Rheinberg, *Fair Play*, p. 21.
18 Bill Frindall, *Guinness Cricket Facts & Feats*, Guild Publishing, London, 1987, p. 192. Flint and Rheinberg refer to another version of a woman (Mrs Lambert) who was instrumental in the introduction of the round arm technique. It is difficult to establish in any final sense the importance of either woman in the introduction of the round-arm technique, but there seems little doubt that some women were keen to play cricket in the early 19th century and achieved a good standard in bowling.
19 J Ford, *Cricket: A Social History*, David and Charles, Newton Abbot, 1972, p. 156.
20 Eric Midwinter, *W.G. Grace: His Life and Times*, George Allen & Unwin, London, 1981, p. 9.
21 Flint and Rheinberg, *Fair Play*, p. 23.
22 Flint and Rheinberg, *Fair Play*, pp 22–23.
23 Jas Scott, *Early Cricket in Sydney 1803 to 1856*, edited by Richard Cashman and Stephen Gibbs, NSWCA, Sydney, 1991, p. 19.
24 Jas Scott, *Early Cricket*, p. 18.
25 Ray Madden, ' "How Delightful is the Sensation": Women and Cycling in the 1890s', BA Hons thesis, University of NSW, 1983.
26 The match, according to Agnes E McDonnell and Mabel E Ruddell, 'Cricket: Then and Now' (MCC Library), was played to celebrate the battle of Waterloo. However, it must have been a minor match as it was not mentioned in Jas Scott, *Early Cricket in Sydney 1803 to 1856*.
27 Betty Butcher, *Sport of Grace: Womens Cricket in Victoria: The Beginning*, Sports Federation of Victoria, Melbourne, 1984, pp. 4–5.
28 McDonnell and Ruddell, 'Women's Cricket', p. 5.
29 Frindall, *Cricket Facts & Feats*, p. 198.
30 Ray Crawford, 'Sport for Young Ladies', *Sporting Traditions*, vol. 1, no. 1, p. 67.
31 See Chapter 2.
32 Sr M O'Donoghue, *Beyond our Dreams*, Jacaranda Press, Brisbane, 1961, p. 45 quoted in Pauline Harvey Short, 'Married Vs Maiden': The Development of Australian Women's Cricket from 1874 to 1934, unpublished essay, MCC Library.

Chapter Two

1. Sonja Lilienthal, 'Tea, Talk and Tennis', pp. 42, 45.
2. Veronica Raszeja Wood, 'A Decent and Proper Exertion: The Rise of Women's Competitive Swimming in Sydney to 1912', BA Hons thesis, University of NSW, 1990, p. 28.
3. Quoted in Lilienthal, 'Tea, Talk and Tennis', p. 19.
4. Wood, 'A Decent and Proper Exertion', p. 98.
5. Wood, 'A Decent and Proper Exertion', p. 29.
6. Butcher, *Sport of Grace*, p. 18.
7. He became President of the North Melbourne Club in 1911 and was Secretary of the VCA in the 1930s.
8. Agnes McDonnell reported that her club, Coldstream, played mid-week games regularly.
9. Quoted in Butcher, *Sport of Grace*, p. 17.
10. Lilienthal notes (p. 37) that women at the University of Melbourne were 'practising tennis every afternoon' by 1887.
11. Lilienthal, 'Tea, Talk and Tennis', p. 22.
12. McDonnell and Ruddell, 'Women's Cricket', ch. 2.
13. The Patrons included W A Watt, a future state premier; H Byron Moore, one-time Victorian Racing Club Secretary; T W Sherrin, sporting goods manufacturer; W C Spowers, proprietor of the *Argus*; and Rev. (later Canon) E S Hughes.
14. Long essay, MCC Library p. 5.
15. *Sydney Mail*, 16 March 1910.
16. *Town & Country Journal*, 28 February 1906.
17. *Town & Country Journal*, 14 November 1906.
18. Clare Papasergio and Janice Moy, *The History of Women's Cricket in Western Australia 1930-1980*, 1981.
19. McDonnell and Ruddell, 'Women's Cricket', ch. 4.
20. *Sydney Mail*, 28 March 1906.
21. *Sydney Mail*, 6 April 1910.
22. The side for the first match was: Agnes Paternoster (c), May McDonnell, Maisie Cavanough, Louie Bone, Flo Spinks, Leon Goodwin, May Fielden, Bub Stewart, Tess Youlden, E Seekamp, Freda Burmister, Ethel Kemp, Lizzie Stewart. The side for the second game was: Rita Sawyer, Effie Girwood, E Bailey, Ruby Symonds, Nellie Percival, Edith Cox, Clarrie Goodwin, Vera Rattigan, Agnes Macintyre, Olive Curtis, May Fielden, Beattie Bone.
23. McDonnell and Ruddell, 'Women's Cricket', ch. 7.
24. McDonnell and Ruddell, 'Women's Cricket', ch. 2.
25. It has been argued (Long Essay p. 10) that the peaks and troughs in women's cricket coincided with upturns and recessions in the economy. It has been suggested that in harsh times individuals 'seek simple and relatively inexpensive pursuits such as sport'. It is certainly true that the AWCC was established and the first international tour was organised during the Great Depression and that from 1930 there was considerable growth in clubs and competitions. However, this explanation seems to underplay the growth in women's cricket organisations in the late 1920s which created the platform for the AWCC.
26. Unsourced newspaper clipping from Christine Garwood.
27. *Australian Women's Cricket*, vol. 1, no. 1, March 1938.
28. The officers at the time of the inaugural meeting of the AWCC were: Miss M Mills (Chair), M Peden (Secretary), Miss E Pritchard (Treasurer). Interview with Margaret Peden, 1980 (tape with Ann Mitchell).
29. Butcher, *Sport of Grace*, p. 29.

Chapter Three

1. Ray Madden, 'Women and Cycling', pp. 87-88.
2. Helen King, 'The Sexual Politics of Sport: An Australian Perspective', in R Cashman and M. McKernan (eds), *Sport in History: The Making of Modern Sporting History*, UQP, St Lucia, 1979, p. 74.
3. Madden, 'Women and Cycling', p. 86.
4. David Frith, *Pageant of Cricket*, Macmillan, Melbourne, 1987, p. 35.
5. Flint and Rheinberg, *Fair Play*, pp. 19-20.
6. Butcher, *Sport of Grace*, p. 4.
7. *Sydney Mail*, 13 March 1886.
8. 'Cricket Chatter', *Australasian*, 13 March 1886.
9. Agnes McDonnell scrapbook quoted in Long Essay, p. 8.
10. Flint and Rheinberg, *Fair Play*, p 86.
11. McDonnell and Ruddell, 'Women's Cricket', ch. 3.
12. Flint and Rheinberg, *Fair Play*, p. 87.
13. *Australian Women's Cricket*, vol. 1, no. 1 (March 1938).
14. Flint and Rheinberg, *Fair Play*, p. 88.
15. Flint and Rheinberg, *Fair Play*, p. 88.
16. Communication from Betty Butcher, 12 March 1991.

Chapter Four

1 Interview of Peggy Antonio and Nell McLarty by Mary-Lou Johnston and Marion Stell, 1 July 1990, tapes held at the National Museum of Australia.
2 Papasergio and Moy, *Women's Cricket in Western Australia*, p. 3.
3 Antonio and McLarty interview, 1990.
4 Max Howell, Reet Howell and David Brown, *The Sporting Image: A Pictorial History of Queenslanders at Play*, UQP, St Lucia, 1989.
5 Howell et al, *The Sporting Image*, p. 46.
6 Papasergio and Moy, *Women's Cricket in Western Australia*, pp. 12–17.
7 Papasergio and Moy, *Women's Cricket in Western Australia*, p. 17.
8 Papasergio and Moy, *Women's Cricket in Western Australia*, p. 3.
9 The basic wage for a female in 1934 was £1 17s per week.
10 N Rheinberg, *Barclay's World of Cricket*, Willow Books, London, 1986, p. 612.
11 *Women's Weekly*, 1 December 1934.
12 *Women's Weekly*, 8 December 1934.
13 *Referee* of 20 December 1934 reported an attendance of 8 617 and a gate of £346 8s for the two days.
14 *Sydney Morning Herald*, 17 December 1934.
15 Marjorie Pollard, *A Diary of the Matches Played by the Australian Women's Cricket Team in England, 1937*, p. 4.
16 10, 700 (4 days), 11, 000 (3 days), 11, 053 (4 days).
17 Phyllis McCorquodale. 'The Lure of the Dance', BA Hons thesis, University of NSW, 1984.
18 Quotation from 'Fair Play', a film produced in 1988.
19 *Referee*, 22 November 1934.
20 Pollard, *A Diary*, p. 18.
21 Pollard, *A Diary*, p. 40.
22 Flint and Rheinberg, *Fair Play*, p. 96.

Chapter Five

1 Sydney *Sun*, 2 April 1946.
2 There were some exceptions to this rule. Women who had represented Australia were granted membership in their own right prior to 1978.
3 Unsourced magazine article, Ann Mitchell scrapbooks.
4 Sylvia Faram, then a student at Abbotsleigh, recalled that American sailors introduced the game at her school.
5 Unsourced newspaper clipping, Dawn Rae scrapbooks.
6 Papasergio and Moy, *Women's Cricket in Western Australia*, p. 11
7 Leonie M Randall, 'A Fair Go? Women and Sport in South Australia 1945–1965', BA Hons thesis, Flinders University, 1986, p. 18.
8 Unsourced newspaper article by Phillip Christensen, Ann Mitchell scrapbooks.
9 Unsourced clipping, Ann Mitchell scrapbooks.
10 See Chapter Four.
11 The award (weekly) wage in 1959 for women was £10 1s.
12 Randall, 'A Fair Go?', p. 18.
13 Ibid, pp. 40–1, 43.
14 Papasergio and Moy, *Women's Cricket in Western Australia*, p. 6.
15 Flint and Rheinberg, *Fair Play*, p. 59.
16 Unsourced newspaper clipping, Ann Mitchell scrapbooks.
17 Joan L Hawes, *Women's Test Cricket: The Golden Triangle 1934–84*, Book Guild, Lewes, 1987, p. 176.

Chapter Six

1 Anne Summers, *Damned Whores and God's Police*, ch. on 'The Sporting Life', Pelican, 1975.
2 Lois Bryson, 'Sport and the Oppression of Women', *Australian and New Zealand Journal of Sociology*, vol. 19, no. 3, pp. 413–20.
3 Donna Edman, 'The Commercialisation of Women's Sport: Netball as a Case Study', B Soc Sc thesis, University of NSW, 1986, p. 62.
4 The All Australian Women's Basketball Association changed its name to 'netball' in 1970 when it became the All Australian Netball Association.
5 Leonie Randall, 'A Fair Go?', p. 1.
6 The number of registered players in each sport was listed in the Australian Sports Directory, published by the Australian Sports Commission. The leading five sports in 1990 were: tennis, 560 000; cricket 550 000 male and 8 992 female; Australian football 474 990; soccer 360 156 male and 21 000 female; netball 359 351.
7 Edman, 'The Commercialisation of Women's Sport', p. 75.
8 She was married in 1971 and then referred to herself as Rachael Heyhoe Flint.

9 The basic wage for women (weekly) in 1971 was $39.10. £600 (sterling) was roughly equivalent to $A1 200.
10 V Jenkins, unsourced newspaper clipping, Ann Mitchell scrapbooks.
11 With a 'no decision' result against International XI Australia finished five rounds with 17 points as against England's 16. Had Australia won its second last match it would have entered the final match with 20 points.
12 Unsourced newspaper clipping, Ann Mitchell scrapbooks.
13 Flint and Rheinberg, *Fair Play*, p. 170.
14 Unsourced newspaper clipping of 16 February 1975, Ann Mitchell scrapbooks.
15 Jim McAuley, Unsourced newspaper clipping, 16 February 1975, Ann Mitchell scapbooks.
16 Unsourced newspaper clipping, Ann Mitchell scrapbooks.
17 *Wisden* 1977, p. 990.
18 The other two matches were at Canterbury and Trent Bridge.
19 *Sun-Herald*, 26 September 1976.

Chapter Seven

1 Elizabeth Coles, 'Sport in Schools: The Participation of Girls', Social Development Unit, Ministry of Education (NSW), 1980, p. 42.
2 *Sydney Morning Herald*, 31 January 1991.
3 Australian Government Printing Service, Canberra, 1985.
4 The staff of WSU in 1988 consisted of: Robbie Swan, Media Consultant; Ray Sneddon, Marketing Consultant; Donna Edman, Secretary; Helen Oldenhove, Program Consultant.
5 *Sydney Morning Herald*, 10 July 1987.
6 The award wage (weekly) for women in 1985 was $215.50.
7 *Cricketer*, March 1984.
8 In Kanga Couples eight to twelve children are divided into pairs who take turns to bat and bowl; In Kanga Co-op there are two teams of six to eight players on each side; in Kanga Cricket there are two sides of eight to twelve players.
9 *Cricketer*, October 1984.
10 *Cricketer*, February 1987.
11 Although this figure was listed in the *Australian Sports Directory* of 1991, it appeared that some of the initial enthusiasm for this game was waning. Some centres were closing down.
12 Many other state teams, such as Victoria, had taken on a state coach by this time.
13 *Cricketer*, February 1986.
14 *Women, Sport and the Media*, AGPS, Canberra, 1985, p. 97.
15 *Cricketer*, February 1987.
16 *Between Overs*, 1986.
17 *Cricketer*, October 1986.
18 *Between Overs*, November 1990, reported a 10 per cent increase from the support of the previous year to cover such costs.
19 *Cricketer*, October 1985 and April 1986.

Chapter Eight

1 *Panorama*, 1991, p. 40.
2 Sandy Gordon, 'The Drop-Out Phenomenon in Organised Sport', Department of Sport and Recreation (WA), 1989.
3 Helen King, 'The Sexual Politics of Sport', p. 68.
4 The only restriction was that viewers watched only the final session of play when a Test was played in their own city.
5 'Couchman over Australia', ABC Television Program, 'Women and Sport', March 1991.

Chapter Nine

1 These are mixed sports in which the proportions of men and women are not specified. While the majority of participants would have been male, there was certainly some female participation.
2 *Sydney Morning Herald*, 6 January 1991.
3 Kersi Meher-Homji, *Between Overs*, vol. 14, March 1991, p. 5.
4 Ken Dyer, *Girls' Physical Education and Self-esteem: A Review of Research, Resources and Strategies*, Commonwealth Schools Commission, Canberra, 1986.
5 He was Executive Officer for the NSWPSAAA in 1991.
6 *Sydney Morning Herald*, 31 January 1991.
7 AWCC, *Annual Report 1990*, Appendix 3.
8 Gary Bromley, Anita Judd and Rodger Warren.
9 The Australian totals were: 4/301 decl. and 6-111 decl.; 3-237 decl. and 0-67; 3-307 decl. and 1-53.
10 The term was so widely accepted that the magazine started in the 1930s was known as *Australian Women's Cricket*.

Select Bibliography of Woman and Sport in Australia

General works on women's sport:
Australian Sports Commission and the Office of the Status of Women. *Women, Sport and the Media*, AGPS, Canberra, 1985.
Bryson, Lois 'Sport and the Oppression of Women', *Australian and New Zealand Journal of Sociology*, vol. 19, no. 2, March 1982, pp. 413-20.
——, 'Why Women are always Offside', *Australian Society*, vol. 4, no. 6, June 1985, pp. 33-34.
Coles, E *Sport in Schools: The Participation of Girls, a Discussion Paper*, Social Development Unit, Ministry of Education (NSW), 1979.
Crawford, Ray 'Sport for Young Ladies: The Victorian Independent Schools 1875-1925', *Sporting Traditions*, vol. 1, no. 1, pp. 61-82.
Dyer, Ken *Challenging the Men: The Social Biology of Female Sporting Achievement*, University of Queensland Press, St Lucia, 1982.
Encel, S, N MacKenzie, and M Tebbutt, *Women and Society: An Australian Study*, Melbourne, 1974.
Fitzpatrick, Jim 'Australian "Cylistes" in the Victorian Era', *Hemisphere*, vol. 24, Jan/Feb. 1980, pp. 12-17.
Hodges, Lena *N.S.W. Women's Hockey 1908-1983*, NSWWHA, Sydney, 1984.
Howard, Ann *Women in Australia*, Sydney, 1984.
Howell, Max, Reet Howell and David Brown, *The Sporting Image: A Pictorial History of Queenslanders at Play*, University of Queensland Press, St Lucia, 1989.
Howell, Reet and Max *Aussie Gold: The Story of Australia at the Olympics*, Brooks Waterloo, Brisbane, 1988.
King, Helen 'The Sexual Politics of Sport: An Australian Perspective', in R Cashman and M McKernan, *Sport in History: The Making of Sporting Traditions*, University of Queensland Press, St Lucia, 1979, pp. 68-85.
McCrone, K E *Playing the Game: Sport and the Physical Emanicipation of English Women, 1870-1914*, University Press of Kentucky, 1988.
Mangan, J A and R J Park (eds), From *'Fair Sex' to Feminism: Sport and the Socialisation of Women in the Industrial and Post-Industrial Eras*, Frank Cass, London, 1987.
Mitchell, Susan and Ken Dyer, *Winning Women: Challenging the Norms in Australian Sport*, Penguin, Ringwood, 1985.
Phillips, D 'Australian Women at the Olympics: Achievement and Alienation', Sporting Traditions, vol. 6, no. 2, May 1990.
Stoddart, Brian *Saturday Afternoon Fever: Sport in the Australia Culture*, Angus & Robertson, Sydney, 1986.

Theses
Edman, Donna 'The Commercialization of Women's Sport: Netball as a Case Study', B Soc Sc Hons, Uni of NSW, 1986.
Lilienthal, Sonja 'Tea, Talk and Tennis: An Early History of Women's Sport at the University of Sydney 1882-1918', B Educ. Honours thesis, University of Sydney, 1987.
Madden, Ray ' "How Delightful is the Sensation": Women and Cycling in the 1890s', BA Hons thesis, University of NSW, 1983.
Randall, Leonie 'A Fair Go? Women and Sport in South Australia 1945-1965', BA Hons thesis, Flinders University, 1986.
Wood, Veronica Raszeja 'A Decent and Proper Exertion: The Rise of Women's Competitive Swimming in Sydney to 1912', BA Hons thesis, University of NSW, 1990.

Women and cricket

Books
Butcher, Betty *Sport of Grace: Womens Cricket in Victoria: The Beginning*, Sports Federation of Victoria, Melbourne, 1984.
Flint, Rachael Heyhoe and Netta Rheinberg, *Fair Play: The Story of Women's Cricket*, Angus & Robertson, London, 1976.

Hawes, Joan *Women's Test Cricket: The Golden Triangle 1934-84*, Book Guild, Lewes, 1987.
Joy, Nancy *Maiden Over: A Short History of Women's Cricket and A Diary of the 1948-49 Test Tour to Australia*, Shorting Handbooks, London, 1950.
Papasergio, Clare and Janice Moy, *The History of Women's Cricket in Western Australia 1930-1980*, 1981.

Journals and reports
Australian Women's Cricket, 1938
AWCC, *Annual Reports*
Between Overs, 1984-

Unpublished
Boyle, Sallie-Ann Women's Cricket in Australia: a Resource Guide, RMIT, 1989 (MCC Library)
Author unknown, Long Essay (MCC Library)
Harvey-Short, Pauline 'Married Vs Maiden': The Development of Australian Women's Cricket from 1874 to 1934 (MCC Library).
King, Rosemary Frances, A Brief History of Anglo-Australian Women's Cricket (MCC Library).
McDonnell, Agnes E and Mabel Ruddell, Women's Cricket: Then and Now (MCC Library)
Webber, H The Beginning's of Ladies' Cricket (MCC Library).

Tour accounts and souvenirs
AWCC, *English Women Cricketers: 1958 Australian Tour.*
English Women's Cricket Tour of Australia 1968-69: Souvenir Test Match Program.
Pollard, Marjorie *A Diary of the Matches Played by the Australian Women's Cricket Team in England*, 1937.
WCA, *Report of the Australian Women's Cricket Tour in England*, 1951.

Archival material
Minutes of the VLCA
Minutes of the AWCC, Archives of the University of Melbourne

Scrapbooks
Vera Cutter
Mollie Dive
Molly Flaherty (Australian National Museum)
Ann Mitchell
Hazel Pritchard (in the possession of her son, Terry Scanlon)
Dawn Rae
Coralie Towers

Tape
Interview of Peggy Antonio and Nell McLarty, 1 July 1990, by Still and Co., National Museum of Australia.

Films and video
Australian Bicentennial Authority and Film Australia, 'Fair Play: The Golden Eras of Women's Test Cricket' (1988).
Marilyn Dooley, National Film and Sound Library, 'The Game is Up' (1991).

Index

Aberfeldie Park 161
Abbotsleigh 32, 37, 94, 117, 119, 166
Acacian Club 32
acceptance 9, 201, 206
Active 149, 176
Adelaide 47, 83, 85, 115, 121, 151, 162, 180, 211
Adelaide High School 118
Adelaide Oval 103, 105, 110, 157
Adelaide Teachers' College 118
administrators 115, 117–18, 170
affirmative action 196
Aggarwal, Sandhya 156
Ahmedabad 156
Albert Park 32, 71
Albion Park Race Course 23
All Hallows' School 23
Allansford 21
Allen, Monique 178
Allitt, Mary 121, 125
American Army 112
Amos, Elizabeth 122
Annandale Club 91
Anne, Princess 132
Annetts, Denise 117, 165, 166, 172, 192
Ansett, 150
Antonio, Peggy 71, 73, 91, 94–5, 97–8
ANZ Youth Sport Scholarship 169
Archdale, Betty 62, 85, 94, 101, 117, 157, 189
Armidale 145
Armitage, Helen 170
Ascham 37
Ascot Vale 32
Ashes, The 104, 108, 121, 125, 157–59, 162
athletics 10, 29, 175, 185
Atalanta Girls' Cricket Club 23
Auckland 183
Australian Bicentennial Authority 150, 171
Australian Broadcasting Commission 110, 161, 174, 177, 179, 195
Australian Broadcasting Commission Sports Award 176, 192
Australian Capital Territory 169, 170, 206–07, 209
Australian Capital Territory Schoolgirls' team 209
Australian Capital Territory Women's Cricket Association 170
Australian Cricket Board 150–52, 154, 194, 198–99, 210
Australian Cricket Club 16
Australian Dairy Corporation 154
Australian Government 154, 176, 180, 209

Australian Sports Commission 149, 150, 167, 170, 176, 178
Australian Sports Directory 183, 199
Australian Women's Cricket 71, 74, 83, 118
Australian Women's Cricket Council 32, 35, 44, 46–48, 50, 59, 62–63, 65, 66, 67, 71, 82–84, 95, 99, 110–11, 119, 137, 139, 143, 145, 150–51, 153–54, 162, 169, 170–71, 192, 199, 202, 206, 210
Austen, Jane 13
'Australia' 9, 20, 56
Avoca Fire Brigade 21

Bakewell, Enid 125, 132–34, 141, 146
Bakker, Peter 162
Bangalore 137
Barbados 134
Barker, Edna 117, 125
Barlow, Lurline 118
barracking 44, 72, 86, 119, 122
baseball 113, 199
basketball 46, 61, 71, 77, 128, 182, 184, 194, 195, 199, 211
Bassendean/Bayswater Club 114
Bathurst 22, 106
Belgrave 82
Bellambi 75
Benaud, Richie 111
Bendigo 18, 54, 159, 185
Betty Wilson Shield 123
Between Overs 150, 208
Black, Mrs 40
Blackham, Jack 10
Blackham, Miss 20
Black Rock, Ladies of 35
Black Rock Oval 73
Blackpool 97
bloomer costume 17, 52, 54
Blue Mountains 22
Bodyline series 45, 85, 94, 99
Boggabri 38
Bombay 156
Boomerang Club 32
booms, sporting 9, 43, 50, 99, 112, 147, 194, 201
Border, Allan 162, 179, 192
Boson, Mary 176
Bouel, Rose 83
bowls 29, 68, 199
boxing 13, 201
Bradman, Sir Donald 45, 99, 111
Brailsford, Dennis 11
Bratton, J S 13
Bray, Elaine 141

Brewer, Joyce 91
Brierley, Christine 202
Brigatti, Maureen 116
Brighton 72
Brighton Club 32, 40, 41, 84
Brisbane 47, 90, 120, 145
Brisbane Exhibition Ground 88
Brisbane Girls' Grammar School 23
British Broadcasting Corporation 105
British Ladies' Football Club 58
British sport 10–15
Brittin, Jan 157, 159
Broadbent, Jo 211
Brocklebank, L 50
Brown, David 77
Brown, Karen 165, 166, 173
Brunswick Club 73
Bryce, Quentin 179
Bryson, Lois 127
Buckstein, Ruth 99, 166, 171
Budget Company 150
Bundaberg Club 25
Burke, Nell 58
Burrell, Elizabeth Ann 11
butch image 66, 187–91
Butcher, Betty 32, 45, 65, 137
Butterfly Club 36

Calcutta 136
Camberwell Club 210
Cambridge Club 47, 76
Cameron, Jean 38
Campsie 134
Canberra 149, 169, 171, 176
Canberra Club 75
Canberra Schools Commission 148
Canty, Elaine 176
caps 54, 59, 62
Cardinals 80
Carey Grammar School 206
caricature 12, 31
Carlstein, Peter 162, 170
Casey, Ron 183, 185
Catholic Club 75–76
Catholic Sports Association (CGSSSA) 206
century, first Australian Test 103
Challis, Natalie 152
Channel 9 16, 195
chaperone 40
Chappell, Ian 145, 194
charity games 1, 2, 5, 25, 50, 73, 102
Cheerio Club 62, 95
Cheeseman, 'Curley' 34
Cheeseman, Jenny 178

242 INDEX

Chief Minister's Trophy 170
Christ, Joyce 119
Christie, Laura 58
Church of England Girls' Grammar School 35
Church of England Ladies' Cricket Association 34-35, 43
City Club 76
City Girls' Amateur Sports Association 71, 75
Claremont Club 38, 47, 76
Clarence River 82
Clarendon Club 71-2, 74, 99
Clark, Belinda 155, 211
Clark, Jackie 162
Clemes College 23
Clifton Hill 72
clubs 10, 14, 26, 32, 38, 72, 99
Clymer, Mrs 2, 41
coach, Australian 162
coaching camps 170
Coldstream Club 32, 37, 39
Cole, June 45, 84, 110
Coles Store 76
Colgate-Palmolive team 102
Collett, John 53
Collingham and Linton ground 163, 165
Collingwood Club 72, 73, 99, 113, 116, 122, 134
Combined Catholic Colleges 206
Combined High Schools 149, 205-06, 210
Commonwealth Bank 175
Commonwealth Games 183
Commonwealth Schools Commission 204
Compton, Denis 132
Coniston Club 75
Conlon, Eddie 73
Coolgardie 38
Cooroy Show Grounds 77
Cope, Harry 38
Cornish, Marie (nee Lutschini) 156
Corrimal Club 75
costume 15, 17, 19, 51-69, 77, 94, 125, 185
costume reform 52, 59
'Couchman over Australia' 177, 183
country cricket 77-82, 145, 161, 206
Country Week Carnival 82
Craddock, Myrtle 108
Crawley, Aidan 134
Cricket Academy (AIS) 151-52, 180
croquet 16, 29, 31, 51
Crow, Sue 207
crowds 2, 5, 7, 9, 11, 15, 19, 21, 38-39, 41, 70-2, 85, 87-8, 91, 95, 97-9, 103, 105, 109-11, 113, 117, 121-22, 132, 137, 140, 156, 159, 172, 194
Crowley, Senator Rosemary 196
Crowther, Jill 84
Croydon Club 36
Croydon Villa Club 78
culotte, 62, 64-5, 69, 189
Cutter, Vera (nee Rattigan) 45
cycling 17, 28-29, 51-52, 201
Cygnets 114

Dandenong 32
Dandenong High School 74
Darlison, Elizabeth 175
David Jones 73
Davidson, Alan 120
Davis, J C 93-94

Dawson, Trish 157
De la Hunty, Shirley 196
Deane, Elsie 73
Deane family 6
Deane, Rosalie 2, 3, 6, 7, 9
Debnam. Dot 71
decline in women's cricket 43, 109, 111-13, 121
Denholm, Lyn 125
Deniliquin 85, 117, 125
Department of Education (NSW) 202
Depression, Great 45, 63, 72, 91
Derby, Countess of 53
Derriman, Philip 175
Devonport 23, 39-40
Dickinson, Miss E 27
discrimination 149
Dive, Mollie 101, 103, 105, 108, 109, 110, 204
'dolly-bird' image 185-87
Donnan, Nellie (nee Gregory) 2, 35, 41, 46
Dorset, 3rd Earl of 11
Douglas, Lord A 13
Doull, Judi 135
Dow, Ruth 118, 120
drop out ratio 196, 204
Duggan, Mary 109, 119, 122
Dunedin 121
Dunlop Tyre 32
Durack, Fanny 28, 30, 52, 185
Durrant, Ruby 28, 40
Duvernet, Sgt 112
Dyer, Ken 204

East Melbourne Ground 20, 32, 42, 57
Edgbaston 122, 132, 140
Edney, June 158
Edulji, Diane 156
Edwards, Miss A 38
Elliott, Percy 80
Emerald 82
Emerson, Denise (nee Alderman) 157-61, 165
Emo Club 32, 39
Emu Plains 38
England 6-7, 9-10, 20, 28, 46, 49-50, 55-56, 62-63, 66, 76, 89, 130-32, 134-35, 137, 140-41, 143, 145, 147, 155, 157-66, 170-71, 195
equal opportunity 179
Equal Opportunities Commission 139, 152, 196
'Equity in Sport' 149, 185
Errington, Graeme 206
Essendon Club 32, 45
Eumavella Club 39
Eva, Helen 176
Evans, Godfrey 132
Evans, Louise 176

factory teams 45, 73
'Fair Play' 150
Faram, Sylvia 45, 65, 117, 119
Feige, H L 46, 48, 62
Fellows, Annette 157
femininity, notions of 12, 29-30, 52, 59, 62, 185, 189
feminist 37, 127, 128, 148, 180
Fernlea Club 1, 2, 3, 5, 14, 18, 20, 54, 75
Fielden, May 41
Film Australia 150

'Fit for Play' 149
Fitzsimons, Peter 212
Flaherty, Molly 62, 97, 104
Flemming, Jane 178
Flint & Rheinberg, Fair Play 15, 44
Flint, Rachael Heyhoe 105, 130, 132-33, 139-40, 146
Flintoff-King, Debbie 178
football 10,16, 29, 117, 182, 175, 180, 187, 189, 194, 199
football, women's 31
Forget-Me-Nots Club 21, 32
Forrest Lodge Club 75
Forrest, Sylvia 105
Foys 76
Francis, Bev 128
Frankston High School 74
Fremantle 47, 114
Fremantle Rovers 76, 81
Fremantle Suburban Club 76
Frey, Margaret 74
Friendly Societies' Ground 39
Friends' School 23
Frindall, W 13
frisquette 2
Frith, David 53
Frykberg, Ian 195
Fullston, Lyn 154, 156, 158-59, 161, 164, 173

Gabba 16, 105, 157, 158, 208
gambling 11, 72, 95
Gandhi, Indira 137
Garvoc 21
gate entry 11, 91
gates 99, 103
Geelong 82
gender and sport 9-10, 12, 187, 189, 200
George, W 98
Geraldton 78, 80-1
Geraldton Women's Cricket Association 63, 79-81
Gillette Cup 140
Gillott, Sir S 37
'Girls, School and Society' 148
Girls' High School 23
Girls' School Tennis Association 36
Glebe Club 58
Gloucester 14
goldfields 38, 56
Goldsmith, Joyce 125
Goldstein, Vida 26, 28, 37-38
golf 10, 12, 16, 51, 194, 199
Golley, F 40
Gordon, Anne 125, 140
Gordon, Sandy 182
Goss, Zoe 165, 191, 207, 211
Goulburn 38, 75, 82
government support 110, 122, 126, 136, 147, 149-50, 167, 198, 202
Grace, Martha 13
Grace, W G 13, 18
Graham Park, Gosford 159, 189
Gray Nicolls 64, 150
Green, Betty 85
Greenwood Secondary College 206-07
Gregory family 2, 9, 10
Gregory Alice 3
Gregory Lily 1-3
Gregory Nellie (later Donnan) 1-4
Gregory sisters 38

Griffiths, Sally 165
Grover, Miss M 38
Growden, Greg 158
Gugeri, Noel 79
Guildford 164
gymnastics 29, 185, 187

Haggett, Belinda 165, 211, 212
Halbish, Graham 152
Hamilton, Duke of 11
Hampton High School 74
Hand, Gerry 133–34
Hargraves, Billie 74
Hawke, Bob 154
Hawthorn Club 76, 82, 114
Hayward, Jack 130, 131, 134
Hayward, Steve 110
Hazelbank School 75
Headingley 105
Health Promotion Foundation 206
Helensburgh Club 75
Henry Buck's 73, 99, 122
Heyhoe, Rachael (later Flint) 122, 125, 126
Hide, Molly 98
high schools 74, 149
Hill End 18
Hill, Lorraine 141
Hoare, Des 117
Hobart Girls' Cricket Association 23
Hobart Ladies' College 23
hockey 35, 46, 59, 77, 82, 109, 112, 117, 119, 183, 199, 204; club 36
Hockley, Debbie 162, 173
Hodges, Carole 157, 172, 173
Holmes, Patricia 95
Holmes, Tracey 176
Holt, Richard 10, 12
homosexuality 12, 189, 191
Honeyball, Nettie 58
Hookes, David 180
Hopetoun Club 32, 50
Horan, Tom 54
House of Representatives Standing Committee 149, 176, 179, 182
Hove 163, 166
Howard, Sally 155
Howell, Max and Reet 77–8
Hudson, Amy 73, 91, 101, 103, 108, 109
Hughes, Rev. E S 34
Hutton, Sir Leonard 132, 180
Hyde Park 15, 32
Hyderabad 143

Ideal Kookaburras 76
Illawarra Women's Cricket Association 75
Imperials 80
Independent Girls' Schools Sports Association 206
India 65, 134, 135, 137, 141, 143, 145, 155, 161, 195, 202, 211
Indian Women's Cricket Association 134, 143
indoor cricket 155, 173, 199
indoor soccer 199
intercolonial competition 6–9
International XI 130, 132, 155
interstate competition 9, 37, 39, 44
Ireland 166, 171
Ireland, Flo 112
Ironside, Fred 1, 2, 38, 40
International Women's Cricket Council 35, 45, 66, 68, 134, 135, 137

Jacobs, Jen 156
Jamaica 130, 131
Jamaican Women's Cricket Association 130
Jarrett, Pat 94
Jegust, Marie 47
Jenkins, Miss 18
Jenkins, Vivian 133
Jennings, Margaret 139, 141, 145
jockeys, female 128–29, 204
Johnson, Connie 81
Johnston, Lesley 135
Johnston, Norma (nee Whiteman) 106
Jones, Bronwyn 154
Jones, Mavis 109
Jubilee series 157, 162, 174
Junee 85
junior cricket 204, 206
junior interstate competition 169

Kalgoorlie Club 38
Kambala School 36, 37
Kanga cricket 152–55, 170–71, 198, 204, 207
Kanowna Club 39
Karasz, Sue 152
Katoomba 22
Kellermann, Annette 16, 28, 53
Kelly, Ros 178
Kennare, Jill 155–61
Kent 13, 53, 95
Kew 72
Kew Club 32
King, Helen 52, 185
King's College Oval 119
Kingsgrove Sports Centre 64
Kinneburgh, Mancy 74
Knee, Miriam 45, 99, 111, 122, 125, 131, 132
Knight, Barry 135
Knox, Ken 112
Kuring-gai Club 32, 62, 75–6, 113, 202, 212
Kutcher, Lorraine 125

Labor Social Club 73
Ladies' Stands 16, 104
Lahore 5
Laker, Jim 112
Lancashire 14, 97
Lancaster Park 156
Lane, Don 182, 191
Lane, Tim 192
Larsen, Lyn 158, 161, 166, 179
Latrobe 40
Laughton, Dot 189
Lawry, Bill 179
Laws, John 182
Lear, Megan 157
Lee, Helen 122
Leederville 47
Leslie House 23
Leslie, Olive 83
Lewis, Hayley 176, 183
Lilienthal, Sonja 35
Liverpool 134
Loongana Club 32, 39
Lord's 98, 105, 106, 128–29, 134, 139–40, 163, 180
Lord's Taverners 207
Loreto 206
Lowerson, J 12
Lucknow 156

Lullham, Amanda 176
Lumsden, Jan 140
Lutschini, Marie (later Cornish) 139

Maclagan, Myrtle 89, 91, 95, 98
Macquarie University 206
Mac Roberston High School 74
Maccabeans 114
Madden, Sir J 37
Maitland 126
Maitland Park 81
Maitland, West 7
male culture 10, 127, 212
male dominance 128, 129
Malvern 32
Manchester 14, 112, 145
manliness 10, 12, 16, 182
Marchioness of Salisbury 11
Maribyrnong Club 32
Marie Cornish Knockout competition 205
marriage 81, 116, 189
Marsh, Rod 145, 179
Marshall, Kirstie 178
Martin, Denise 157, 159
Martin, Mary 44
Maryborough 25, 78
Marylebone Cricket Club 105, 108, 134, 139
masculine traits 31, 59, 66, 94
Masters, Roy 187
Matthews, Christina 156, 164, 170, 180, 184, 209, 211
Maudsley, Henry 12
May, Patsy 139
May Mills Trophy 117
Mayfield Park Club 32
Maylands Club 76
Mayor's Park 72, 122
McConway, Jill 158
McCredie, Kath 117
McDonnell & Ruddell, 'Women's Cricket' 35, 37, 40, 43–4
McDonnell, Agnes (nee Paternoster) 37, 49, 56
McDonnell, May 20, 56
McGregor, Adrian 129
McKay, Jim 185
McKenzie, Graham 117
McLarty, Nell 62, 71–3, 91, 94, 99, 142
media coverage 2, 15, 35, 52, 65, 84, 86, 91, 93, 95, 99, 110, 134, 158, 173–74, 183, 185
media criticism 2, 7, 8, 9, 20, 21, 26, 30, 57, 66
media support 19, 71
medical profession 16, 29–30
medical theory 12
Meher-Homji, Kersi 202
Melbourne 2, 7, 20, 32, 34–5, 37–45, 55–6, 59, 62, 65, 73–4, 76, 82–3, 85, 113, 115, 145, 152, 160, 171
Melbourne Continuation School 35
Melbourne Cricket Club 85
Melbourne Cricket Ground 21, 91, 103, 105, 110, 151, 170–72
Melbourne Ladies' Cricket Club 84
Melrose 40
Memerambi 78
men's cricket 40, 45, 111, 210
Merton Hall 35, 58, 73
Methodist Ladies' College, Adelaide 118
Methodist Ladies' College, Melbourne 22

Meuleman, Ken 117
Mia-Mia Club 32, 39
Midland Club 114
Midwinter, W 20
Midwinter, Miss 20
Miller, Rae 46
Mills, L C 45, 48
Mills, May 116–17
Milner, Lady 56
Minister for the Environment and Sport 150–51
minor sports 184, 195, 196, 200–01
Mitchell, Ann 65–67, 136, 140, 141, 143, 162, 189, 192, 200, 210, 212
Mitford, M 13
mixed cricket 77–78, 155
Moffat, Sally 155
Monaghan, Ruby 75
monarchs, female 10–11
Montego Bay 139
Moreland 32
Morpeth 7
Mortimer, Kerry 141
Mrs Hazelton's team 102
Mt Keira Club 75
Mt Kembla Club 75
Mummery, Dot 110

Napier, Wendy 158
Narrabri 38
National Development Officer 152, 170, 173
National Executive Director 152, 170, 175
Navena Club 36
netball 112–13, 128–29, 152, 187, 195, 199, 204
Netherlands, The 65, 171
New Delhi 136, 156
'New Woman' 27
New Zealand 22, 46, 49, 62, 66, 98, 101, 103, 104, 110, 113, 116–17, 119, 121, 126, 130, 132–35, 137, 141, 143, 155, 156, 161, 162, 169, 171, 173, 211
Newcastle 7
Newman, Dawn 125
Nirranda 21
Normanhurst School 37; Club 146
North America 112, 137, 194
North Sydney 36
North Sydney Oval 110, 119, 125, 171, 195, 211
Northampton 63, 78, 81, 97; LCA 81
Northcote, Sir J 104
Northern Rivers 75
novelty factor 5, 9, 20, 21, 24, 25, 38, 100, 137, 174, 201
Nowra 145
NSW 6, 7, 8, 9, 16, 18, 22, 35, 38, 40–2, 44–5, 47–8, 55, 61, 67, 73, 75–6, 82–3, 85–6, 95, 98, 104, 112, 113, 115, 117, 125, 145, 159, 169, 170, 171, 204, 207, 208
NSW Cricket Association 75, 151
NSW Cyclists' Touring Union 52
NSW Department of Education 149
NSW Government 149
NSW Ladies' Amateur Swimming Association 28, 53
NSW Ladies' Singlehanded Tennis Tournament 36
NSW Schoolgirls' Association 169; Championships 206

NSW Softball Association 113
NSW Women's Cricket Association 2, 32, 35, 46, 66, 75, 90, 91, 102, 109, 126, 134, 137, 139, 145, 169, 202
Nunn, Glynnis 180

O'Hara, J Still 22
Oberon 22
Old England 132
Oldfield's team 73
Olympic Club 116, 131, 137
Olympic Games 28, 30, 35, 52, 84, 129, 183, 192
One-day international 158, 160
O'Neill, Pam 128
Open tournament 170, 175
Orange 145
O'Reilly, Bill 104, 179
Oval, The 98, 105, 108, 122, 132, 140, 163
Owens, Jenny 165
overarm bowling 13, 21

Packer, Kerry 194
Paisley, Una 101, 103, 104, 119, 121
Palmer, Anne 91
Papasergio and Moy, *Women's Cricket in WA*, 76, 78, 81, 112, 119
Papworth, Melissa 152
Parker, Grant 206
Parramatta 8
Parrish, Tracey 176
Paternoster, Agnes (later McDonnell) 37, 41, 44
Paternoster family 37
Peden, Barbara 32, 91, 94, 117
Peden, Margaret 32, 45–47, 62, 75, 90–91, 95, 117
Pelaco team 73, 84
Penguin 40
Penleigh & Essendon Grammar 206–07
Penrith 38
Perth 38, 76, 78, 80, 81, 83, 85, 113, 121, 141, 158, 162, 171
Phillips Industries 150
Philpott, Peter 175, 191
Picton, Muriel 125, 126
Pioneers, The (PVLCA) 37, 49
players 77, 155, 171, 173, 199, 202
players, English 134, 136
Pollard, Marjorie 97–98
Poona 134, 136
Port Kembla Club 75
Potter, Jackie 132
Pratt, Kerryn 176, 178
Pratten Park 159
Preddey, Ruth 29, 35,38, 46, 75, 84, 86–87, 93
prejudice against women 16, 44, 113, 128, 137, 174, 180, 197, 199
Presbyterian Ladies' College 35, 73
Presbyterian Ladies' College Croydon 37
Presbyterian Ladies' College Melbourne 58
Presbyterian Ladies' College Pymble 67–68, 109, 117
Preston Club 44–45, 59
Preston Girls' School 74
Preston, Kingsley 105
Price, Karen (later Hill)141, 146, 153, 155–58, 170, 173
primary schools 153–54, 205, 207
Pritchard, Edna 58, 95

Pritchard, Hazel 95, 97–98
prize money 179, 182
Probable Intercolonial side 6
public acceptance 9, 43
public criticism and neglect 9, 110, 126
Puma 150

Qantas 150
Quairading 117
Queen Elizabeth Oval, Bendigo 159
Queen's College 23
Queensbury, Marquis of 12
Queensland 23, 44, 47, 61, 77, 82–83, 89, 93, 95, 111, 116, 169, 207, 208
Queensland Ladies' Tennis Team 59
Queensland Women's Cricket Association 46–47, 62, 111, 145–46, 155, 208

radio 45, 99, 105, 158,182, 183
Rae, Dawn 116–17, 131
Rambler's Club 74
Randall, Leonie 118, 128
Rangaswamy, Shanta 156
Rattigan Vera (later Cutter) 42
Ravenswood School 158
Raymond's team 73, 84
Read, Karen 156, 161, 170
records 22, 139, 140, 165, 171, 211
Reeler, Lindsay 156–58, 164–65, 171–72
revival 101, 119, 126,145–46
Rheinberg, Netta 84, 141, 163
Richmond Cricket Ground 172, 179, 195
Richmond Girls' School 74
Richmond Racecourse 41
ridicule of women cricketers 9, 12, 30
Riviere School 37
Robinson, Cecilia 108, 121
Robinson, Julie 141
Rockhampton 24
Rockley 22
role models 13, 45
Rothman's Nation Sports Foundation 135
roundarm bolwing 2, 13, 21, 57
rounders 71
Rowell, Ailsa 208
rowing 10, 29, 35, 200
rowing, women's 61, 128
Rowlandson, Thomas 12
Royal Park 32
Royals 80
Ruddell, Mabel 37
rugby, women's 212
Russell-Clarke, Peter 155
Russell, Capt. 47
Ruth Preddey Cup 35

Sabina Park 139
Sainsbury, Erica 162
Sandringham 35
Sans Souci Club 58, 75, 91
Sargeant, Anne 178
Scarborough 108, 122
SCEGGS Darlinghurst 37
SCG 1, 2, 5, 7, 9, 16, 47, 86, 103, 104, 105, 110, 119
Scharlieb, Dr M 29
Schmidt, Joan 108
school sport 149, 204, 206, 207, 209
Schoolgirls' Championships (NSW) 206
schools 10, 15, 22, 29, 35, 74, 93, 99, 112
Scotch College 129

Index

Scott, Rose 28, 30
Seafoams 21
secondary schools 118, 207
Secondary Schoolgirls' Competition (WA) 117
Semco team 45, 73
Senate, Australian 26, 37
Sex Discrimination Act 152, 196
sexism 16, 104, 113, 133, 149, 179, 185, 187
Shea, Jack 79, 81
Sheffield Shield 49, 86, 90, 99, 111, 159
Shell Company 68, 150, 169 171, 175
Shell Rose Bowl 162, 169, 211
Shell Super Clinics 150, 169, 170, 208
Sherring, Neil 204
Sherwood Club 32
Shevill, Essie 75, 89, 91
Shevill, Rene 75, 89
Shiell, Alan 129–30
Simmons, E 32
Simpson, Bob 162
Sirocco Club 1, 2, 3, 5, 14, 18, 20, 54
Smith, Heather 176
Smith, Kath 88–89, 91, 93, 95, 97–98
Sneddon, Ray 150, 152, 155, 167, 170–71, 174–75, 197, 198–99, 202, 210
Snowball, Betty 91
Snowflakes 21, 32
soccer 149, 199, 200
social games 17, 21, 36, 38, 58, 74, 76, 113, 134
Sofala 18
softball 112, 113, 117, 128, 136, 199
South Africa 135, 162
South Australia 26, 40, 44, 46, 49, 67, 80, 85, 95, 105, 112, 117, 145, 155, 169–70, 189, 196, 207
South Australia Women's Cricket Association 46, 83, 116
South Melbourne 160
South Perth Club 114
South Sydney Club 75
Southampton 95
Southgate, Jan 157, 158
spectators, male 86, 93, 97, 99, 105
Spence, Peter 154
Spillane, Debbie 176
sponsorship 67, 122, 126, 130, 139, 147, 150, 153, 161, 163, 167, 175–76, 178, 210
sport, competitive 16, 17, 28, 113
squash 199
St Elmo Club 45
St James's Club 32
St John's (Elsternwick) Club 32
St John's (Melbourne) Club 32
St Kilda Oval 110, 119, 121, 125, 135
St Paul's Club 32
St Peter's Club 44
Stackpole, Keith 152
Stanton, Anne 46
Starling, Avril 158
Stead, Janice 135
street games 71, 75, 115, 117
Streeton, Richard 133
Subiaco Club 114, 157, 207
suffragettes 27, 133
Summers, Anne 127
Summers, Susan 47
Sunbury 140

Sunday play 135, 140
Sunflowers Club 32, 39
Sunshine Technical School 74
Surrey 11, 53, 98
Sussex 11
Swanton, E W 98
swimming 10, 16, 28–30, 52, 58, 81, 112, 185
Sydney 1, 2, 6, 7, 9, 14, 15, 18, 20, 22, 28, 38, 40, 43–44, 47, 49, 54, 58, 83, 85, 103, 115, 169, 171
Sydney Club 6
Sydney Girls' High School 35
Sydney Ladies' Club 7
Sydney Sports Ground 71
Sydney University Oval 82
Sydney University Women's Cricket Club 32, 66, 76, 109, 113
Sydney University Women's Sports Association 36, 66, 94, 109
Symonds manufacturing 64

Talbot, David 133
Tally-Ho Club 32
Tamworth 145
Tarana 22
Tasmania 23, 39, 40, 42, 49–50, 130, 207, 208
Tasmanian Women's Cricket Association 43, 130, 145, 170, 208
Teachers' College 75
Telecom 150
television 105, 156, 158, 161, 163, 172, 183–84, 192, 194, 197
tennis 7, 16, 31, 35, 36, 51, 53, 66, 81, 111, 112, 117, 129, 180, 185, 187, 194, 199, 204
tennis, women's 175, 191–92
Thebarton Oval 110, 125
Thirroul Club 75
Thomas, Lorna 104, 132, 145
Thomas, A E 102
Thompson, A G 150
Thompson, Raelee 134, 140, 142, 146, 157–60
Thomson, Jeff 146
Tiddy, Josephine 152, 196
Tighe, Karen 176
TNT 150
Tonkin, Annette 162
Toowoomba 58, 61, 78
tour, costs of 83, 110–11, 116, 131, 133–34, 137, 139, 150
tournament, interstate 40, 47, 49, 61, 82–83, 115–16, 129–20, 135, 141, 146
tours, international 46, 66, 76, 80, 82, 83ff, 95, 99, 109, 162
Towers, Coralie 115–17, 121
Tredrea, Janette 140–41
Tredrea, Sharon 99, 140, 142, 143, 156–57, 171
Triffit, Jacqui 208
Trinidad and Tobago 130
Trott sisters 20, 21
Trott, Albert 20
Trotting Girls' Club 47, 76
trousers 53, 58, 62–63, 65–66, 189
True Blue Club 7

Under-15 competition 207
Under-18 competition 169, 170, 206, 207

Under-19 tournament 169
Under-21 tournament 117, 169, 170, 206, 207
Under-23 side 161, 169
Under-25 side 134, 135, 161, 169
underarm bowling 13, 16, 21, 86
University of Adelaide 118, 204
University High School 74
University of Melbourne 26
University of NSW 149
University of Queensland 185
University of Sydney 26, 27, 35, 36, 75, 94, 109
University of Western Australia, 156, 182
universities 10, 28, 35

Varley S 3
Verco, Peta 156–57, 159, 207
Vice Regal Club 62, 75
Victoria 6, 7, 8, 9, 10, 18, 21, 23, 28, 32, 37–45, 47–49, 55, 67, 73, 75–76, 82, 85, 93, 95, 103, 110, 117–18, 126, 145, 162, 169, 170, 207, 208
Victoria Park 39, 42
Victoria Park State School 73
Victoria Parliamentary team 21
Victorian Cricket Association 85
Victorian Institute of Sport 152
Victorian Ladies' Cricket Association 28, 32, 34, 35, 37, 43, 45
Victorian Women's Cricket Association 44–45, 50, 84, 104, 118–19, 137
village cricket 11, 13, 15, 53
voting rights 26

WACA 85, 105, 110, 117, 121, 141, 157, 169
Wahroonga 23
Waldron, Dot 46, 48
Walford School 118
Waratahs, The 75
Warner, Pelham 98
Warrnambool 21
Wasps, The 36
Watmough, Chris 141, 158
Wattle Club 35
Watts, Tracey 176
Waverley Club 32
Webb, Danny 110
Wellington 103, 139 High School 206
Wells, H G 27
West Indies 65, 130–31, 134–35, 137, 141, 143, 167
Westbrook, Ruth 122
Western Australia 38, 44, 47, 49, 62, 76, 78, 81, 83, 85, 95, 105, 111–12, 115–17, 145, 157, 162, 170, 212
Western Australian Women's Cricket Association 47, 49, 63
Western Girls' Club 76
Western Star Butter 154
Westgarth High School 117
Whatmore, Dav 152
White Heather Club 14, 55–6
Whiteman, Norma (later Johnston) 106, 108
Whoopee Club 75
Wicks, Kathryn 176
Wilde, O 13
Wilkie 120
Wilkinson, Jan 131
Willes, Christina 13
Willeton Oval 162

Williamstown High School 74, 137
Willows Club 114
Wilson, Betty 72–73, 99, 101, 103, 104, 108, 116, 119, 121, 122–23
Wilson, Bev 132, 134, 139, 159
Wilson, Cecilia 136
Wilson, Debbie 157, 159
Wilson, Edith 22
Wimbledon Ladies' Championship 36
Wisden 6, 14, 98, 141, 146, 163, 165
Wollongong 75–76
'Women and Coaching' 178
Women Sport and the Media 149, 176
Women's Cricket Association 59, 62, 106, 130, 163
Women's Federal Political Association 26
Women's Sport Unit 149, 176, 196–97
Women's Weekly 35, 71, 84–6, 93–4
Wood, V R 30
Woodville High School 118
Wool Corporation 150
Worcester 108, 163, 165
World Cup 67, 111, 116, 130–34, 141–43, 147, 151, 155, 171, 195
World War I 101, 201
World War II 46, 91, 93, 94, 99–101, 111–13
Wylie, Mina 28, 30
Wynyard 40

Yabba 87
Yass 18, 38
Yorkshire 105
Young England 130, 133
YWCA 45, 47, 73, 82, 84, 111, 113, 117, 119, 126, 140